NEVER BEFORE, NEVER AGAIN

EDDIE ROBINSON WITH RICHARD LAPCHICK

NEVER BEFORE, NEVER AGAIN

❖

The Stirring Autobiography of Eddie Robinson,
the Winningest Coach in the History
of College Football

St. Martin's Press *New York*

THOMAS DUNNE BOOKS.
An imprint of St. Martin's Press.

NEVER BEFORE, NEVER AGAIN. Copyright © 1999 by Eddie Robinson with Richard Lapchick.
All rights reserved. Printed in the United States of America. No part of this book may be used
or reproduced in any manner whatsoever without written permission except in the case of brief
quotations embodied in critical articles or reviews. For information, address St. Martin's Press,
175 Fifth Avenue, New York, NY 10010.

Book Design by Leah Carlson Stanisic

Library of Congress Cataloging-in-Publication Data

Robinson, Eddie.
    Never before, never again : the autobiography of Eddie Robinson /
Eddie Robinson & Richard Lapchick.—1st ed.
       p.   cm.
    ISBN 0-312-24224-7
     1. Robinson, Eddie. 2. Football coaches—United States Biography.
3. Afro-American football coaches—United States Biography.
I. Lapchick, Richard Edward. II. Title. III. Title: Autobiography
of Eddie Robinson.
GV939.R58A3 1999
796.332'092—dc21
[B]   99–36158
                                       CIP

First Edition: October 1999

10 9 8 7 6 5 4 3 2 1

For Doris, who has made my ride through
life sweet, meaningful, and complete.

—EDDIE

For my children, Joe, Chamy, and Emily,
who provide me with infinite hope and happiness.

—RICHARD LAPCHICK

CONTENTS

I want to thank so many people who have helped make me into the person I am, which eventually led to the writing of this book. Since the book is about my life, then so are the acknowledgments.

I have spoken at length in this book about my wife, Doris, our children, Lillian Rose, and Eddie, Jr., and our grandchildren. They are my bedrock.

Our home has been both Grambling and Ruston. The people in both communities have made us feel so very welcome. The people of Louisiana have been so giving to me, my family, and my school.

So many writers have said such wonderful things about me and our program. Their kindness has been so appreciated.

I want to thank all the professors at Grambling who delivered the education that I promised to all the young men I recruited. I need to tip my hat also to all of Grambling's administrators, from the presidents on down through the ranks, who over the years gave us the support we needed to be innovative and stay on top of our game.

My fellow coaches in college sports were all at once great rivals and great friends. The American Football Coaches Association brought us all together on a national level, while SWAC gave us our competitive edge with our primary rivals. So many rich traditions were built there.

I had some incredible assistant coaches who I must thank for helping our team achieve so much over my fifty-six years at Grambling. We ended up with Ernie Sterling, Melvin Lee, Eddie Robinson, Jr., Dennis Winston, Robert Smith, Glen Hall, Al Mohammed, and Matt Reed, but there were coaches throughout all those years who helped create the great teams we developed.

They included Billy Manning, Ed Stevens, Ron Taylor, Fred Collins, Steve Dennis, Eugene Hughes, George Small, Marty Steward, Lee Flentory, Jessie Applewhite, Leroy Hawthorne, Tom Williams, Otis Moore, Hugh McKinnis, Fred Hobdy, I.V. Billis, Douglas Porter, George Glenn, Jerry Hardaway, Jeremiah Davis, Julian Spence, Oree Banks, Whitney Vancleve, Clifford Anderson, Leonard Griffin, and everyone's coach, Collie Nicholson, who was our voice as sports information director.

The teams were, of course, made up of our student-athletes and we had so many great ones. Each one of them helped us earn the victories, and I will always be in their debt. Working with them each day was one of the greatest joys of my life and they give me confidence for our nation in the new millennium.

As for the specifics of this book, I need to thank Werner Scott and Karl McDonald for getting this project going. Then I salute my special friend, George Steinbrenner, for writing the foreword and the Reverend Jesse Jackson for writing the afterword. Having them associated with this book has lent honor to me and my family.

Last but not least, this book has given me the opportunity to begin what I know will become a lifelong friendship with Rich Lapchick, who has helped me in numerous ways as my coauthor. Rich's own background helped him understand so many things about my life and helped me frame it in the way I wanted to tell my story.

PERSONAL THOUGHTS AND
ACKNOWLEDGMENTS OF RICHARD LAPCHICK

One of the greatest joys of my life has been having the honor of coauthoring *Never Before, Never Again,* the autobiography of Eddie Robinson, with him. It is an incredible story of a man believing he could do what others said he could not.

Eddie Robinson's coaching career at Grambling in deep, rural Louisiana lasted through 11 presidents and three wars. Grambling has been home to Coach and his wife, Doris, for fifty-eight years. They have been married that long and he coached for fifty-six years—all at the same institution! When he retired in November 1997, many people in America stood up and took note for the first time of the winningest coach in the history of college football. In the African-American community, he was very likely the best known coach in America and was surely the most beloved while institutionalized racial barriers kept Robinson a secret from most of white America outside of the world of sports.

Initially a coach in a segregated society, Eddie Robinson helped football transcend race in the America he loves and treasures. It is my hope that this book will help Americans of every color and in every corner of our country discover the full meaning of the life of this great son of America.

At a time when so many coaches and players seem ready to extol their own virtues, Robinson is reluctant to discuss any of his victories or records. I had to drag game stories out of him because he wanted to talk about his players and fellow coaches as men. He wanted to talk about life and philosophy, which was a pure pleasure for me to listen to. Nonetheless, getting him to talk about himself was very difficult.

After achieving one of sports' most incredible records with his 400th win in 1995, Coach Eddie Robinson said, "I wish I could cut up all of these victories into 400 pieces and give them to all the players and assistant coaches I have had. They are the ones who truly deserve the credit." Now that I know him I see that these words were coming straight from his heart.

The stories about his retirement brought new exposure for Coach in communities where his messages of tradition, loyalty, family, and racial understanding are desperately needed. Eddie Robinson began to become a household name after every major newspaper and TV station featured him on multiple occasions throughout the 1997 season. Viewers and readers caught glimpses of his wisdom and his wit. But his story has never been fully told before now.

Never Before, Never Again will finally completely open America's consciousness to this great American leader who happened to be a coach and happened to be African-American.

Never a public crusader for civil rights, Coach courageously challenged racism in his own way by proving that a black man could be a great football coach and, simultaneously, build the tenacity and determination of those in his charge as he led adolescents into manhood. Thirty years later, many of today's civil rights leaders hail Eddie Robinson's life in the same breath as that of Jackie Robinson's. Rev. Jesse Jackson's afterword is an affirmation of this fact.

In 1941, he assumed the role of mentor, role model, father, and counselor to his student-athletes both on and off the field. Grambling and college coaching have never been the same. Nor have the thousands of young men who played for Coach Robinson. He guided the once obscure Grambling State Tigers to national and international acclaim while helping to produce championship teams and players. Yet the career-related accomplishment of which Coach is proudest of is that eighty percent of his players graduated in a sport where the national average during his tenure had been less than forty-five percent. At a time when most head coaches today delegate caring for student-athletes to assistants, Coach Robinson spent fifty-four years personally going into the athletic dorm with his now famous cow bell at 6:30 A.M. each weekday to be sure his men were awake and ready to go to class. Coach has proven the power of an individual to make a huge difference in the lives of young people.

Of all of his accomplishments, he maintains that his greatest achievements are that he has had only one wife and one job for over fifty-six years. Robinson came to Grambling in 1941 just months after marrying Doris, his sweetheart since he was fourteen! The marriage is still going strong.

They still hold hands sixty-five years after they first met. I've seen it and it is moving. I have been told on many occasions, "Listen, Rich, I have to go now to have lunch with Doris," or, "It's time for dinner with Doris." At first I thought he might just be tired from hours of talking to me. But then we would always pick it up at 10:00 P.M. and go until 1:00 A.M. For years I believed I didn't know any man who loved his wife as much as I did. I may have met him that first night with Coach.

In spite of the racial barriers that surrounded his life, Coach somehow maintains a positive attitude about opportunity in America for people of all colors. Coach believes: "We are in a position to do a lot of good and that's the real importance of this work. America offers more opportunity to young people than any other country in the world."

My life with my father gave me an added and very special perspective from which to write about Coach. I am the son of Joe Lapchick, the Original Celtic center who became a Hall of Fame coach for St. John's and the Knicks, where he helped to integrate the NBA. I saw the pressures, victories, and defeats firsthand growing up with a bigger-than-life sports figure in my home.

Like Coach, my father dealt with the issue of race in sport for most of his playing and coaching career and is considered a pioneer on this issue. For many, St. John's University was more identified with my dad at one time than with any academic programs, just as Grambling was identified for many with Coach.

Finally, my father was mandatorily retired from St. John's before he was ready to stop coaching in 1965. There was great public pressure from the press and from fans to let him stay. I watched the pain and the ultimate triumph as only a son could see it. I believe I understood Coach Robinson's ordeal when his desire to coach one more year at Grambling seemed to conflict with the institution's desire for him to retire.

I have been lucky enough to be the recipient of numerous humanitarian awards, including the Arthur Ashe Voice of Conscience Award and the Ralph Bunche International Peace Award. Nothing, however, has given me more honor than being associated with Coach Robinson on his life's story.

After our first evening together, I called my wife, Ann, at 2:30 A.M. I told her that my greatest regret in my life was that she and my children had never met my father. I said now you will get that chance, because Coach Robinson reminds me so much of my dad. I can think of no higher compliment to pay Coach. It has been wonderful for me to get to know him so well.

I feel equally lucky to have been able to spend so much time with Doris, both in person and on the phone. During Coach's last game in the Superdome, Doris was supposed to go from the family's box to the field. I was asked if I could take her down the long corridors in a wheelchair. As we moved through the almost all-black crowd, tears of joy rolled down my cheeks. I am sure many wondered what this white man was doing with Doris and why I was crying. I had spent many hours taking my own mother around in a wheelchair. Eddie and Doris had brought me back to my own mother and father and not only rekindled so many memories of the past but inspired so much hope for the future.

We all have the capacity to be dream makers, be it for the world, our nation, our city, or for even one other human being. We can make a difference. For the sake of our children, we have no choice. Eddie Robinson has done that for eight decades.

Coach's vision is of a world where our children can play with each other without worrying about whether or not their play-mates look like or think like themselves. He lived a life that showed him those possibilities.

I am also in debt to several people who assisted me with this autobiography. Werner Scott had the faith to think I could help Coach, while Karl McDonald assisted me in getting some key elements. Scott Waxman helped bring Coach and me together with the people at St. Martin's, where Pete Wolverton was always available to help make this a better book. Larry Lundy has been a treasure with continuous encouragement to complete this book.

Lennox Chase and Miles McLean helped me search the press before I met Coach. Carolyn Lovell helped me transcribe the seventy hours of tapes. My wife, Ann Pasnak, read the text and made many useful suggestions. Bill Curry, Keith Lee, Father Bill Talentino, and James Hutchinson also read the draft and made comments. Philomena Pirolo helped with the technical work and final packaging.

In the end, none of us could really add to or diminish the importance of this story. We were all merely vessels to expound on the life of one of the greatest men I have ever known. I hope you enjoy reading it as much as I enjoyed helping to write it with Coach.

FOREWORD

In recent years as principal owner of the New York Yankees, which is arguably the greatest team legacy in all of sports, I have been called upon to speak of men who have transcended the very sport of which they were such a major part; Ruth, Gehrig, Mantle, and so very recently, the Yankee Clipper—Joe DiMaggio.

Now, I find myself once again speaking of a man who has transcended the very sport which he has been such a major part of. There is a significant difference though—this man will be able to read my thoughts of him, and that is very important not just to me but to everyone who may spend a few short minutes reading what I have to say.

"The Coach," Eddie Robinson, is just that. Others are and will be coaches, and I have proudly worn that title myself, but in my forty years of involvement in sports, high school, collegiate, and professional, I can truly say that there are very, very few who deserve the title of "the Coach." His life is best described by the words of Ralph Waldo Emerson,

"Do not go where the path may lead, go instead where there is no path, and leave a trail."

Eddie Robinson spent a lifetime devoted to the development of young athletes, not to just become great football players, but to become great Americans. He is a living monument to the premise that all men are created equal and that while there may be times when other unfortunate human beings seek to deprive them of those rights, they must never cease to strive by example to prove those poor souls wrong.

"The Coach" brought records that few can even dream of: fifty-seven years as the head coach of a sport at one single university, 408 victories, and over 200 players who went on to professional football, and all of this from a little school in Grambling, Louisiana (just four miles west of Ruston, in case you didn't know).

Because of what this "great" man (and I never use the term freely because few men can truly qualify) has accomplished in his lifetime, every true American who believes in this great nation should be proud to read this story of "the Coach" and his beautiful and wonderful companion of fifty-eight years, Doris. Smile, laugh, even cry, for you will enjoy every minute of the life of the greatest American I have ever known!

—George M. Steinbrenner III

NEVER BEFORE, NEVER AGAIN

INTRODUCTION

For years people have been telling me, "Eddie, you need to tell your story." I could never see doing it because that would seem to say that I think I am so important.

I still feel that way now. I love people. I like to think that when I meet someone I give them some of me to keep, that they get to know me. I coached my last student-athletes at Grambling in 1997. They were good kids. They got to know one side of Eddie Robinson.

But I now realize that they won't get to know all sides of Eddie Robinson. It's not that I'm so important, but the things I have seen and lived through might be helpful to these young men and those who will follow them at Grambling. I want to use my perspective as a witness to eleven presidents, three wars, and the civil rights movement to talk about that piece of American history. So here I am, writing this book for all those I can never coach. There are many others who I think will find my outlook useful—the thousands I did coach, the students and alumni of Grambling State University, the parents of those students, fans of black college football, and fans of football in general, black Americans and white Americans. Ultimately, I am writing it for all Americans.

But my primary audience, as it has been all my life, is young people who might benefit in some way from my experiences and perspective.

I know life isn't easy for young people now. They face all these challenges that my generation didn't have. When I was growing up in Jackson and Baton Rouge, children weren't killing each other; crack didn't exist; I never head of steroids; most families had a mother and father. Many of today's student-athletes were raised in poverty and despair. They know that some white people will decide who they are just because of what they look like. Yes, indeed, life is hard today.

My momma was a domestic; daddy was a third-generation sharecropper. They separated when I was six. Neither graduated from elementary school. I lived in a two-room house and slept on the floor most nights. The bathroom and the kitchen were outside. I had to work throughout my childhood, in high school, and in college. Virtually all the white people I knew were people I worked for or my parents worked for. I was raised in a segregated society that placed legal limits on what and who I could be.

But I was determined that I would do my very best to get what I wanted out of life. I knew only what I knew, not what I had missed out on. Despair was never part of my life. It was never easy . . . still isn't. But I have had some kind of life. I can't say I have any regrets. That's what I want these young people to know. It may be hard, but nothing is impossible.

They said I might not be able to finish high school. By 1941, I called Leland College my alma mater. In 1997, they called me "Dr. Robinson" at Yale where they gave me an honorary degree. I still can't believe that!

They said I would never be able to reach my third-grade dream of coaching football. I saw a coach then; he looked so good and his boys seemed to worship him. The fact that he was their hero was written all over their faces. That was the life I wanted.

Seventy years later I ended a fifty-six-year ride as a college head coach!

So many of my players come from broken homes. I did too, but I tried to show them what is possible in a loving relationship. I started courting Doris in the seventh grade. I knew she was the one then—and she is now. We hold hands. I go home every day for lunch and dinner. Our love is as strong now as it was when I took her to hear Louis Armstrong play at the Temple Roof Gardens. I make sure my players see us together. Now the readers of this book can feel what Doris and I have together. I hope that the example of our love can serve as a source of hope and inspiration for those who think strong families are not so possible.

They say blacks and whites can't get along. I wondered myself growing up. But now I know what is possible. Being accepted so readily by my white coaching colleagues was only the beginning. I guess winning so many games and being at Grambling so long made others give me a second look. Now I can go in any hotel or restaurant and white people simply say, "How're you doing, Coach Rob?" That's a real good feeling to know they have come to trust me and that can help break their stereotypes of blacks in general. Maybe if Grambling wasn't so successful, we wouldn't have blacks coaching in the NFL and at the big college Division IA schools. Maybe I wouldn't even have been welcomed in such a friendly way in the hotels or restaurants. But people in Louisiana—blacks and whites—know I did whatever I said and that I worked hard. I am welcome. We do get along. But we have to communicate first so we can trust each other, get to know one another.

I hope this book will also break stereotypes of some white people. Two come to mind right away. I know some people don't have a positive impression of George Steinbrenner. Not me. George has become one of my best friends. He has been so generous to me, my players, and to Grambling. I can share a meal with George or folks from Ruston (rural Louisiana).

Coach Bear Bryant is another. He was always so good to me whenever we met. Who would have thought I would have been asked to pay tribute to Bear Bryant near the end of his life?

When I was a child in Jackson, Louisiana, would anyone have dared to tell my father that I would have had discussions with a series of American presidents? Or heads of state? We are all people. We have to realize that we are just people. Same God . . . same nation . . . same world.

As many of the formerly all-white colleges integrated, I was told it would be the end of Grambling football. Since that integration took place, our team has traveled to Japan and has established huge national games in New York, Dallas, and New Orleans. Grambling football is far better known today than before integration came.

So this book is, in part, for all those young men I will not have the privilege to coach. But I am, of course, writing for those I did coach as well. Without them, no one would have been asking me to write this in the first place. Some of the greatest who ever played the game have been part of what we have built here. From Tank Younger onward, our guys have made their mark in the NFL. They, too, did a lot of things people said couldn't be done: Tank was the first NFL player to come from an Historically Black College. James Harris didn't listen to the chorus that sang "no black NFL quarterbacks" and became the first. Then there was the ultimate when Doug Williams quarterbacked Washington to the Super Bowl championship. Man, that was really something.

Four other Grambling greats made the Pro Football Hall of Fame. Willie Davis was the first and now is a powerful businessman. Grambling teammates Buck Buchanan and Willie Brown were inducted in the 1980s. Charlie Joiner was selected in 1996. More than 200 Grambling grads played in the NFL!

We also had some who didn't play football as well as Tank, James, or Doug, but who have played the game of life in ways that have made Grambling a better university and the world a better place. More than eighty percent of my student-athletes graduated.

I am writing for their parents as well. They trusted me with their babies. I cannot imagine any bigger responsibility. That is something I have tried to preach to my coaches. They saw me go into the dorm at six-thirty every morning to be sure the guys were up for class. I could have been home with Doris at that hour, but I knew the parents expected me to act in their place.

I want to provide some history of Grambling State University. While it is a great American university, this history will be even more special for our friends and alumni. It has been my second home; its students and faculty have been my second family. I love this school and its people. Grambling embraced me when I was working at a feed mill for twenty-five cents per hour. I have been grateful for the opportunity ever since. I stayed here because I wanted to be among those who stood up for and with America's Historically Black Colleges and Universities. I never wanted to be anywhere else.

As I meet young people today I see they have no real sense of America's social and political history. I have been at one place all that time—on a black campus in the rural South—that's a pretty unique view. I want to help the reader to see the challenges and turmoil of the civil rights movement from that perspective. While I am a sports figure who worked the football fields, like everyone else, I always kept my eyes on the prize of the struggle.

You can bet that the issue of race affected sport just like it did society. I want the readers to know that, in my own way, I challenged racism by proving that a black man could be a good football coach, that he could build the tenacity and determination of those in his charge as he led adolescents into manhood.

We made extraordinary statements to break stereotypes: Buchanan was the first Grambling player picked in the first round of the NFL draft in 1963. Grambling won seventeen SWAC

Championships and nine Black National Championships. The Howard Cosell documentary on Grambling in 1968 had black and white sports fans calling me a "great football coach." As we traveled across the South, we tried to use Grambling green (dollars) to quietly integrate hotels and restaurants. None of my players or coaches were seen at demonstrations in the 1960s. We made our own. The civil rights movement was helping to change the laws. Our goal was to help to change attitudes.

Before Grambling football's successes, many whites believed we (blacks) could not coach because we didn't have the necessary intelligence and leadership qualities. Our successes sent a message to all society: We could coach, we could be college presidents and CEOs of corporations.

Well, I am ready to begin now. You'll learn a lot about football on these pages. Football has been the focus of my entire professional life. Football and its people have been great to me. People have called me a "great coach." Some have called me a "great black coach." All my life, I have simply wanted to be a great American. If football helped me achieve that, then I am once again grateful for this wonderful game.

That is why I am, in the end, writing this for America. I know that probably sounds a little crazy for a man who has spent fifty-six years on an almost all-black campus to say. Before meeting me, some people expect me to be bitter or angry. They talk about the racism I experienced as a child; about being raised poor, about winning so many games and only getting one feeler from the NFL about a job there, no offer for a head job from a Division IA school (the predominantly white colleges with big football programs), being paid a fraction of what some other coaches get.

How often have I heard some young man ask, "Coach, do you hate white people for the hard road you had to go down?" I tell them, "Son, I am the luckiest man in the world. No way that all white people hate all black people. I have met too many who may have been taught to hate or thought they should. But I had the chance to meet them as equals. In the end, most of them treated me just fine, treated me like a man." Maybe it's easier to hate and to blame. It's a lot healthier to love and forgive. But you have to live by your principles.

This is what our 400-plus wins really mean. In America, we can do anything, overcome any hurdle and win—whether it be games, respect, or civil rights. It is our destiny as a people and a nation. We need victories on all three fronts. I hope my life helped move us ahead and will continue to try to do so in the years before me.

I have now completed my last season coaching on the sidelines. From here I want to go to the people of our great country and tell them the lessons I have learned from sports and life. I have tried to give back all my life. That has not stopped with my last game. The game of life is bigger and more demanding. Now that my football career has ended, I have started my new position in the game of life. I am ready.

1.

GROWING UP ONLY KNOWING
WHAT YOU KNOW

The tears were flowing down my face, which was buried in my wife Doris's, shoulder. Together when my career started fifty-six years earlier at a school with 175 students, we had to be together when it ended with more than 70,000 people in the Superdome shouting, "Eddie! Eddie! Eddie!" Someone pulled me and said, "Coach, it's President Clinton on the phone for you." I took the phone, gazing out at this huge crowd while trying to wipe away the tears. "Coach, this is President Clinton. I want to tell you how proud America is of you and what you have done in your incredible coaching career at Grambling. You are a great American."

I wish my parents had lived to see that day, a day no one could have predicted when I was born in Jackson, Louisiana, in 1919. Like his father and his granddaddy before him, my dad, Frank Robinson, was a sharecropper. My mother, Lydia Stewart, was a domestic worker. We didn't have much, but I didn't really know that for a long time.

Daddy stood 5'11" and was stocky. He was always in motion, walking fast wherever he was headed. Although he was stocky, Daddy was a really good athlete. His skin color was the same as mine. I guess I had a lot of Daddy's genes.

A real family man, he would do what he thought was right. He took in my cousins, Preston and Lester McKinley, the children of his sister who had moved to the Mississippi Delta after her baby daughter died.

Daddy was not a leader in the community but he listened and followed people he respected.

Momma was as tall as Daddy and had a medium build. I remember she always worked hard and never complained when I was little.

I was named for my Uncle Eddie on my Daddy's side. I didn't know him well when we lived in Jackson but became real close later. Uncle Eddie was a barber and a carpenter and was also a very sharp dresser. Eddie invariably looked good; even as a little boy I recognized that.

I was the only child, even the only grandchild, for a while and got special treatment. On both sides, the only grandchild!

The house where I was born is still there and was a typical house for our neighborhood with a tin roof. Boy, you had to get accustomed to that when it rained; you'd just sleep away with that sound as it beat down on the tin high above your head. The house had two big rooms and a kitchen. Lester and Preston lived in this house, which was the home of my paternal grandparents, Robert and Biner Robinson.

It was a full house with three kids, my parents, and grandparents. Some slept in beds and some slept on the floor on pallets. At that time young people just loved to sleep on the floor. We didn't know any better. The house had a fireplace and a kitchen that was actually outside. You had to walk across a little boardwalk to go from the house to the kitchen. The outhouse was just beyond the kitchen.

We always ate well because we raised food. Most of the people in our family worked. My maternal great-grandfather, Ned Davis, was pretty well off. He had a horse and a syrup mill. As a child I never understood how he lived so much better than other black folks in the area.

Some of my earliest memories were going to the mill. A long pole was hitched to the horse which just walked round and round. They would throw the sugarcane in, and it would mash it up. It was fun to watch. It looked like the horses didn't mind the work and my Great-granddaddy treated the horses well.

He would turn the horses out, let 'em run free. I loved these horses. Old Charlie and Pete were my favorites. Pete was a big gray horse who was so gentle that we could catch him eating grass. We could take a chair to him and even fall down a couple of times and he wouldn't kick us. I was four years old when I finally got up there on Pete's back. I felt like I was on top of the world. Pete would just keep on eating, and I kept on sitting out in that sun.

Sometimes he would run and I'd just ride. It was something I'll never forget. I loved that horse. I heard people say that the horse had been with Great-granddaddy a long time. Finally, he had just turned him out in the fields. No more work. We would feed him at times. But he mostly just ate the grass.

There was a pond on Great-granddaddy's land where the livestock and horses would drink. One day this old horse went in and Grandpa saw me trying to make him drink water. He laughed so loud that all the animals turned toward him. I was irritated when he said, "You're young now but the longer you live you're gonna learn you can take a horse to the water but you can't make him drink." Now I have heard that so many times since, but that day I was humiliated. Today I know I learned from it.

Most of my Momma's people worked at a sawmill. They sometimes called it a planter mill, and it was where they got the lumber ready for building.

Harry Stewart, my grandfather on my momma's side, had a farm where he and his wife, Sissy Stewart, raised cotton. I picked it some as a child, mostly fooling around. But the real pickers weren't fooling. Grandpa Harry and Grandma Sissy worked until they seemed exhausted. I could see how hard they worked, especially in the boiling sun. That image sticks with me today. When I learned more about cotton and the history of race in the South, those days on the farm got added meaning for me.

Long after I left Jackson I started to come back in the summer to pick cotton. It wasn't so much for the money. I wanted to use the hard work as a way to build up my body to get ready to play football. The other pickers couldn't understand me then. But I was using the remnants of slavery and sharecropping to my advantage instead of being used by others.

I was playing lots of football in the ninth grade. I'd go back to Jackson in August and pick cotton. It just amazed the other pickers that I could go out and pick as much cotton as anyone, but I was on a mission, trying to get in shape for football practice. I'd get out there and race them and win. I could fill those sacks and pick cotton with the best of them. I did it each summer during my years at McKinley High and also when I played for Leland College. But no one else knew what I was trying to win for. It was personal.

Moving to Baton Rouge

I was six years old when my Daddy left Jackson because he didn't want to farm any more. He was ready to break the cycle of sharecropping as the Robinson family's livelihood. He went to Baton Rouge—about twenty-eight miles from Jackson—where he eventually got a job at the Standard Oil Company. Daddy worked there until he retired. Having worked so many years with my own son as my assistant coach, I now realize I don't exactly know what Daddy did at Standard Oil. I know he left real early each day and got home real late each evening. I never went to work with him in all those years.

Something happened between Grandmother Biner and her husband, Robert. They called him "Charlie Red." He was a tough man who was always using profanity. Grandma finally realized that they just could not get along anymore.

I think it had a lot to do with me. Grandpa would beat me badly if he didn't think I was working hard enough. I don't know what he expected of a four- or five-year-old, but he beat me as if I was a grown man. I don't think Grandma could take it anymore. I think that was also part of the reason Daddy wanted to move away, although Daddy could also use a belt on me.

My Daddy sent for me as soon as he had secured living quarters. So Grandma decided to pack us up and we'd go to Baton Rouge together, without "Charlie Red," and that was it. We went there to live with Auntie Lucie Robinson and my Daddy. Auntie Lucie's place became known as the "stopping point" for everyone in the family who wanted to move to Baton Rouge. I was ready to start the first grade.

I will always remember the morning we left. Lester and Preston begged Grandma to stay in Jackson. They were crying as we walked out of the house, and we could still hear them wailing when we were a few blocks down the road.

It was a brutally hot summer day. I was young so I didn't really care. But I could see the sun pulling the energy out of Grandma's body. We were carrying the few clothes we had in bags and sacks. We must have walked almost ten miles to Ethel, Louisiana, the next little town to catch the train going to Baton Rouge. Ethel was south of Jackson. We were talking all the way. Grandma had some spirit and she kept me going. Later she confessed that she was fearful for the entire ten miles that Grandpa Bob would chase her down and bring her back.

Life really got going once we got to Baton Rouge. I lived there until I graduated from college. But at age six, with parents who never graduated from elementary school, I can't say that going to college was on my mind.

My Momma had already gone to Baton Rouge but was no longer with my Daddy. It was very difficult for me to learn that they were going to split up. I cried for hours each day and begged them to stay together. After they split up, I would visit Momma each Sunday. Momma and Daddy almost never saw each other in Baton Rouge.

Daddy had remarried a woman named Ann Floyd before I moved to Baton Rouge. She was a teacher in the McManus Kellers Quarter in Jackson. Ann was educated and had the special status in the community that was shared by other teachers. Looking back now, I realize that the black community always placed a very high value on teachers because teachers represented hope for our children to do better. She read constantly and inspired me to read something other than the sports section. Ann was very good to me, but I still wished Momma and Daddy were married.

Daddy kept me on the straight and narrow path. He used the belt on me whenever he thought I had done wrong. I always said Daddy had the fastest belt in Baton Rouge.

Daddy got us a place in the Eaton Park section of Baton Rouge so we could move out of Auntie Lucie's house and also so he could send for Lester and Preston. Eaton Park was in South Baton Rouge. It was great to be reunited with them. This was where I started to play ball. We hadn't played ball in the country, but I quickly grew to love sports.

My Momma was making $4 a week in Baton Rouge, where she continued to do domestic work for white people. While Daddy didn't have a lot of money, Momma had hardly any. However, there was always plenty to eat when I stayed with her. Momma would bring food from the homes she worked in. I ate better than anybody in my neighborhood. I've been sort of ashamed to say this. When I was there with my Momma, a lady she worked for told my Momma, "Now you haven't forgot Eddie. Did you get food for him?" Momma never forgot.

I went to two different Catholic schools in the first grade in Eaton Park. My first day at my new school was so humiliating. Of course, I didn't know anyone. You know how kids are. I remember because I was the only one walking around at that time with my ABCs pasted on a piece of cardboard. I had no other books. I remember being so embarrassed with the other guys. I hurried up and got that changed by getting Daddy to buy me all the school materials I needed. I don't think he could afford them all at once, but he sacrificed so my embarrassment would end. Of course, as a young boy I didn't recognize that it was a sacrifice, but now I see clearly how sacrificing things for me was a big part of the lives of both my Daddy and my Momma.

Mrs. Janette Rucker was the principal of the second school I attended. We were living in one of her rental houses. She handled me the same as anyone else. Mrs. Rucker had two sons, Lawrence and Wormack, who became my friends. We did everything together, including seeing my first movie for a dime and buying peanuts for a nickel.

The town was all buzzed when *King Kong* came. Everyone wanted to see it, especially Lawrence, Wormack, and me. They persuaded me to sneak into the Grand Theater to see *King Kong*. I didn't really want to do it but the peer pressure was too great. We snuck in through an exit door. An usher saw something and checked everyone's tickets. We got busted. I was so embarrassed, but I really learned something about peer pressure that day! I thought much harder about decisions in the future. I didn't want to face my daddy's disappointment.

I started second grade in the Scott Street School, which was a public school. Needless to say, it was segregated. There was never any thought then that black parents could send their children to a school with white kids. All the teachers were black; all the students were black. I knew what I knew, and had no other expectations at that age.

Meeting Coach Kraft

I went to the Scott Street School for the second and third grades. Then I went to Perkins Row from the fourth grade through the seventh grade. I finished up at McKinley High School in the 11th grade. That was the final year of high school at that time.

Third grade changed my life. It was that year that football became my obsession and I fell in love with football. The reason was the high school football coach, Julius Kraft. He was a real showman, who could talk and sell his team to anyone. He would bring the McKinley High football players in their uniforms on a Monday or a Wednesday to the Scott Street Elementary School.

We didn't have an auditorium at Scott Street so they would bring us out in front of the school. Coach Kraft sat on the steps with his guys, while we'd all be standing out there. Coach could tell so many stories about the kids. He made us laugh.

Then he would describe each of his players, telling us what all these guys could do. This one was fast, that one could catch the pass, this one could really tackle. I remember he had a back they called "Blue Heaven." Boy, he scored more touchdowns than you could count. He could really run with a ball. I never knew his name, only "Blue Heaven."

Coach Kraft yelled out to us, "Hey! Come here. This is Blue Heaven and he's gonna score when you come to see our games."

Then all the kids in school would buy a twenty-five-cent athletic card. With that and ten cents we could get into each home game. Without the card, it cost forty-five cents. Coach had us ready for these games, and I never missed one after that first encounter.

When we got to McKinley, we would also see other aspects of what education could bring: we saw a dance recital, chorus, and, of course, other sports events.

But that Julius Kraft, he was really something. He had been the center on the Bishop College team in Marshall, Texas. Kraft stood 6'4" and was a lean 190 pounds.

Julius Kraft was a chemistry teacher and a businessman who ran his own store. He directed plays with students. People paid to see them, and he always put the money back into his programs.

I dreamt about football and education everyday after the first time I saw Coach Kraft. I knew then that I wanted to coach and read everything I could get my hands on about football. When I went to the McKinley High School games, I tried to get close to the bench to hear what Coach Kraft had to say. When I was in the fifth grade, Coach Kraft leaned over to me near the bench one Saturday and said, "Boy, you ought to be a good football player someday!" That was all I needed to hear, and that lived with me until I made the team.

By the time I was in the ninth grade, I was organizing street leagues for the neighborhood kids in Baton Rouge. There was no McKinley team for two years because of the Depression and I wondered if I would ever play. During those two seasons, Piper Coleman and I went to see Southern and LSU play on Saturdays.

Piper asked me one day if I wanted to see an LSU game, and I told him that I did but I didn't have any money. Piper said he knew a way to sneak in. We didn't even realize that in those days blacks could not buy a ticket. It was a few years before LSU set up a small section for blacks. The next day we were out in front of my house and I was telling a bunch of the boys about the game.

My dad overheard me and asked me how I got into the game. I told him and that belt came off. He skinned me and told me he didn't mind me going, but he said the next time I went I was to tell him and that I ought to find some way to make some money to pay my way in.

Herman Lang, who worked at LSU, lived in our neighborhood. I went to see him and Piper and I told him what we wanted and asked if he knew any way to get in to see the games. He told us he needed some help lining the field in the morning and bringing towels and equipment out to the field in the afternoons. That's how I got to see LSU play.

When the football season ended, I worked in the cafeteria at LSU. That's where I got to meet Abe Michael. I remember him walking through the cafeteria one day in the summer when the students got up and gave him a standing ovation. That's when I decided I wanted to be a good enough player to earn that kind of respect.

In the spring before my junior year, Coach Kraft got together a little money and invited some of the guys for tryouts and told us to bring old clothes. We didn't even have a football. We were out there practicing just running and practicing tackling and blocking.

I remember all that spring Coach said he could get together only enough money to buy twenty-two shirts. That meant only 22 guys would make the team. That was serious motivation, and man, I worked hard.

Finally, when school started in the fall, we were having an assembly and Coach had all the guys interested in being on the football team come up to the front. I could see he had the box of twenty-two jerseys.

I think the first one he passed out went to James Green. He was 6'2", 210 pounds, and could run like the wind. He gave out twenty-one uniforms and there was only one left. I did not have a jersey.

Finally, Coach asked who could pass the ball? I told him I could. He asked who could punt? I had punted only one time, but I said

I could. I told him I could direct all those fast players he had. He walked by me once and again, and I was so nervous I was sweating.

Finally he threw me number 22 and that was the biggest thrill I've ever had in football. It turned out to be the beginning of more than sixty years in the game. I have had many great things happen to me, but if Coach Kraft hadn't tossed me that uniform, I might have never been involved in football.

So in the fall of my junior year I was the starting quarterback and my dream was at hand. I had made Coach Kraft's team and had a chance to be a leader right away. If I was becoming a student of the game, Coach Kraft was the real deal. He studied it and taught it at the same time. He always cut winning college plays out of the newspaper. He especially liked the systems at Tennessee and Minnesota, and their plays became ours at McKinley. No one taught blocking and tackling better than Coach. The Louisiana State (LSU) coach came to see us and called us the best blocking high school team he had ever seen. He came to study Coach Kraft's system and learn from it because LSU couldn't recruit blacks.

I tried to do whatever Coach asked, but I remember one game he called one play and I ran another for a touchdown. Coach Kraft was really mad, yelled at me, and when I put my hand out to reach for him, Coach Kraft smacked it hard. However, I always wondered if he was really happy inside that we scored that TD.

Years later when I was coaching at Grambling, McKinley came to play some high school near Grambling. I said, "Coach, what about that play? Should I have done what you said?" Coach Kraft responded. "No, I thought about that a lot of times. You made the right decision, but I was the coach so I needed to show my authority."

The years I played at McKinley were like a dream. We had two straight unbeaten seasons, and I was the quarterback in every game. It was no vacation but it was something. We practiced in street clothes because we had no practice uniforms. But we lit the place up on Saturdays for two years.

McKinley was a big school for that time with about 500 to 600 students, with more girls than boys. We knew we were lucky because there were a lot of blacks in those days who didn't even go to school. It was pretty heady stuff, but my father kept me in line at home while my best friend since the fourth grade, George Mencer, kept me straight at McKinley by making me focus on my studies. He was my seatmate. Two of us sat at each desk. George and I sat together right through high school, and he was my stabilizer and helped me to mature.

At the time of my graduation, I was not one hundred percent sure which college I would attend. Leland College was not all set because I thought I might have been going to Southern to play for Coach Arnett Mumford. He was a very fine coach who had visited McKinley when I was in the tenth grade. I wanted to be recruited by him but wasn't so I went to Southern myself for about ten days. Feeling unwanted, I left Southern and went to Leland. Coach Mumford came to Leland to ask me to come back, but it was too late. So Leland it was!

We had Class Day right before graduation from McKinley. We all dressed up. A girl named Amy thought she could see the future. Amy dressed up as a fortune-teller on Class Day. Parents loved to hear her predictions. My mother, father, and stepmother were all there. Momma said, "I'm your Mom and you're my baby no matter what this girl says!" Dad said, "Tell us what he's gonna be."

The "fortune-teller" said, "I see a big crowd . . . 101,000 in a stadium. It's the Rose Bowl. The band is playing. Eddie, there's Eddie. I see him. Listen to what he has to say after the kickoff. 'Hot peanuts, soda, get yours right here!'" Everyone fell out.

Contact with Whites

Baton Rouge was like any other southern capital city with all segregated schools, including all the teachers. Blacks only went uptown to buy clothes or to work for white people or in a hotel. My life through my high school years was almost exclusively with other blacks.

My very earliest contact with white children was through my mother when she was a domestic worker back in Jackson. The white families usually had children. I would go to work with her sometimes since I knew the people she worked for and their children.

I started working at a early age for an icehouse in Baton Rouge after becoming friends with the son of Mr. George E. Eldridge, the owner. My cousin Lester was pulling ice for this company full time. He had quit school against my Daddy's wishes. Daddy wanted him to graduate, especially after Lester's brother, Preston, had died of pneumonia.

The ice was made at night in two big tanks and put into cold storage. The guys would take it out in the morning for delivery and sales. Mr. Eldridge sometimes brought his boy, George Jr., to work. At that age we were playing football, just throwing something up and catching it. Mr. Eldridge sat around there a long time with his boy until George Jr. finally got up with us to play. When we brought him back, boy, they didn't know him. We were playing in a potato patch and they had just plowed it up. I believe his daddy gave him an earful when he got home, with him looking like a muddy mess. I don't think his momma had seen him look like that before.

After that day, I would be around with Eldridge's boy quite a bit. We talked a long time. His daddy was always afraid of fights and feared that we would fight with his boy. Then he found out that we could play and didn't fight and that the other guys would come around and they could also play and wouldn't fight. We were playing football and doing things, catching ball on the side. I could see that Mr. Eldridge was happy that I seemed like a good influence on George Jr.

I needed a job so I asked Mr. Eldridge to give me one at the ice company. I knew he would agree and that started a long career there. Maybe I should have known that if I could work for an iceman for ten years as a boy, then fifty-six years at Grambling would be a cinch. Loyalty was a quality that my Daddy talked about all the time, and it became part of my life.

They would have a box on the outside where they would have 12.5-pound, 25-pound, and 50-pound blocks of ice. The people at that time would have a back bumper on their cars. They'd come in and buy twenty-five or fifty pounds. We'd put it on the running board on the outside. They don't have that on cars now.

Well, when Mr. Eldridge gave me the job, that cut me down on the football time with George Jr. But he'd come to work with his daddy and help me do my job all day. It made me laugh; still does. Finally, he asked his daddy for a job, and boy, I never saw a man as happy as his daddy.

I was a boy when I saw this and it really struck me—the fact that George Jr. wanted a job working down where I was putting ice on the back of the bumpers. It wasn't that the work was fun, but I think he wanted to be with me.

George Jr. wanted to continue working with me when I finally got the job going out riding on the ice wagon. But somehow Mr. Eldridge didn't ever let him have that job then. I was pretty sure his father did not want him to be out in "bad neighborhoods."

From the upper elementary school years at Perkins Row, I worked with ice all summer, making $3.50 a week. It went to $4 a week, but they would hold back fifty cents so I could buy my clothes to go to school.

I worked for them every summer till my last year in college, but the jobs changed. When I was in college, Mr. Eldridge's company got the contract to put coal in the schools to get ready for the winter.

Now I had worked for him a great number of years by then, from elementary school 'til I was in college. I wanted the job with the coal deliveries because it paid more money.

I was at Leland but for some reason a guy from Southern applied and Mr. Eldridge gave the job to him. I was driving all those years, and he didn't give the job to me.

I went in and told him I wanted to talk to him, and he agreed to see me. When he called me, he asked, "What did you want to see me about?" I told him, "I called you because all my life I've been working for you. I've worked here at the box, I worked on the ice wagon, I've done about everything you have around here. I'm in college now and you have the contract to put the coal in the schools for the winter. You hired another boy from another school, another guy who's never worked here, to drive the truck. I just want you to know that I don't want to work for you this summer," Eldridge said, "What you mean?" I said, "I thought I should have been considered because I worked for you, and you've never had any trouble with me."

Well, I compromised with him when he told me, "I want to tell you something. Of course you know I don't have to do this, but I just want to tell you I made a mistake." At that age, I wasn't sure I would ever hear a white man say that. I laugh at thoughts like that now, but then white people were often disrespectful to blacks and that was almost expected. But Mr. Eldridge was always different.

Something had happened—an agency or somebody had contacted him to place this guy in a job. Eldridge had the coal driver's job and he gave it to this young man named Woodson from Chicago who was an outstanding football player at Southern University. Woodson was working for clothes to go to school and for spending money. I guess I wasn't as good a football player as he was, but I certainly could drive a truck. Mr. Eldridge told me, "You're right. You've worked for me for a great number of years and if you can give me an opportunity to get free of the commitment—it might be next summer—the job will be yours as long as you want it."

When I accepted his explanation and his offer, I got the job the next summer and kept it for the next three years.

One of the most frightening missions I've ever been on was when I was in tenth grade. My Mother was working for a family when something happened to the woman's mother. The man of the house, as usual, was working out of state. The woman had to go to her mother, and she took her son and daughter out of school. She convinced my Momma to let me drive them to Alabama from Baton Rouge.

That was when I grew up to be a man since I realized that I had this man's family in the car. I didn't think of them as a white family, just as a family. No one else had a license, and I recognized the responsibility that I had in my hands. Momma told the lady I could do it and I did! I took them there and brought them back; but when I got back, I decided I would never do it again! While it was too much responsibility for me at that age, it was very rewarding to know I did it.

Momma and Daddy

I had lived with my Daddy since I moved to Baton Rouge. He told me that after the 11th grade I could go and stay with my mother if I wanted to and I did. I also needed clothes and spending money, but mostly I wanted to help my Momma.

I felt real comfortable with my mother because I could bring my friends home and know they'd be welcomed. Ann Floyd, my stepmother, was a fine lady and she cared for me. The thing that was really important to me was that she and my Daddy got along so well. But she wasn't as flexible or as adjustable as my Mom. With my Momma, I could bring a guy home and she would bring us food from work.

I don't know how to explain it, but it was different at Momma's. There was no money or "things" like there were at Daddy's. When my friends came over, they saw that, but they liked it at Momma's. Her house was rich in other ways.

We were real happy living together, and I really worked hard to help her. I trimmed hair almost every Saturday to help my mother out and get some spending money. She knew most of the guys who came by for the cut.

I had learned to trim hair from my namesake, Uncle Eddie, while I was still in high school. Eddie had moved to Baton Rouge sometime after we did, and that is where I really got to know him. I loved the way he dressed.

Uncle Eddie acknowledged that he wasn't much with the books, but he could cut hair. He made a decent living doing this and "taught me a living" that I could use forever. He gave me the clippers and he spent time teaching me to use them. I was cutting for fifteen and twenty cents a head, less than the real barbers, so I always had customers because I was good and I saved the guys money. So I constantly had a little money for me and for Momma.

I knew I didn't want to be a hair cutter all my life, but the money sure helped then. Uncle Eddie used to laugh when he would come into the house and see me always trimming somebody's hair. He continued to kid me, "I told you I'd give you something you'd have forever."

I had many jobs. I worked at the fish market where the money was good and came quickly. The problem with that was I was going to school, which I had to cut to work a half day each Friday 'til noon.

You'd just cut class and go around there and help get the shrimp ready and put them in bags. The job was available because Friday was a busy day with people coming to buy shrimp. At twelve noon I could leave with fifty cents, which went a long way at that time, in my pocket. If I could make a dollar a day that was something!

2.

TEENAGE LOVE, RELIGION, AND RACE

I also needed the money to take out Doris, my sweetheart.

I wanted Doris to be my girl as soon as I laid my eyes on her at a party in the seventh grade! I had not come with her that night, but I took her home. At age thirteen I didn't have marriage on my mind, but I wanted her to be my girl as soon as I first saw her.

Clifford Haynes was doing some matchmaking, trying to patch up a quarrel between Doris and her boyfriend at that time. Clifford and I would become teammates at McKinley before he eventually played at Southern University.

But I didn't want any patching up that night since I just wanted Doris to be my girl. Doris was so pretty and well-dressed. Everybody liked her ways: she was funny and smart and could carry on a conversation about quite a few subjects even in the seventh grade. She told me right off that she wanted to go to college so I assured her that I did also.

I met her folks and was immediately impressed. I had actually known her Momma, Lillian Mott, when she had been my teacher at the Perkins Road School. Nobody in my family had gotten out of elementary school and her family was well-educated. Doris's Daddy was a brakesman on the Illinois Central. They were always so nice to me. Doris's mother and her aunties were teaching school in Wilson, Louisiana. Her Auntie Inez had risen to a supervisor level and traveled across the state. Doris didn't have any sisters but had an older brother, John, who was born to her Daddy and his previous wife.

In the beginning, movies were the thing. The first time I took her to one I was shocked by the cost. Both of us were used to going with an adult when it cost only ten cents. When we got to the movie, the lady told us we had to pay twenty-five cents each. "You know, you are coming to the movie with your boyfriend and so you can't come in for a dime. That is for children and you're not a child if you have a boyfriend." So I gave Doris my quarter and told her to go in. I waited for some of my boys to come, and I put the deal on them to get the rest of the money. My guys finally came by and I got in the show, too.

But I didn't want to have to go through that again. That made Friday's fish catch of fifty cents perfect for the show each week and meant I was going to miss that half-day of school. The things we do for love.

Doris's daddy didn't really let anybody else drive his car but me. That impressed me a lot that he trusted me so much. Not that I used his car much since Doris and I walked pretty much everywhere. But I guess there is no doubt that from the very beginning my relationship with her parents was just something that brought us even closer together. In addition to the movies, most of our dates were at parties at our friends' homes.

Temple Roof Gardens

As we got a little older, we were able to go to the Temple Roof Gardens. Now that was something. Over the years, we heard all the big bands there. They had people like Jimmy Lungsford, Cab

Calloway, Louis Armstrong, Count Basie, Ella Fitzgerald, the Mills Brothers, Fats Waller and all these great guys coming into Baton Rouge to play at the Temple Roof Gardens. Boy, this place would really be packed.

My girl's mother would let her go with me, and that was a big thing to take your girl to the dance and hear all of the big bands at that time. The dances would start about 9:00 P.M. and go until 1:00 A.M. I lived about five blocks from Doris, and since I didn't have a car I'd just stroll around to her house at about 8:00 P.M. and we would go with our friends. I had to work to get the money for these nights and Uncle Eddie's "trade" usually paid my way into the Gardens.

The building was interesting. It was a very large structure with a movie theater inside. The dancing took place on the upper floor, where Leland and Southern also played basketball. That's where I got caught up in basketball.

It was something. Bands from the North would come through the South and they all knew about this place, the Temple Roof Gardens. All the big ones came; everyone did. It was the place to be, and all these people would come and play. When I first started going they weren't jitterbugging but were doing ballroom dancing. I was thinking I could really dance, that I could really put some shoes on the floor. I was the star quarterback.

When they had Hoagy Carmichael playing "Stardust" for a dance number, your girl had to dance with you. Now if your girl didn't dance with you for "Stardust," she wasn't your girl anymore. So whenever "Stardust" was played, Doris was on the floor looking for me. And it was crowded, and I'd be looking for her and you'd be telling your friend, "Well, I just saw your girl over there waiting on you," and you're standing over there so we'd just find each other and dance the whole dance together. In her arms, I would dream of our life together. There was always romance in the air whenever I held her at the Gardens. We were together and that's what really mattered. There still is romance in the air, and being together still is all that matters.

Sometimes if we had enough money left, we'd get a sandwich when the dance was over. What we did after wasn't so important. But man, that dancing was really the only thing that was happening.

I didn't know nothing about drugs. Those things that they're doing now, they weren't around. If they were, we didn't know about them. I don't know what we would've done had people been smoking marijuana. Even today, I don't know how it smells. I know I need to know, but I just don't. Some of my assistant coaches had been around it enough to recognize it, but I know there wasn't any in our neighborhood when I was coming up.

I didn't go the whiskey way either because my relatives made a wager that I couldn't even drink a quart of whiskey. I was the big man so I did it and nearly died. I didn't know what I was drinking but I knew I didn't want to do that anymore so that didn't ever come up when we went to the dances.

In any case, I had to be in early on all but the dance nights, so I couldn't ever get caught up with that kind of thing. My Daddy watched me closely so I wouldn't get in trouble.

Later the dances changed—the jitterbug was coming in. Glenn Miller was playing and all these guys doing the one o'clock jump. We got all the new stuff and just looked forward to that. Mostly we went on Monday nights or Friday nights; we did more in the summer, and man, everybody went to the dance. My mother, now she really wanted to get out there. But if she went to the dance that just messed up everything.

The Temple Roof Gardens—that was our entertainment. I wish young people had a place like that now.

We wore out a lot of shoes between the dancing and walking to and from the place. Later on in college my cousin had a car that I drove, but in high school it was all walking. And we loved it.

Well, now Doris never had a chance to court anybody else. I didn't give her any breathing room. I don't know if she wanted it. I hope not 'cause we've lasted nearly sixty years as man and wife.

I always knew she was the one for me. I'm so glad that we feel about each other the way that we do. Its been good for the kids. They need to see how their Daddy treats their Momma and the Momma treats their Daddy. This is the good way to learn how marriage is supposed to be.

My mother seemed to have loved Doris the first time she saw her. Doris would come by the house and visit my momma often, even when I stayed with her on weekends but especially after I moved in with her in the eleventh grade.

At one point in high school, Doris's Mother thought that we might run into trouble and/or that we might get married. So she put Doris in a boarding school in Leland, which was about 13 miles from Baton Rouge, but that didn't really change anything. I was right there all the time, and we were still courting whenever she came home.

She was always so wonderful to me. Fortunately it was early on when she expressed how she felt about me. I always knew how I felt about her. We talked about our dreams for a family and for our careers. Doris was as sure that she wanted to teach as I was sure I wanted to coach. Her Momma's career in teaching had a big influence on her own hopes. As our high school years went by, I could see how she related to children. She was always caring about them and reaching out. It was always clear that Doris would be a perfect teacher.

Looking back now, it seems amazing that we both knew what we wanted at such an early age and that we both really followed our dreams. None of our other friends from those days at McKinley were as sure as we were. I know how lucky we are.

Her mother didn't have to worry about us getting married early because of the promise I made to myself that I would wait until I graduated from college before I would get married. I wanted to do it for my family. Doris's people also always expressed the importance of finishing college to me. But mostly my Momma wanted me to finish and so that was it.

Doris and I saw each other just about every day. We were a couple—no girls bothered me and no boys bothered Doris. Everyone knew the deal, but Doris worried about other girls chasing me since I was the captain of the football team. I knew the girls knew about us and left me alone, but she was always thinking the other girls were going to pay attention to me.

Coach Kraft threw our relationship our only curve ball on the day that he picked me for the McKinley football team. Coach got me all messed up with Doris. He gave me number 22 for my uniform, which was the number of a cheerleader! Doris didn't like that at all, because she couldn't understand why I had the same number of another girl. Now we laugh about it.

All during high school we would work hard in the summer so we would always have that picture show money and have that dance money. Those were great times we had together.

We were always busy and none of us got involved with smoking or drinking. I never drank after that challenge to my manhood. I did try to smoke but stopped after my father almost caught me. I was always looking over my shoulder for my Daddy. Once I was in the bathroom smoking and heard him closing in on me, coming to the bathroom. I ate the cigarette and was trying to fan that smoke out. I was through with that and any future cigarettes.

My Daddy was a real good influence on me this way. I lived around people and I saw a lot of people drinking but it just never appealed to me. My Daddy didn't drink and my Daddy didn't smoke. It does mean something to have that kind of example. When you come into the world, your parents need to set an example for you to follow. In high school I sometimes just feared his reaction if he found out I had done something he didn't like. Now

I see he wasn't trying to strike fear in my heart but to set an example I could live by. My Daddy taught me so many things.

We Got Religion!

Same thing with your folks going to church. I was a great church-goer, who didn't have to be convinced to go to church. Quite a few of my friends liked to hear the preachers preach and we tried to imitate them. We had a preacher named Reverend Hall at the Newark Baptist Church in Baton Rouge. He had a medium build, but his voice was powerful and he made an ordinary church extraordinary.

He was the first man I had known who could preach. It was the same each week: The church was full when Reverend Hall started but he would preach so powerfully that it emptied out and then filled up again before he was done. People loved him even when he talked too long.

We had a real bad man in Baton Rouge who was a prizefighter. Even his name was rough: Bully Gaiter. He ran the gambling house, and nobody would want to mess with this guy who was known to cut and shoot people. His own face was scarred. His bowed legs looked like they couldn't carry him, but they did. He was one tough man!

I went to church with my grandmother in those days. One Sunday I turned around and saw Bully in the back of the church, looking hard and mean. But what gave Reverend Hall such great stature with me was he made Bully Gaiter cry with his sermon that day. Man, he was preaching about living the just and good life while Bully was standing in the back of the church. I couldn't believe it when I realized Bully was crying, holding a handkerchief out to wipe away the tears. The reverend got to Bully. I told my grandmother, "Momma, look, Bully is crying." She said, "Well, yeah?" as if she didn't get it. I said, "You don't understand Momma, Bully is the toughest guy on the block, but Reverend Hall got Bully crying." Man, she started to cry, thinking that Bully's soul had been saved. I'll tell you, it was really something.

It was the same each Sunday. The church would be packed because people wanted to hear him preach. Every time he shouted, a sister would shout back and stretch out—passed out cold. It would take about three people to carry her out. Each Sunday he'd shout enough that about twenty or thirty sisters went down. The church was eventually empty because three or four carried each one out. There was nobody in church but the benches after they'd taken them out. The men would revive the sisters, walk them around the church, and bring them back in. The church filled back up as they all returned. And Reverend Hall, he'd keep going no matter what was happening.

I remember telling people that he could preach the church empty. Boy, we would really follow those guys who could preach, and Reverend Hall was something else. I will always remember him.

When Reverend Hall moved from Newark Baptist, I joined new St. John's Baptist with my grandmother. St. John's was Reverend Billups's church.

When I was in the fifth grade, a lot of the guys—someone counted 103—started hanging on the corner. We didn't have a playground so we'd just stand around. We'd hang around until that sun was about to go down. We weren't doing anything bad, but nobody liked us being there. Reverend Billups did something about it. There was a Chevrolet dealer in Baton Rouge who promised Reverend that if he baptized the 103 guys and cleaned out the corner, he would give him a car. He did and they really gave him a car. But it wasn't a simple thing. How he did it came up twenty years later when Reverend Billups visited me at Grambling.

We were all trying to get baptized—we all wanted to get religion. You had to get an "experience with God" and they would take you into church. But the time was running out, so we'd slip off from each other and pray. When you felt the spirit, you'd get up to tell everyone in church of the experience that made you know you got religion. It's what they called "determination."

Piper Coleman was my buddy. Piper is deceased now. Back then, we were lucky to have one Sunday shirt apiece. He thought this particular Sunday was going to be his day for getting into the church. But his shirt wasn't ready on Thursday night so he told his momma to get his shirt ready before Sunday because he'd have religion and he was going to need to wear the shirt. His momma was telling him, "You don't know if you're going to get it." Well, anyway we were trying hard to get it, but she was right; we never really knew.

Now it looked like the time was going to run out on me. Reverend already had ninety converts, and I wasn't among them yet. I was trying to see if I could have just dreamed anything that I could have gotten up in church like these other kids had done. But I stopped dreaming and I couldn't get anything to tell them.

They could sing these songs in church, "Please don't let this harvest pass," and Reverend would stand up and say, "Don't let me leave you; come on, come on up here." Boy, I'd just be crying when he said, "You got to believe."

So I said I just want to live a Christian life and be a good person. Reverend, who was young himself, said the Lord accepted me. As soon as it happened, they would take you and tie a white bandage around your arm. That meant you were a new convert.

Boy, when I got mine I stood over there with those other guys. One of them was Howard and he had been converted right before me. He could whip any of us because he was so physical. Howard was really built and must have weighed about 210 pounds, and we all were around 130. He looked like he had been eating and we hadn't been. Then Reverend went behind me, as he did with all new converts, and asked me to tell the sisters and brothers why I had religion. When I told them, my arm shot up. I was not real happy standing there.

Next was Abner Armstrong, who lived next door to me. As Abner walked up, he said, "Church, I want to tell you all I got it, and I want to let you know." One sister said, "Tell it, brother."

Howard was a funny guy who always sat right down in front of the person who was professing to the congregation. He was making faces at you while you were trying to tell the church. The congregation couldn't see him making faces so you're trying to tell the church you got it, trying to profess your religion, and keep a straight face.

I was out there trying to look like a young angel, as if I had never been into anything. When Armstrong got up, Howard was right in front of him. Abner began, "I just wanna tell you why I know I got it." Then he began his story with his chance to be in the fold: "Tonight, when I was coming to church, I walked out of my house and turned and came up there in the street."

Well, Howard was repeating everything that he was saying, but he was making it funny and poor Abner was trying to keep from laughing. I had to put my hand over my mouth. Howard said quietly, "You had to turn left because if you turned right you couldn't have made it to the church." This was the undertone that day. Five of us had professed, and we were standing up there trying to keep from laughing. Armstrong went on that he "saw God when he passed Julia Street and crossed over Railroad Avenue." Howard mumbled, "You couldn't have passed over it; you had to have passed under it." Now all of this was going on in church while this boy was professing.

Howard was tearing everybody up. Armstrong finally went on, "Well, I got to South Boulevard and I turned right." Howard jumped in again with, "You couldn't turn left 'cause if you'd turned left you would have gone over the East Boulevard." By then some of the elders heard Howard and started to laugh. Then everyone got real quiet.

Armstrong kept going. "After I turned down South Boulevard, I crossed the railroad track." Howard couldn't let it pass saying, "You had to go across it because you couldn't go under it." I was trying to fight this laugh, but I couldn't keep it in. You can't imagine how funny this was for us at that age.

By Abner's account, after the railroad track he was about a block away from the church. He said he knew he got religion because he "saw the lights" as he got near the corner where he would turn to be on the street where the church was located.

A sister said, "You know those were automobile lights," loud enough so that everybody was laughing. But Abner Armstrong got his religion that day since it wasn't as much about an epiphany as it was about getting up and proclaiming that you believed. Like the rest of us, Abner believed. I always wondered what the preacher thought or if he was so holy he didn't even hear anyone but Armstrong.

Reverend Billups came to Grambling about twenty years later to our church there. Doris and I still go to the same church. He was preaching when he suddenly told the congregation, "I'm going to ask a question . . . nobody will understand what I'm talking about but one person . . . Coach Robinson, do you think those automobile lights coming around that corner for Armstrong were a sign from God?"

I had my answer. Reverend tore me up even more than Howard.

The Reverend loved sports but the women in the church never let him play. I always taunted him, mainly so the women would give in, but they never did. I still don't know why they wouldn't let him play.

I was a pretty good pitcher. Reverend would joke that he would kill my sinker and curve. I'd say, "Come on," but the sisters didn't want the preacher to play baseball. I taunted him to get the bat. He wanted so much to show that he could really hit the ball, that there was another side to the preacher man.

James Johnson, the fastest kid on the block, was at the church picnic the last time I challenged Reverend Billups. As a high school football player, no one could catch Johnson once he caught the ball, and six points were ours almost automatically.

James had this speech impediment. That morning we were having a Sunday school lesson about how strong Samson was. I don't know if I'm really correct about this but I think Samson took the jawbone of a jackass and killed a lion. Our teacher, Miss Rose, was just going off with a great lesson on what Samson had done and what he could do. We were all excited to learn this, especially the boys. Then the teacher noticed that James had been totally quiet during the discussion. She asked James, "Is anything wrong with you?"

James answered, "No ma'am, there is nothing wrong with me," and so she went on to talk more about Samson and all he did. When she asked the class what we thought about all of this, James jumped in with, "You are a-a-a-a-asking me wha-wha-what I th-th-think about Samson. I believe he's all right, but I want to tell you one thing. You said he did all that but he ain't so hot. If you think he's so-ss-so good, put him in th-th-th-the ring with Joe Louis. Joe would beat his damn brains out."

Man, we lived through high school with great times. Just about all these guys went to college—either to Southern or Leland. Many had outstanding professional careers. But we must have seemed a little bit crazy to the adults, especially the sisters at the church.

Joe Louis

But James Johnson, as funny as the incident was, didn't bring up Joe Louis out of the thin air. He was a real hero. Every Black person I knew followed his every move. Joe Louis was the star in our constellation. He belonged to us, showed us we could lead the world.

Heck, as a teenager, I wanted to be a boxer myself. I was secretly training to do this until I got caught by my father and was told I could not fight anymore. I didn't want my father's anger, which would sting more than any boxer's punch.

I knew Joe Louis built his momma a house. Man, that made me want to be a boxer real bad because I wanted to build a house for both my Momma and my Daddy. I walked around town with boxing gloves strung around my neck and practiced at the service station on 13th Street. It was a big hangout. I watched the newsreels of Joe Louis over and over to pick up his moves.

My boxing skills paid off in one of my proudest moments with my Dad. There was a street fighter in town, a real bully who insulted my Dad to get me mad. It worked but he didn't know I could fight and I beat him badly. My father found out about it. We were walking home together one afternoon and didn't say much to each other during the three-block walk. Then he said quietly, "Well, you beat him, huh?" I said, "I've been boxing and he didn't know." It was a great day for me. My father always looked at me differently after that. My stepmother later told me that Daddy bragged about my fighting for his honor.

My Daddy was so special to me. Even though he was tough on me and beat me whenever I got out of line, I know I wouldn't be who I am today if he didn't have a disciplined home for me to grow up in. By today's standards, it seems like the wrong way, but I will always be thankful for his ways.

He always wanted to teach me a lesson with each beating. That was the worst part. He would hit me a few times, then stop and ask me if I understood why he was hitting me. I just wanted him to whip me and get it over with. I didn't want any conversations. Now I realize the conversations were what drove the point home.

Like all black people, Daddy and I had Joe Louis in common. I know a lot of white people also liked Joe Louis, especially after he beat the German boxer, Max Schmelling. That was the very first time I had ever heard a black person called an "American." The announcer said, "The American is entering the ring." That moment still lives with me today. I waited another three decades before I was called an "American" for the first time. I had to leave the country for that to happen, just like Joe Louis. For me, I was called an American when we were in Tokyo to play. White people are often called "great Americans." If you are black, it seemed to me at the time like you had to leave the country to be called what you always had been.

Black people loved Joe Louis because he always said the right thing and was our role model. He would have been great in any business or profession, but he *was* a boxer. Joe Louis sold more radios and newspapers in the black community than any other person. I bet there wasn't a black family in America that didn't buy a radio sometime during his career.

His fight nights were big social events in the black community. Even if we had radios in our houses, many of my friends gathered somewhere to listen. In the early days, the fights were not broadcast live but were read line-by-line.

They were intense moments. I still have a scar on my hand from the time he lost to Max Schmelling. I was cranking up a Model-T Ford and smacked my hand because I was thinking about the fight and not paying attention to what I was doing. It was a good thing for the rest of my body that he almost always won. Plain and simple: I loved Joe Louis. He was my hero!

Race Relations in Baton Rouge

The different reactions of white and black America to Joe Louis began to open my eyes since I surely had not thought much of the issue of race at that time. It's almost like it's hard to miss what you never had. We had come up with segregation all our lives, and nobody had ever told us it was wrong. We accepted it and you just grew up with the thing. That was what it was like and we stayed where we were supposed to stay.

But other things happened besides Joe Louis to make me think about race. I would question myself about why would they put a house where the ladies were prostitutes in the black neighborhood. Of course, the whites did it so nobody would know what was going on. But we knew because it was right there in front of us.

They moved "the house" right into our neighborhood. Why would you have a house there and not in the other part of the city where the whites lived? White men would come to this particular house. I believed they had some connection with the city police, who didn't bother the white men and white women. In an all-black neighborhood, no blacks dared go near this place except to clean it. Like all the public officials, the police were all white. That was Baton Rouge at that time and these were just some of the facts that you just accepted.

I didn't ever see it too much, but the police had a reputation for manhandling black people. However, something happened to me as a young man that stays with me even now. I was scared.

It happened when I was working on the ice wagon on North Street in Baton Rouge. We would deliver the ice to people's homes, usually dropping it at the back door after they told us how many pounds of ice they wanted. Some had standing orders of twenty-five pounds per day and would leave the back door open, for no one was afraid of robbery back then. If no one was home, we would just go in and put the ice in the icebox. Of course, there were no refrigerators at that time. Customers bought tickets, which were discounted if they bought a book of them. We'd just take the right number of tickets and go on.

A lady called the icehouse to report that her husband's watch was missing after I made a delivery. She said it was left either on or near the icebox on that particular day.

Normally, we'd finish our deliveries and leave the white neighborhood about five o'clock. Then we'd come back to the icehouse to make sure we'd covered our territory. When I got back on that day, a police officer was there in his car, told me to "come here," and asked me where the watch was. I said, "What watch?" The officer said an "old watch up on Long Street."

I told him, "I don't know about any watch," and he told me he didn't believe me. Mr. Eldridge, my boss, told the officer, "I don't believe he has the watch because he's been working 'round here for years . . . we never had any person accuse him of doing anything like that."

The officer insisted on taking me uptown by the house to face the lady so she'd be sure I was the right person.

I had never been in jail but I had heard from the guys that if they got you up there to the police station, most times people would admit to a crime, even if they didn't do it. Now I couldn't prove it because I had never been up there, but I had heard about it enough.

Mr. Eldridge kept telling the officer that I didn't have the watch, but the policeman insisted that he take me to headquarters. So I got in the car with him, going to headquarters.

I was scared because of the reputation of the police with black folks. Yes, sir, I was very scared. I had heard a whole lot of things and didn't want to end up at the station or they might have beaten something out of me that wasn't there. I told him I didn't even know the color of the watch and I didn't have any reason for taking a watch. He wasn't listening but did go by the woman's house on Long Street on the way to the police station. What was she going to say? I had also heard that some white people lie to the police to get black folks in trouble. I felt I was in deep trouble and she was going to hurt me even more.

The woman came out and told the officer that her husband had called back when he remembered where he had put the watch. I took a deep breath and turned to the officer, hoping that would be the end. It was, but it made me think about all the guys who were taken to headquarters. I continued to hear the talk about the police but always remained grateful that I didn't experience it myself.

You'd never know where the police would be or when they would show up, but we did know we didn't want to be around when they came. We'd be playing on the street corner. Hey, we were kids and sometimes made too much noise. A guy would tell a joke and we'd laugh. Sooner or later the police would be coming and, boy, you would have to pick up and run. They could clean the corner up real quick. When they got near the corner, they'd turn on the sirens and, boy, I guess James Johnson would have some competition in the hundred-yard dash. Maybe the police were trying to make us good athletes. They gave us plenty of practice on the streets.

My Daddy was always aware of all of this. He always told me what could happen and what he didn't want to happen to me. While he was sure to tell me the darkest side of race relations, my Daddy said other things about race that also made sense, especially as I grew older. He knew that many blacks had come to expect whites to treat them badly—an insult, a slight, or something that would hurt and sting long after the white person had passed by. He believed that sometimes the expectation gave them the result that they thought would come. In other words, a white individual might see a black person looking at them in a certain way and react with a behavior that might not have happened otherwise.

Daddy always told me to treat anyone, no matter what they looked like, the way that you want him to treat you. That was pretty simple, but it really is true and works most of the time.

If he doesn't react to that, Daddy said, "Don't you get mad the first time, Eddie. You keep working at it. You got to work at it. Someday, you'll get to be 'the man,' Eddie. Then you'll be in a position of power. So treat him the same way you want him to treat you so when you get in power you'll know how to treat folks well."

Daddy would tell me, "Don't ever take advantage of anyone. It's wrong and it's not going to make life better. You can't tell a guy how he should treat you, but if you keep treating him well, sooner or later he will get it."

He preached patience to me because he knew how easy it would be to lose that patience. It is always easier to get mad and act out against someone who doesn't treat you right. After all these years, I now know how much more rewarding it is to see people change because you were good to them. Acting out might give you a moment's satisfaction, but then it's over. Reaching into someone's heart, that will stay with you until your last breath.

My Daddy was a smart man, smarter than many I have met who had a Ph.D. or law degrees. He knew we were all going to have to live together in America. Daddy knew that if we were going to continue to be the strongest and most powerful nation in the world, somehow we were going to have to come together and understand each other.

While he educated me on such things, I certainly noticed on my own things like the house of prostitution and how the police treated blacks. Those things had been happening ever since I had been in the world, and I just accepted it. I only questioned it when I later read about race in school, where I started finding out more.

I read the most about it at Leland College during my years there.

Leland didn't have many students—maybe 3,000. My childhood friend, George Menzer, was at Leland. We now had single seats for the first time after sitting together in double seats for so long in grade school and at McKinley. He was a receiver and I was a quarterback, both at McKinley and at Leland. We lived in the same neighborhood in Baton Rouge. It was a natural friendship.

We had a great time at Leland, where George continued to be a stabilizer for me. I wasn't a bad person but I was just maybe a little louder than he was and I just made some wise remarks that he didn't make. We talked about so many things and I learned a lot from his thinking. We remained close friends and teammates throughout high school and college. We majored in the same field, English, at Leland. Then George went into the army as a second lieutenant. That's when we were separated for the first time since fourth grade.

When I was at Leland I was fortunate enough that a cousin of mine let me use his car to drive from Leland about twelve miles to Baton Rouge. A couple of buddies rode with me and they paid me a dollar a week. That took care of the gas until I got out of college. I would go to my Mom's and cut hair each weekend to help with expenses.

Coach Ruben Turner may not have been as famous as Southern's Coach Mumford but he taught me plenty about football. Coach Turner knew I wanted to be a coach, so he told me I had to be a student of the game. He began preaching about clipping articles from the newspaper and going to coaching clinics every year. He really hit hard on going to the clinics. I knew then that if I did become a coach that I would seek out the coaching clinics as often as possible.

Coach Kraft taught me how to play football, while Coach Turner taught me to learn about football by studying the game. By the time I graduated from Leland, I thought I had two degrees.

Race and Economics: Looking Back at Ned Davis

In 1985, we were being honored in Baton Rouge, Louisiana, for breaking Bear Bryant's record for most wins by a college football coach. It was just such a big surprise that they would do this. I never had problems with the people of Baton Rouge and I always went back to see my family, especially my grandparents on my Momma's side, while I was coaching. Right before the salute to me that night we were just talking with some of the people who were going to be attending. I told them I've just got one question I wanted to ask: How was my great-grandfather, Ned Davis, able to have a syrup and sugar mill at that time when no other black man in the community had anything like it?

There was an elderly white gentleman in the crowd. He said, "Eddie, now that's easy to answer about Ned Davis."

I said, "Sir, I sure hope you would answer it for me because he has land up there now that the whole family is still living on. It's a big piece of land for the other great-grandchildren to live on. Since he left, nobody has accumulated that much land."

He said, "Your great-grandfather had a trade as a well borer, and we all had to have water. Ned Davis wanted the syrup mill. So it was just a fair exchange to let him have the mill and then he got the water for us. It was just that simple." Sometimes economics overruled race.

3.

THE EARLY YEARS AT GRAMBLING

The Wedding

Doris and I decided to slip off and get married without telling anyone. We were shy about our intentions, partially because of our circumstances.

Here we were just out of school. Doris had tried to work for the railroad but didn't get the job. I was working in a feed mill for twenty-five cents an hour and knew I needed another job. After many years together, Doris's parents had separated just about the time we graduated. Suddenly we were both from broken homes, yet we were convinced that we had what it would take to be happily married.

We thought this should be a private moment between the two of us. We knew we were going to get married ever since the beginning of high school, yet we had fulfilled our mutual promises to each other to finish college first. We knew the war was coming and that America would soon be involved. Doris had always talked about a June wedding and it was June. We really didn't care about money and felt that our love was all we needed. It was pretty much all we had to work with in June of 1941. Common sense prevailed and we realized that we needed to tell our families. They were just too important in our lives. So we told our parents and got their blessings.

On June 24, 1941, we walked to the ferry with a friend who would be our witness, went across the river, and found a preacher in Port Allen, where we got married. As we returned on the ferry, we talked about the future. We talked about starting our own family, how many children we might have and when we would have the first one. We talked about being able to take good care of them and making sure they got all the love they needed from both of us. We talked about taking care of our own parents and about returning all the love and support they had given to us throughout our lifetimes. We knew we would live near them. Doris was every bit as close to her mother and father as I was.

She emphasized that she wanted to teach. Trying to get a job with the railroad was an attempt to fill a gap just like my own job at the feed mill was, hopefully, a holding pattern on my way to a coaching job. We both knew that segregation limited our opportunities. If Doris was going to get a teaching job, it would have to be in an all-black school. I knew I was limited to a black high school or college job myself and that I would only be able to coach against other black schools. The main thing was we wanted to be educators.

Back home as Mr. and Mrs. Robinson, we didn't tell many people at first and most of our friends didn't know our plans. After we got married, some found out.

The Feed Mill

When I had finished college I took a job working at the Kamback and Burkett Feed Mill. That was one of the toughest jobs I had ever had because it was August and the heat was brutal.

The weevils would be crawling everywhere. Man, they were disgusting enough to look at, but when I put a sack of corn on my shoulder, the weevils would jump on me. I could feel their little legs crawling on my arms and neck. Sooner or later, some managed to get under my shirt and all over my back and shoulders. As they mixed with my own sweat, they became even slimier than they were. They were sickening and the work itself was pure hard labor, as those sacks were heavy.

I had gone to this feed mill because I was getting married and needed a job. I had to work, but as a new college grad this job was not what I had thought of when I marched at commencement a few months earlier.

This feed mill was right in front of my house, and I watched when these eighteen-wheelers came to the mill, full of corn. All the old guys took the day off when they saw the trucks pull up because they knew how hard the next few days would be. That was my opening to make some money. When I got that job at that feed mill it didn't matter if they had ten trucks of corn because I needed the work. That was how it was at that time in Baton Rouge.

I worked at the feed mill from the time I graduated until I got a call about the job at Grambling. The way that happened was that Doris was at Grambling at a workshop while I was working at the mill. Mrs. Grace Jackson, who was Doris's aunt, called Doris's mamma to get the message to me about the open job at Grambling. To this day I remain in Aunt Grace's debt.

President Jones Rescues Me from the Weevils

Mrs. Jackson had met President Ralph Waldo Emerson Jones, who told her he remembered me because I had played at Grambling that year when Leland fought hard but came away with only a 0–0 tie. We had whipped Grambling pretty good at Leland the year before.

I finally got the message from Doris, and I called the president about an interview.

He told me that I didn't have to travel to Grambling because he was coming to Baton Rouge for a board meeting. President Jones told me he lived in Scotlandville. He didn't know that his sister, Arthesta, who was around our age, was one of our best friends. We went to the dances together.

I looked up a little history of Grambling football before the interview. President Jones was the coach himself from 1926–32. Then there were three coaches in the next three years: Ira Smith, Joe Williams, and Osiah Johnson. Finally, Emory Hines was there from 1935–40. Hines had moved on to Southern University as an assistant line coach and baseball coach. He had played at Southern for their head coach, Mr. Mumford.

Located in a lush, hilly part of the state, Grambling is between Shreveport and Monroe. The town, which now has about 10,000 people, grew up primarily to accommodate the university. It is a virtual metropolis now compared to when I took the job in 1941.

The school had opened in August of 1904. A group of farmers and church leaders in Grambling contacted Booker T. Washington at Tuskegee to request a recommendation for president. Grambling had been a predominantly black farming community settled in the Era of Reconstruction by former slaves and their children. Dr. Washington nominated Charles P. Adams to lead the school. Charles Adams was our first president and led Grambling until Ralph Waldo Emerson Jones became our second president.

The campus has never been one of our best recruiting enticements. Many outsiders call it drab, with a series of two- and three-story brick buildings. There are a few grocery stores, cafés, and laundromats around the campus that serve the students. In any given month of the year, the grass will probably be more brown than green. In 1941, Doris and I would never have guessed we would spend the rest of our lives here.

When President Jones came to Baton Rouge I got dressed up for the interview. The dress of those times was what we called "drapes" or "zoot suits." I was ready with my drapes and the long coat.

When I got to his house, I took that long coat off, folded it over my arm, and went in to talk to him. I told him how grateful I was to get the chance to coach at Grambling. Dr. Jones shot back that he hadn't made me an offer and said straight-up that he didn't think I could lead the football team to win. The interview was going nowhere fast and I didn't know what to do, so I tried to get off the subject and start a more casual conversation.

I had seen President Jones play baseball—he was a pretty good pitcher. So we began to talk about baseball and he became more relaxed. We talked about our favorite players in the Negro Leagues and compared who we each had seen play.

Sometimes I think that if it had not been for baseball, I may not have gotten the job. He asked me if I liked to play baseball, and I answered, "Yes, sir." I loved the game but before we got married Doris didn't because I would leave her to play baseball on Sundays. We would go to Appaluchas and all these other places. By the time we'd get back at eleven or twelve midnight, it would be too late to come calling on Doris. From her point of view it was a lost day. I said if he wasn't coming to town I would have been with my baseball team, since it was Sunday. Then he got excited. "You play baseball?" I told him, "Sure I play baseball."

I was starting to feel more confident with the president when, out of the blue, he challenged me with, "I'll strike you out," and I responded that I would knock his best pitch out of the park. I hadn't bothered to think of where we could find a park.

Man, the discussion got so heated. When I look back now I

can't believe how this went: This was an interview for a job I would love which would get me away from those weevils. I cannot believe I acted like I did, but suddenly we were on our way to a field with the necessary baseball paraphernalia.

Finally, I realized that I was trying to get the job, and he had the job to give. So I switched over when I thought I might hit his pitching hard. I didn't know if I could hit him, but I didn't want to take any chances.

President Jones hired me after telling me one more time that he was still going to strike me out. It seemed like an unusual way to hire someone, but I think Dr. Jones thought it was a good way to see my character.

I later found out that he had already spent a lot of time on my case, and I was really impressed when I learned how he'd gotten information on me before the interview. Dr. Jones went into the streets: He went to the people who knew me, the people in the barbershop and everywhere he could think of to ask about me. He asked older people and younger ones to get it from both sides. He spent hours in the barbershop, asking them what kind of person I was. He was really on his job.

As we were parting, I told him what kind of team I was going to get him and how we were going to have a great program. Then I asked him if he would send me to the coaching school at Northwestern University. If I was going to coach, it was about time to go to a coaching school. Coach Turner from Leland was willing to drive me to the school if I could take the train to Chicago. He would pick me up in Chicago and then take me to Evanston, where Northwestern is located. The president gave me the green light to go.

I had never thought about Grambling—that's probably about the last place that I thought that I might have been coaching until the job came open. But when it came open, I was really excited because I knew how much I wanted to coach. And none of the people I played with at Leland got college coaching jobs right after school, so I also knew how fortunate I was.

I was married to the woman I loved, had a college degree, a college head coaching job, and was off to coaching school. I knew that day that America was a great place. I never forgot that or doubted it since then. And no more weevils.

Doris was so happy when I told her the news. Our lives were coming together. It was the beginning of another journey, but to get to life's journey I had to go through Chicago. For a boy from rural Louisiana, that seemed pretty awesome. I had never been far away from home myself and was a bit intimidated by my images of the big-city life, but nothing was going to hold me back.

Small-Town Boy Goes to Chicago

I got my money and put it in my pocket. Then I pulled my pocket out through my open fly and wrapped some rubber bands around that money. That way when I put my hand in my pocket it would stop before I could feel the money. I did that because I figured people were so bad in Chicago and here I was, a small-town boy. I had to hide my money, as if I was carrying a fortune in my pocket. I guess to me the $120 or so that I had in 1941 was a fortune.

I waited for the train outside of a rickety wooden building that we called our railroad station. There was no ticket window or stationmaster. The sign read GRAMBLING, LA. And the train never stopped unless you flagged it down to make it stop for you. In 1941, that was all we needed in Grambling. That would change for the better as the university grew and later for the worse after federal cutbacks.

It was a long way to Chicago. I slept halfway through the night and woke up early thinking about some things. When I popped my hand in my pocket. I couldn't feel my money. I jumped up screaming, "I've been robbed; I've been robbed."

I was looking and running around until I realized that the rubber band was keeping my hand from going all the way in that pocket and that the money was down there. This small-town boy felt even smaller and was so embarrassed, but I never would let on why because I did not want to invite someone to really take the money.

Coach Turner met me at Illinois Central Station and took me out to Evanston, where he was staying at the YMCA. We went straight to the clinic where they had Fritz Crisler, who was the coach at Michigan; Carl Slavley, who coached at Cornell; and other great coaches who were teaching there. I was in awe of these legends, and I was ready to learn from them.

The Clinics: Meeting White Coaches for the First Time

Most of the people at the clinics at Northwestern were white. Sometimes there might have been two or three, rarely four or five blacks but never a whole lot. This was the first time I was in a situation where I was with whites as an equal. This thought came to me for the first time early in my final season as a coach. I found myself reflecting a lot on things like this in my last season. So the Northwestern clinic was the first place I had gone like that, but it never fazed me that I had not been with whites as equals before because it was the way it was. I had always been able to get along with people, but it seems strange now to realize that getting along with people up to his point in my life meant getting along with other blacks. We had no alternatives.

Jackie Robinson: Early Groundbreaking

One of my earliest memories of the clinics was from my first year at Northwestern. There were, of course, many teaching seminars. But part of the time we watched the coaches prepare for a benefit game that was between an NFL all-star team and a team of college all-stars sponsored by the *Chicago Tribune*. I thought about it so often in 1997 as I watched the tributes to Jackie Robinson in the 50th anniversary year of his breaking baseball's color barrier. I wish the love America seems to have for Jackie now was clearer to him while he was still with us, but that's often the way it is with great people.

Many people forget that baseball was probably the sport that he excelled in least. He was also a great basketball and football player in college. When I first saw him, Jackie was a football college all-star at UCLA, and I was about to start my first year as a coach at Grambling.

Of course we noticed each other at that game in Chicago. It would have been hard not to see each other since I was one of two black coaches at the clinics that year, and the predominantly white schools had hardly any black players in 1941. Who would have thought that this football player would go on to help change a nation? Again, this was my first time in mixed company in which I was being respected by whites. Not knowing much about Jackie's youth, I thought UCLA might have been the same for him. No way either of us were thinking of America in the bigger picture in 1941. At least I know I wasn't; we were just two guys named Robinson. It sure is fun to think about it all these years later.

Jackie had a reputation that he would always do what he thought was right. As far as I knew in 1941, that meant in sports. Might have been what everyone meant then. But there's that sports-and-society relation again that I just didn't see then. The coach of the college team was Fritz Crisler, who had a tough disposition with players: If you didn't follow his line, you weren't going to play much.

The coaches at the clinics attended all the practices. As a black man, I waited anxiously to see if Jackie and Coach Crisler would make a good team or have fireworks between them. We didn't have to wait very long as we were standing out there watching the practice.

The college guys were working on punt returns, and Jackie caught the ball on the ten. The defensive team was bearing down on him and Jackie took the ball back into the end zone. He burst out of the end zone, looking for a hole or a key block. There weren't any and he made it to the eight-yard line.

The coach was furious and was ranting and screaming at Jackie. No coach had ever talked to me like that; I don't know what I would have done. He shouted at Jackie, "You don't ever do anything like that. Don't ever back up into the end zone. Don't try to do that!" I don't know if this had anything to do with a white coach handling a black athlete for the first time. I never talked to Jackie about it, but later I heard him talking about things like this and wondered what was on his mind that day in Chicago. As he frequently did, Jackie Robinson gave part of his answer on the field in the next sequence.

But before that Coach Crisler was not ready to let go. He was snorting and his whole body was just shaking since there was no, "Yes sir, Coach," response from Jackie. He turned to the coaches on the sideline and railed, "The more you understand this game, the more you learn that there're just some people who can do some things and other people can't."

I don't know how the other coaches reacted. I wasn't the head coach. I was a student there learning to be a head coach. My turn was coming, and I was learning something right then and there. As Coach Crisler may have stereotyped Jackie Robinson, I knew I would work hard from that day so I would not stereotype anyone.

I tell you, some of the things he was saying about Jackie were rough, too rough. And I knew the guy that Coach Crisler was talking about could carry it all the way out of the end zone for a touchdown. I looked hard at both, wondering what would happened next. Would this take the spirit out of the player and give the coach the total power he seemed to need? Or would it serve to enrage the player? If it did that, would it elevate his game or destroy it?

Fritz Crisler walked away and was working with another player at the 50-yard line when they kicked that ball again. Jackie Robinson got the opportunity to respond when he caught the ball right around the two. I glanced up to see if Coach Crisler was watching. He had moved onto the field to get a better view of the results of his lesson. Now Jackie had the ball. There was no hesitation as he retreated back into the end zone.

I looked back to the 50-yard line where Coach Crisler's whole body was shaking as he watched Jackie run across the back of the end zone, pursued heavily by a defensive team that the coach was no doubt rooting for at that moment. If they nailed Jackie for a safety, Fritz Crisler's tirade would have been punctuated by an exclamation point.

But there was going to be a different mark made on that play and my whole coaching career by my fellow namesake. Jackie moved toward the goal line seemingly going straight at the defense, then cut away with such speed that by the time he passed the 10-yard line there was no doubt he was going the full ninety yards left for the score.

By the time he crossed the 20, I looked up the field. Coach Crisler was quiet. His body had stopped shaking, and he was well off the playing surface. To this day, I don't know if he was elated or humiliated by that 100-yard, electrifying run. This was only the first ground that I saw Jackie Robinson break.

Pappy Waldorf: A Coaching Role Model

Later that day I had the chance to talk to Linn "Pappy" Waldorf, who was the coach at Northwestern. He was another coach teaching at the clinic. I told him that I liked Coach Crisler and was learning from him, but that his "my way or the highway" attitude bothered me.

Pappy told me that what had happened between Coach Crisler and Jackie was "the kind of thing you need to keep in mind. All of those ball players are not the same and you see that now. There are more ways to skin a cat. One boy might do it one way; the next one might do it differently. The question is, does he get the job done? So, as a coach, you need to decide, do you want the six points or don't you want them?" I told Pappy I wanted them, and he told me I was ready to go coach.

Pappy was one heck of a good coach and I liked him a lot. It was getting near time for me to leave Illinois, so I went to say good-bye to him two hours before my train for Louisiana was leaving. I'll always remember what he told me—it still lives with me today. When I got there he was putting some of the things into the lockers and he didn't quite hear me when I said, "Hey, how are you doing, Coach Waldorf?" He never looked back but said, "What did you say, Eddie?" I said, "What did you say, Coach?" Coach repeated, "What did you say, Eddie?"

I was so surprised that he seemed to know my name. Pappy Waldorf was a well-known man in the coaching business and somehow he had absorbed the name of a guy who had yet to coach his first college game.

I asked, "How do you know my name?" Coach replied, "You've been here a whole week haven't you?" I felt so good that he knew my name that I knew from that day on I wanted to know everyone's name. It's obvious that players are people and not numbers but I have seen coaches who don't bother to learn the names so they call out the numbers. I promised myself that I wouldn't call my players by a number. I felt such respect from Coach Waldorf, and as a result, I have always given that to my players.

The System

Then I asked Coach the biggest question on my mind. I knew I could play, but I wasn't sure how to coach. I wanted to get my guys to respect me from the first minute they met me. They didn't have to have the awe displayed by me when I met Coach Kraft of McKinley High School in the third grade. But they did have to respect me. What would I do if they didn't? How would I get it?

I said, "Coach, I've got a little question I want to ask, and I hope you'll answer it for me. Coach, what advice would you have for a young coach in his first year who hasn't even reported to the job?"

He took a long time to answer and started with a question begging for more time. "A coach who never coached before . . . his first job?" Another pause. Now I was nervous that I shouldn't have asked such a basic question of such a great coach. I held my breath as he started to talk again, "Well, I guess, Eddie, my advice would be for him to get a system."

At first I thought he was being sarcastic and I reiterated, "System? I'm talking about myself, Coach, but how am I going to get a system . . . ? I haven't coached and I'm going to the job the first time. How can I have a system?"

At last I realized that Coach Waldorf was serious when he answered, "Well, that's easy to do. Did you play college ball, Eddie?" I said, "Yes, sir," He said, "Did you use plays?" I said, "Yes, sir, we had plays." Pappy then said, "Well, that's a starting point. Now at the clinic, did you see any plays you liked here?" I said, "Yes, sir, I liked your plays."

Now I was with him, hanging on every word. "Well, if you

liked mine, you probably liked something from Fritz. So I'd say to you, get the plays that you used in college, and if you liked anything here, I would take them. And I'd get back to your school and I'd get a mimeograph. The first time I met with the team I would give everybody a copy of my plays and tell them that this is my system. That's a good way to get your system."

That was another lesson. The simplest ideas, the most obvious ones that were filled with common sense, are frequently the best ideas. Man, I couldn't wait to catch the train and come to Grambling, where I could get me a system. I ended up using some of Coach Turner's plays from Leland College along with Coach Waldorf's plays.

I worked the plays while I was on the train coming back, and when I got to Grambling, they had a mimeograph. The first day I met my team I told them, "That's my system." They've been playing my system ever since.

The Clinics: Lessons for Life

That's the thing . . . play your system. You've got to have a system. Boy, I remember all those old guys. They just had so many good thoughts on what you could do with your team. I learned so much each summer and continued to go to that clinic until the agents got into football. They broke up the all-star game because they impressed upon the college all-stars that they could get hurt in this game with the pro team and ruin their careers. That ultimately wiped the game out. But I went for a good twenty years to that clinic.

I just like to see what the other guy is doing and test it myself. Sometimes you can take this material and beat him with it. You know you might even do a little more with it and make it better. But I was always trying to make Grambling football better. No matter how good we were, I knew we could always be better. Learning new things reinforced all of my strengths as a coach and that is important no matter how long you coach. But in my case, as long as I've been around, it's even more important.

I felt very accepted by the white coaches at the clinics right from the start, but Pappy Waldorf stood out from the others from the first time we met. I didn't think about it then, but later I realized how important it was for me that my first substantial contacts with white colleagues were good ones. Man, I don't know what it would have been like if the clinics were run by a segregationist. The fact that I was there at all told me that was not going to be the case. But just like changing the Jim Crow segregation laws in the South didn't change everyone's attitudes on race, my mere presence at Northwestern didn't mean everyone accepted me, certainly not that everyone liked me.

This clinic was Pappy's school, so he could set the tone. He'd always take time to talk. He came to Grambling many years later when he was working with the San Francisco 49ers. He'd come to the house and Doris would cook for him and then we would go the office. He smiled when he saw films of our team using his plays because that showed him respect, that I thought so much of him that I used his knowledge of the game. Some coaches might have thought I'd stolen them and become angry, but I knew he wanted to teach the game. He didn't care that I was a black coach, just that I was a coach. Pappy was teaching me that sport—and coaching—could transcend race. I have never stopped thinking about that and how America itself could learn about better race relations if our society was more like our sports.

First Team at Grambling

So I was back from Northwestern, I had a system, and now I was ready for my first team. I was the coach. Then it dawned on me: I didn't have an assistant. Heck, there was barely enough to pay me—my first salary at Grambling was $63.75 per month. But I found out that Jesse Applewhite, the night watchman, had played ball, so I asked the president to let him help.

Everyone at Grambling had several jobs then. It was nothing unusual. Within a few years, I would become the football and basketball coach, plus I coached at the high school, taught physical education in high school and college, was director of the playground, recreation director, part-time dorm director, and baseball coach. I lined the field, wrapped the players, coached every phase of the game, got the officials, paid the officials, looked after the hurt players and carried injured players to the hospital. I had to write stories about our road games because the local papers couldn't—or wouldn't—send reporters to our away games. I had to copy the local writer's style, so I'd take a great article he'd written about a game we'd won, about one we'd lost; then a story he'd written about a blowout and one about a close game; then one where it was a tough defensive game and one that was high scoring. Since I could never know how a game would end, I had to be ready to write about all situations.

Quite a few people knew I coached high school football during the war, but most didn't know I also coached girls' basketball. We lost the state championship in the final game by one point. I enjoyed coaching girls' basketball. They'd really play for you. Those girls played real hard.

However, even with all that on my plate, I never doubted that my primary purpose was to coach football. When I first started coaching, I never thought of how many games I might be able to win over the course of my career. I was happy to have this job coaching. Period.

There were only 175 students in the entire school at that time and only forty were guys. I had enough to play football—barely. We would have between twenty to thirty of the forty guys in the school on the team, and the rest all thought they should be on the squad. They would tell me, "Coach Robinson, I can do this in the 40," or, "I can press this," and, "All I need is a shot; can you give me a shot?"

They'd be at practice everyday—you'd see those little guys over there who said they could "walk on." So I'd take time to talk to them. Since I really believed playing football was good for young people, I hated to turn a guy down who really wanted to play. You really can never know the hidden talent of someone. You think you know by the size and speed you see the first time, but you can't be sure.

Game Time

Right from the start I tried to convince my players that they could win, but we really didn't have such great players that year.

I remember the pain of defeat in my first game against Filander Smith from Little Rock. We lost by a close score, 12–0, and I felt like we could have won it if I had played.

We were letting the game slip away. I was tempted to go in. I guess this was a test of my being an adult and trying to be a good-thinking person, so I managed to stay on the sidelines. It was hard because I knew more about the system than these youngsters did, and I just figured that I could help us win it if I played. Of course, I knew what would happen if it was discovered that I'd played. The authorities made it real tough on a coach who put himself in a game.

We lost to Leland early in the season in a game I really wanted to win badly. We lost the first five games and things looked bleak for us.

We had some guys on our team who could have helped us to win but who were giving me and the team a hard time. Some of the guys were older than I was and some had played against me during the last two years I was at Leland. We beat them at Leland when Coach Turner used the new system that he'd learned at the coaching clinics he attended. We went to Grambling in my last year at Leland. The final score was 0–0 after one of the guys dropped the ball on the last play in the end zone.

This wasn't an easy situation for the start of my coaching career since we were going from equals to me being in charge as their coach.

One of the guys I had played against looked like he'd be a pretty good fullback for our team at Grambling. I wanted to teach him how to spin. Coach Turner had taught it to me at Leland and I had seen Westfall demonstrate it at the clinics that summer. I was pretty good with the spin myself as a fullback, and I was trying to teach it to this boy.

When I would show it to him, he wouldn't do it right. When I would walk away, I could hear him muttering in the background. "I play defensive end. What does this coach know?" Dr. Jones heard about this and told me I would not have any peace until I got rid of some of these guys, especially the older ones. Finally, I was pushed to a point where I had to make the decision to remove three of them from the team. Morale increased right away. The others guys knew that day that I was the head coach and that I took this role very seriously.

At the same point in what had been a dismal season, there was this boy who looked like he was ready to take over as the new spin back. He would spin to the right and hold his body low to hide the ball, which is what I taught him in practice. But when he got in the game he held the ball high, so I sent word in to tell him that our opponent could read him. At first he didn't get it and a boy on the other team put a hit on his face and knocked him out cold. There were no masks at the time, just a bar. He finally came to, and when we put him back in he was running so low. He learned his lesson, and I never had to tell him to go low again. He'd tell everyone how important it was to "listen to Coach Rob!" I had my team.

We had done a lot of work on the fundamentals. We thought we knew what we were doing, but I was new and many of the players were new. There were a lot of miscommunications and errors to work through. We dropped passes and fumbled balls way too much. Finally, we got things rolling the way they needed to be.

Our next game was on November 15 in Austin, Texas, against Tilliston. We won that game in a pretty big way for our first victory that year. We got in control of the game real early and never let up, winning 37–6. We ended up winning three games that year and felt that we were turning the program around as the season ended. But then the unthinkable happened. I'll never forget hearing the news of the bombing of Pearl Harbor on December 7, 1941, as the first season ended. That put everything, including 3–8 records, in perspective. It was impossible to believe but all too real that American soil had been attacked.

Decades later, many people have asked me what I thought of my future as a coach in 1941 after a losing season. Well, at that moment, I was thinking more about the war than the game. But when I did focus on the game, from the very beginning, I thought I could win. President Jones released the pressure before the season began. He had met me when I got off the train from Chicago and told me, "This is your first year and you may not win any games." I'd said, "Well, what do you mean, telling me I won't win?" The president responded, "You've got to learn to coach first." He was that kind of person. I was afraid he was right about not winning that year after the first five games.

President Ralph Waldo Emerson Jones made the greatest impact on my life of anyone other than my father. Here was a college president who had played baseball in the Negro Leagues and was real close to the athletic program. When I started coaching football, we got to know each other real well. He'd come out and coach some football and that was all right with me. Heck, he was the president.

From that year until my last few years at Grambling, I was always confident I could coach our boys to win the big games. Until my last year, I never had any problems trying to win games or thinking about whether I could win. But that first year we came up 3–8. Things just weren't happening for too long until the president gave me such good advice about cutting those players. I never thought about losing my job until a lady came up to me in Grambling's dining hall and asked if President Jones was going to fire me because we had lost so many games. I nearly choked on the food.

But Dr. Jones would never have done that. He built confidence in people. I watched how he developed his relationships with the State Board of Education. He would go and talk to them, and he usually could get what he wanted. Grambling got more than some of the other state schools got. Considering the condition of black colleges in other southern states, that was quite an achievement.

When I took the job the school was not called Grambling State University. It was the Louisiana Negro Normal and Industrial Institute. Everyone wanted that name changed, including Dr. Jones. But the board was moving slowly on this. You don't change the name of a school very often, if ever.

Then one time we were playing Tennessee State on Saturday night. We had a good team, but Tennessee was always tough. President Jones had to get up on Sunday to drive to Baton Rouge for a board meeting on Monday. At the end of the meeting, the chairman asked, "Is there anything else we need to put on the agenda?" A board member joked, "I say we have to put on there that Dr. Jones wants to change the name of his school because he requests it at every meeting. I want to save him that effort today so I'll put it on the agenda."

Dr. Jones got up and said, "You all want to laugh at me, but if you had been at our game when we played Tennessee State you wouldn't be laughing. I wouldn't have any trouble getting you to change it." He told the board that it was a great game and that we fought hard. It came down to the last second and Tennessee State was right down at the goal line. The official was about to blow his whistle as the clock was approaching zero. Our fans were ready to cheer to help our boys but before they could get out, "Hold that line, Louisiana Negro Normal and Industrial Institute," Tennessee State scored and we lost the game. Dr. Jones got the name changed that day!

The Birth of Our Children and the War Years at Grambling

With all the turmoil around us, from starting our careers to the expanding war and the churning of race relations, Doris and I never lost sight of what was most important to us both, especially after Lillian Rose was born on February 7, 1942.

Family life was a regular topic of conversation between Doris and me. The fact that we both came from broken homes made us want to work very hard to be sure we were always together. We did not want to take a chance that our kids would also come from a broken home. We really knew what it meant to have the Momma and the Daddy in the same home. As we got older these were some of the things that we talked about.

From the time we got married we really worked at what we had talked about. I think the fact that we had all those years together before getting married allowed us to be more mature and thoughtful than our actual ages. We had already discussed the family values we wanted to give to our children and to model for them.

As our second season began, the news from the war kept hammering at everyone's consciousness. As the war expanded, it became clear that we might not have enough boys at Grambling to field a team. In fact, for the 1942 season, thirty-three of the sixty-seven men at Grambling were on the team. One was my dear friend, Fred Hobdy, who years later became our basketball coach and succeeded me as athletics director.

That second season, which helped us build such confidence after going unbeaten and unscored upon, became the only great memory of 1942 as our boys went off to war and we shut the college program down at the end of the season for the duration of the war. Grambling's students didn't care too much about football in the beginning. Also, it was the war and the future of the world that they were thinking about. The students really didn't care that much even after the local sports media began to play up our record.

I was amused late in 1998 when I read an article in *Sports Illustrated* called "Absolute Zero" about the 1939 University of Tennessee team that "faced 10 foes, and not one of them scored a single point." The story said that was never repeated in the history of college football. I guess the writer had missed the news about our 1942 season.

With the suspension of Grambling's college football program, I decided to coach the Grambling High School team in the fall of 1943. As that first high school season began, Doris was far into her pregnancy with Eddie Jr. His birth on October 20, 1943, completed our family, which became the rock for both of us. It was our strength as a new family that helped keep our spirits up during the war. Coaching the high school guys kept me occupied.

I had worked with many of the students at the high school when they were still in elementary school. One of them was Tank Younger. His brother, Elmo, was on my first college team. But it was one of the toughest periods for me because I knew my college guys were risking their lives every day in the war. Nonetheless, we had a great high school team. Tank played there for both years I was the coach.

I knew Tank had good football skills from the first time I saw him. He also played basketball at Grambling High. At first he was not aggressive at all. He would run away from confrontations. I asked Tank if he wanted to be a great athlete, and he said, "Yes, Coach." Tank began to walk away when a teammate slapped him in practice the next day. I called a time-out and told Tank he had to stop running away. The other guy would own him until he fought back. On the next play down, Tank hit the guy good. From that day on, he was recognized as the team's leader. He never had to hit anyone again.

Tank was one of the hardest working players I had ever seen. He was a little slow at first. But by his second year on the Grambling High team, he had become our fastest player. I never saw anything like it.

I know we didn't keep the records of Tank in high school, but I doubt if anyone ever broke them. I think they're still trying to break Younger's touchdown record. Heck, Tank scored a touchdown nearly every time he touched the ball. Like most of the guys, Tank played both offense and defense. He was good at defense, but man, he was extra special on offense.

In 1944, we won the North Louisiana High School Championship. Alfred Priestly, the coach of Xavier Prep, the champion from South Louisiana, refused to play us for the state championship. Of course, there were separate white and black championships. Blacks and whites weren't about to compete against each other in Louisiana in the 1940s.

General Douglas MacArthur was in the Philippines fighting for our country while we were playing high school ball. Now it seems silly, but we had a play we called "Douglas MacArthur" and that was Younger's play for a touchdown. We'd go in there and call "the general." That was it. Younger was strong—one of the biggest and fastest guys on the team. He looked like a man out there playing against boys, so we took advantage of that. Tank could run away from defenders; but if one caught him, Tank just ran over him.

During the war years, James Riley, inspired by Tuskegee's great military marching program, started such a program at Grambling. They'd get up in the morning and drill, showing off to the girls on campus. Of course during the war years, Grambling had far more girls than boys. Riley would promote the guys to corporals and sergeants. There were a lot of egos there.

At first, I encouraged them because of the war, but then they got so full of themselves that I decided I'd start my own company. I went over to the girls and talked to them to see if they would join me. I told them I had seen this drilling where they did a series of fancy steps while moving around at the same time. The girls got white skirts, red blouses, red socks, and white tennis shoes. We worked on everything we could about close-order drilling and trick steps. We put it together. We got so good the army bases were fighting to get us to come to perform there. We'd also perform at the half-time of high school games. It was very eerie at Grambling without many men. Not just because there were so few men but because we knew where they were and what could happen to them. Eventually the army took all the college men off the campus except for two guys: one had one leg, the other one had one arm, so they couldn't join the army.

Our military marching meant something and filled a void for me at Grambling by raising our spirits and those of the soldiers we performed for at a time of tremendous national distress. While everyone was concerned about the future of democracy, many blacks had a special concern. We knew America was not perfect for blacks, but we began to read about Hitler's plans for the master race. If America lost the war, then whatever rights blacks had won would likely be lost. We joined the war effort with full force and pride. The history books are filled with stories of our contributions. I am proud of them to this day.

4.

SOLDIERS RETURN AND GRAMBLING
STARTS TO PLAY

Keeping the World Free for Democracy

America mourned the passing of President Franklin D. Roosevelt just before the end of the war. I think that black people were especially saddened by his death. I felt sorry that he didn't live long enough to see victory. I thought he was a fine president and believed he was doing good things for black people.

America was thrilled about our victories over the Nazis and the Japanese. But with so many lives lost in the battle to preserve democracy, the war took its human toll on the entire nation. The war took a special psychic toll on the black soldiers who returned home to see that democracy had still not spread its wings to include them. I know many of my friends expected sweeping changes for blacks after the war ended. After all, they argued, our black soldiers had been fighting against people who believed in racial superiority so how could we resume a legal system like segregation founded on racial superiority?

I had seen enough in my lifetime to know that real sweeping changes were not going to be that easy. I thought that the black soldiers had gone out, had seen what it was like, and had gotten some perspective on what they would really need to do to win the additional freedoms they wanted in the United States. Most of those guys who left Grambling to enter the service came back and graduated. That was an important first step in gaining success.

Vets Dealing with Failed Expectations

But there were so many of the black soldiers who came back and were very disillusioned. There weren't enough jobs to go around for the returning GIs. Like other periods of American history, if you were black, even a black GI, you would not be at the head of the employment lines for whatever jobs there were.

Just a few months after the war ended, more than one hundred black vets marched in Birmingham, Alabama, to register to vote. They had risked their lives for democracy but were told by the local authorities that they did not have the right to vote in their own state and nation. That was a bitter pill to swallow. I felt a real need to reach out to all the vets, but especially to the disillusioned ones.

I understood how disappointed they were, but I knew ending a history of discrimination was not going to be easy. When they left they knew what America was like regarding race. I'm not sure exactly how they thought it would be when they came back, but I know many thought they'd find full democracy here for them.

Obviously, either they were very idealistic, naïve, or hadn't really studied the history of the country and what has gone down for centuries. If they had done the latter, then they really couldn't have expected full change in a few years as a result of war that took place away from our shores.

We need to understand the American system and the Constitution. Of course, in 1945 most of our guys coming home hadn't had an education, so they couldn't understand. From their point of view, they left, risked their lives, won a war against the world's biggest oppressor, the most racist nation we knew about, came home, and expected the America they left to have changed. That was an unreal expectation. But it was theirs and I understood it.

What I'm saying is they didn't understand the system. I think if they understood the system, they would have felt better about it, been ready to live within it and challenge it through constitutional means. I know there are a lot of lawyers who will accept anyone's money to plead a case. Black people want to be heard, to have a voice in the affairs of our nation, and we need to know how to use the judicial system. That's about all we had. If the black vets and others called out to those on the judiciary to use their dignity and sense of what was right, then many people who were on the judiciary would have lived up to the letter of the law. They may not have wanted to in their hearts, but I have seen some remarkable things happen in the courts.

Of course, blacks had not historically been able to use the courts, and there were far too many whites sitting on the courts who had been raised with all the stereotypes about blacks. Nonetheless, I told the returning Grambling vets that they could work for change within the existing system as far back as the mid-1940s. Most would listen. Sometimes they believed me and sometimes they didn't.

I believe everything can change, including the laws, if you're willing to pay the price. I'm an American citizen. As Yogi Berra said, "It ain't over till it's over." If you can love the nation as much as anybody else, I don't think it would be really hard to overcome things. If you would walk that last mile to get that injustice erased, to get it off the record, then you have a chance. If you don't do anything, then things will remain as they have always been.

I think that if people in power took into consideration the circumstances of other people, then things might change more quickly. But those in power never lived it, so it's hard for them to understand the effects of racism.

Back on the Field

I knew what I personally had to do. I was Eddie Robinson, a young, relatively inexperienced football coach with a vision of how we could win at Grambling and how Grambling's education could open up opportunities for so many current and future student-athletes.

When football resumed at Grambling in 1945, I was ready to do that but also to work with everyone, no matter what their beliefs or skin color. The war was over and I felt, more than ever, that I was a citizen of the best country in the world. As an American I wanted to help America live up to its ideals. We were on such a mission when we came to campus for the 1945 football season. But I knew that we had to be successful on the field to achieve our goals off the field. And we had to let people know about our success so we would not be viewed as merely some black college in the deep rural South. President Jones and I talked about how to make Grambling's name nationally known and set our specific goals.

The plan was simple but hardly easy. We had to win. We needed to be sure our student-athletes graduated from Grambling. I needed to continue to learn about the game by continuing my own education. We needed to send a player to the NFL. We had to publicize who we were. We had to develop a unique form of entertainment to complement the football team, and we had to beat Southern. Like the Army-Navy rivalry, the regular season was only a preparation for the real game with Southern. Whoever won that was a winner; the other was a loser.

Most of the players from Grambling High, including Tank Younger, enrolled as freshmen. The 1945 varsity logged a 9–2 record but lost to Southern.

We were only 5–5 in 1946 and some were getting discouraged. We were destroyed by Southern in 1946. But I knew we were building toward something.

First and foremost, we were building a team. When a player approached me and told me that he had to miss a game because his daddy needed help picking cotton, I got the entire team together and we all headed to the fields to help out. The labor made our guys stronger. Their experience helped make them a team.

I had seen President Jones have this effect on the faculty at Grambling. I had much to learn at the institution soon to become known as "Common Sense College." President Jones got us national attention after the war when he helped organize the faculty to ride throughout Louisiana to show poor rural blacks how to have a better life. The faculty helped repair roofs, installed indoor plumbing, and built additions onto what had been shacks. They encouraged the children to think about a college education. Many of those children are now proud Grambling alums. He was building his own academic teamwork on campus and across the state. I never talked to President Jones when I didn't learn something from him that I could apply in my own life.

1947: Grambling Beats Southern and Jackie Robinson Beats Jim Crow

As 1947 dawned, I was wondering if I was going to stay in coaching since I had not met the goals that I had established with President Jones when we resumed football after the war. Grambling's name was not well known and we had not been dominating any teams.

I was losing my temper far too easily. I was fussing all up and down the sidelines in 1946. During one game, I yelled at the officials and was taking a loss out on my own players on the field in front of the fans. Doris was waiting for me at the front door when I came home that night. Doris asked if "that's the way you are going to act? Because if it is, I'm taking you out of coaching!" She didn't say much, but what she said changed me back and gave me the perspective I needed. I never did any of that nonsense again. And Doris never took me out of coaching.

Like many Americans, especially Black Americans, I got an incredible morale boost in April of 1947 when Jackie Robinson took the field for the Brooklyn Dodgers and baseball's color barrier fell. We knew it was coming after his great year with the Dodger's minor league team in Montreal, but it still sent electric shock waves when it happened. Suddenly Branch Rickey, the owner of the Dodgers, became a special man for many of us.

Having seen Jackie in 1941 on the football field, I had tried to follow him closely after that. Jackie's own military experience had not made Grambling's returning vets less disillusioned about the war. The U.S. Army had tried to court-martial him for refusing to move to the back of a military bus at Camp Hood in Texas in the summer of 1944. Jackie had been talking to a light-skinned black woman whom the driver apparently thought was white. People familiar with the circumstances thought Jackie should never have been charged; we were certainly relieved when he was acquitted. As I told the returning vets, you had to know your constitutional rights and use them in court. Jackie Robinson did that. However, not many knew about Jackie when that was happening.

Everyone knew about what happened in April of 1947. Robinson's becoming a Dodger brought new hope for change. That was bigger than life for me or Grambling.

The first huge win of my years at Grambling had to be against Southern in 1947, when Tank Younger just ran over and around them. That was bigger than life in what was then our own, obviously smaller world at Grambling. Southern was big and Grambling was small. Southern had beat us pretty badly in 1946 at their place, and the loss left a bad taste in our mouths.

When we beat them in 1947, it rocked the state. It was the first game we had ever won against Southern. Thus, we served notice of what was going to come in the years ahead.

Tank Younger was a junior. In 1947, Tank was having his greatest year to date. As I said earlier, Tank was one of the hardest working players I had ever seen. Unstoppable in high school, he was able to carry the team. By his third year at Grambling, he was again unstoppable. He made Southern feel the pain. I never saw anyone like him. You could see the frustration on the faces of the Southern players.

Tank scored the first touchdown on a short run. Southern had its own great runner named Snow Taylor. He countered Tank's TD with his own. When he crossed the goal line, he slammed the ball down and tried to stare down John Christophe, our defensive back. Snow told John, "I'm so good that I don't even run like I'm human." John was startled, since Grambling's guys just didn't act like that.

The next time Snow carried the ball, Tank, Christophe, and some of our other guys tackled him hard, causing some bleeding. Tank turned to John—but so Snow could hear him—and said, "Funny, he sure bleeds like he's human."

Tank got almost every first down for us, but Southern was ganging up on him throughout the game. We knew they would so I'd set up plays for our other guys whenever they were overcovering Tank. Tank knew his role was to draw a pack of defenders to him. That set up what may have been our biggest play of the game when Roy Givens, our fullback, ran forty-three yards for the touchdown that sealed the victory for us.

The rivalry was already intense by 1948, and you could just sense how it was going to grow. You could feel the tensions on the field that day, and by the end of the game the emotions on both sides were ready to explode. Unfortunately, a scuffle broke out after one of our linemen hit a Southern back. Suddenly there was pushing and shoving, but players from both sides stepped in to quickly stop the action. It was so brief and so contained that fans in the stands didn't even know that anything had happened.

Southern's coach, A. W. Mumford, thought we weren't playing clean and refused to play us again. I never completely understood what happened that day except that Coach Mumford blamed us, and more than a decade went by—it wasn't until 1959—when we appeared together on the same field. I can't describe how much I regretted that this happened. I guess emotions got the best of us. I knew I had to work harder with my coaches to control our guys. From that day on, Grambling played with emotion and intelligence.

Collie Nicholson Joins the Team

But we were winning, were on the black college football map, and had our first big star in Tank. In 1948, President Jones hired Collie Nicholson to publicize our efforts. Collie, Tank, and President Jones gave us a formidable team. The president's plan was to make Grambling a national school for blacks in the way that Notre Dame was for Catholics. He knew that was a big task because we were located in such a remote part of rural Louisiana. Collie was a Grambling grad, who had caught the president's eye as a marine correspondent during World War II. He was perfect for the job.

We tried to do a lot to let the scouts know Grambling was developing some real players. Collie Nicholson was a great writer. We came to call him "the Man with the Golden Pen." He understood the media and the value of public relations. Collie kept all of the black papers around the country in the know, sending up to 200 press releases out each week. His phone bills were legendary, and he brought incredible prestige to our program. It didn't hurt Collie to have Tank to write about when he joined the Grambling team. He wrote endlessly about Tank and the things he could do.

Collie had a way of writing with enough superlatives to get you intrigued enough about Tank to want to see him. But Collie was so brilliant that he left enough out so that when you saw Tank, he was even better than what you read in Collie's articles. Collie's articles opened the road for all black athletes in this part of the country because he talked about Tank and the others we played against.

One NFL scout told me that he was glad when Collie left Grambling in the early 1980s because he had written so much about our student-athletes that his team felt they had to draft our players. He said that if they didn't draft a player after all Collie had written and somebody else drafted him and he did well, that he would lose his job as the team's scout. Collie's writing brought people to our games. Collie helped establish us as more than a school in northern Louisiana. Collie Nicholson did a whole lot for our program by putting our vision of what we could do in the mind of the public.

Tank Younger Meets the Rams' Eye

Collie helped answer my prayers by making the NFL scouts want to see Tank. I prayed at night that Tank would be somebody we could get into the NFL because no one from Grambling had gone there. I knew how great that would be for Tank, and that it would help us advance Grambling's program.

Schools around us were sending people to the NFL. I was taught early on that to keep up with or beat the competition, you always had to advance. That occasionally required adjusting. We needed a player in the NFL, and by 1947, Tank seemed like the guy who could get there.

There were always challenges for our program, and I was often responsible for increasing the challenges. It was always, "Can we do this?" or, "Will we ever have this?" And if we were going to accept the challenge, then we really needed to meet it.

Tank's parents had moved to California while he was at Grambling. President Jones pretty much adopted Tank during his four years here. Imagine having the university's president as your surrogate daddy? He took good care of him. Tank even called him "Pa." They were very close friends. The fact that the president had coached made him a great friend of athletics, period. He was there so much that you noticed if he was not at a game. And I'm not just talking football. Any game. But President Jones and Tank Younger had a very special relationship.

One year we were all invited to the president's house for Thanksgiving dinner after our game. Everyone had noticed that when he was playing defense, Tank hadn't seemed to hit his opponents as hard as usual. He always got his man but without his usual intensity. I asked him if he was OK at the dinner table. Tank answered. "Coach, I knew how good the food was going to be tonight. I stopped my man on the field, but I didn't want to take a chance on hurting my jaw. I wanted to fully enjoy this meal."

Like all our students, Tank lived in the dormitory. He worked each summer to earn money for clothes and other things. Most of our student-athletes worked all summer on the campus, and they were paid the money at the end of the summer.

By 1947, Younger had served notice to everybody in the NFL that he was a real force. We were 10–2 in 1947. He got even better in 1948 when we were 8–2. The Rams sent Eddie Kotel, their scout, to Grambling. The Rams had read about Tank and knew people who had seen him. They wanted Tank as a free agent.

Eddie came to see us in a season-ending playoff versus Wilberforce. No one could catch Tank that afternoon as he helped us totally control possession of the ball by running for first downs at will. Tank was so strong that even if a Wilberforce guy lunged and caught him, Tank would shake loose. Eddie told me that the

Rams' staff had worked all the game films I'd sent him. Eddie told me that, one-by-one, all the coaches noticed the same thing. They could tell exactly where Tank had run on the field because there would be a pattern of opposing players on the ground where they had tried to tackle him.

After all of this, Eddie told me that the Rams' offer wasn't huge at $4,500 but "it would be better to give him $4,500, with a promise that we will keep him. We know he's good. But if we have to give him $6,000, you know we're gonna be looking hard and critically. If he can't play, we're gonna get rid of him." Tank wanted to play in Los Angeles to be closer to his parents. I knew Eddie wanted Tank and that he was just trying to negotiate the best deal possible for the Rams. So I knew I had to push Eddie Kotel that day.

I told him, just give him the $6,000 and then if he can't play, cut him. I knew he would make the team and be a star. We went back and forth for quite some time, but I always sensed he would come up with the $6,000 so I didn't let Eddie bluff me one bit. The Rams paid him the $6,000, and he surely repaid them with many years as a player.

Not only did they never cut him, Tank stayed in the NFL, mostly with the Rams organization, for nearly fifty years. There are only a handful of former players who had that history. He was a scout and an assistant general manager there and for San Diego. Heck, he nearly broke my record with Grambling. I had to stay here a few more years to stay ahead of Tank Younger. Seriously though, Tank Younger made me proud to be a coach. He was always a student of the game and a student of life. His intelligence was greater than his strength or speed. Like many other Grambling players, Tank continuously returned to campus to see the new guys and talk about the Grambling tradition.

It was a heady time in 1948. Tank was the local story about to become a national sensation. On the international stage, Ralph

Bunche, a Black American, won the Nobel Peace Prize for his work between Arabs and Israelis. President Truman took a huge step with our military forces. Fifty years later we would all like to forget that the armed services during World War II were segregated. Vets understandably made that a huge issue after the war. With the stroke of a pen on an executive order in 1948, President Truman ended segregated units. Our players and alums who were vets all came by the office to celebrate. Tank joined them. An intelligent and perceptive man, football was a big part of but not the only part of his young life.

He was some kind of football player. The year Tank went to the Rams he was one of the best-conditioned people in their camp. Grambling's training regimen in the heat of Louisiana no doubt helped. We were running forties in the August sun. We were running miles and miles.

As great as he was, a lesser man might not have been able to successfully make the transition to the NFL. In 1949, Younger was shouldering the burden of being the first player from an historically black school to seek a spot on an NFL roster.

Tank was picked as Black College Player of the Year in 1948, his last season at Grambling. I told him, "Tank, you've got to go out there and make that team. If you don't make it, there's no telling how long it will be before another black gets a chance. They're going to say they took the best we had and he couldn't make it."

We were all at the railroad station for his departure to Los Angeles. At one time four trains would stop each day in Grambling. Then it got down to two a day. Tank was boarding the afternoon train. Of course, Tank boarded the car for "coloreds only." I was so used to segregation that I didn't even think about it that day. Here was our greatest player headed for the NFL, and Louisiana laws deemed Tank Younger wasn't good enough to sit with the white passengers. But I don't know if anyone thought about segregation that day because we were so happy for Tank.

I will always remember what he did when he got on that train. Somebody asked him, "Hey, Tank, do you think you're going to make the team?" without skipping a beat, Tank shouted back above the noise of the train, "If they're playing football, I'm going to make it. I can't play hockey and I'm not a basketball player, but if they're playing football, I'll make it." The rest, as they say, is in the record books.

He made all-pro as a linebacker and as a running back. In the first year, Coach Clark Shaughnessy played him as a defensive back. But many think Tank made his biggest mark in the NFL on offense. I went to see him play whenever I could, especially when they were coming through the South.

I went to an exhibition game in Little Rock. I saw the Rams' opponents were getting to the Rams' quarterback, Bob Waterfield. He was being rushed hard and was sacked twice. Shaughnessy called a time-out. When the huddle broke, Younger was in the game and I think that was his move to the offense. Younger was a great blocker, and he was helping to get Waterfield a chance to throw the ball by keeping the people off his back. Waterfield threw for a couple of touchdowns.

Tank's adjustment to Los Angeles was made much easier by the fact that he had been visiting his parents there each summer. Tank noticed that the Ram players rarely came out of their rooms to eat in restaurants. We finally realized that they were embarrassed because they weren't quite sure how to eat properly. Tank told me some of the guys at Grambling were also embarrassed. As soon as he told me that, I met with Professor Fidelia Adams Johnson. She was the daughter of our founder, Charles Adams, and was a professor in Grambling's Home Economics Department. That department has taught etiquette classes to our student-athletes ever since.

Tank has always been a look-you-in-the-eye type of guy. It is so fitting that this classy man was our first great player. His greatness started at Grambling but only grew once he left. Tank Younger was a genuine pioneer in football in America.

Radio

Our stature was developing quickly. We got station KRES in Ruston to do a delayed broadcast on radio. They would recreate the game the next day. We first went on the air in 1949. The name of the radio show was *Grambling's Football*. Even with Tank Younger gone to the NFL, we had a good 1949 season with a 7–3–2 record. The radio shows hardly made up for the loss of our great star, but they did add to the excitement of Grambling football. When they put that on on Sunday morning, boy, the young kids were getting up and the preachers were changing the time of their services.

We helped raise the money and KRES did all the production. The students really enjoyed the games being on the radio. It was a source of pride. It made them feel big time.

Like everything else we did, we were trying to keep up with what was going on at the white colleges. We never wanted our students to feel that they were at a college that was something less than the white schools. We worked hard to make sure they knew that.

President Jones and the Grambling Band

Ralph Waldo Emerson Jones was the first person who realized what a marching band and a football team could do together. Back when he was a new faculty member, Dr. Jones was asked to start a band by Charles Adams, who was the president of Grambling at that time.

He showed his economic resourcefulness when he contacted Sears Roebuck to establish a line of credit to begin purchasing the band's instruments. By the time Jones was president, we knew that the Grambling State Marching Band was what he had in mind for the entertainment complement to GSU football.

President Jones put the band out there with the team, and they're been going ever since. That was the beginning of the Grambling State University Tiger Marching Band, doing precision dancing steps to a combination of military music and soul. Now Grambling says it "embodies the spirit of Sousa and the soul of Ray Charles." They have performed with us in Japan and on their own in Africa, in movies and on TV.

The Tiger Marching Band was already terrific when Dr. Jones paid the money to send them to perform at the first Super Bowl between Green Bay and Kansas City. Most white people had never seen a black marching band. He put them on TV in front of the nation, and they just tore the place up. They just really tore it up. People across America now know about it. The NFL later paid Grambling for them to perform at Super Bowls IX and XX. It changed a lot of things when our bands started showing up on television.

Thus another piece of our plan for Grambling was in place by the time Tank played his first game for the Rams. I knew I had to resume my own formal education by getting a master's degree. My own mentors in football had drilled me to keep on learning about the game all my life and career. Each summer at the clinics I would hear about many coaches going on for their M.A. Each year, I would question the guys, and it seemed apparent that the M.A. program at the University of Iowa was the best one. I wanted to be with the best and keep up with them, so in 1950, I began spending the first of four summers at Iowa working toward my masters.

Graduate School at Iowa

I met some great people at the University of Iowa, including Frank Carideo, who was then an assistant coach at Iowa.

Frank Carideo could really kick the football, and he dominated that area in the summer. He had been a punter for Notre Dame. They put up the big nets in the field house. Nobody would challenge Frank as a punter.

I was passing through the field house, and Frank was just kicking the ball to any spot he chose. My friends and I were kicking a ball for fun. Some guy asked me if I could always kick a ball like this. I said "pretty much." He said, "Man, hold tight—we're gonna get something going here."

This guy told Coach Carideo, "You're not the best kicker in town." Coach said, "Well, who is then?" I insisted that the coach should not pay any attention to him. Heck, I was taking a class with Coach Carideo.

Nevertheless, we finally met inside the field house. There were tons of spectators out there to see this showdown. We did some kicking that night. Fortunately, it got dark before anyone could be declared a winner. That was really the best thing that could have happened in that case since I sure didn't want to embarrass my teacher.

I also studied with Dr. Charles McCloy, the most important guy at the University of Iowa. Dr. McCloy did a lot of work in test and measurement in physical education. He made so many predictions that came true. He created the sergeant jump, a test for power in which you squat and then you spring up as high as you could. You then marked the height you jumped on the wall with a piece of chalk.

Respect

Another professor at Iowa was Dr. Tuttle, who taught physiology of exercise. Everybody was scared of this guy. He was tough. He would come to class in his physiology lab and call us the "strong-arm boys" because we were in physical education.

He'd say, "Well, what do you strong-arm boys want to talk about today?" He was always pitting physiology people against the physical education people. I'm not kidding when I say that grown men were afraid of this guy. We knew it was important that we passed his course, so we all kept quiet. When we went to his lab we'd be sitting up like little boys while he lectured with a cigarette in his mouth. You could hardly hear what he was saying.

There was a national physical education meeting at the university while I was taking physiology of exercise with Dr. Tuttle. Miss O'Keefe was teaching me playground supervision and offered us extra credit if we went to the national meeting and asked a question that came out of her class. We had to go anyway because Drs. Tuttle and McCloy required it.

One of the main speakers was Dr. Steinhauser from the University of Illinois. He was a nationally known expert in the physiology of exercise and had written a book on the subject. Dr. Steinhauser gave a lecture on the "second heart," which I didn't know anything about. In physiological terms, he was referring to the skeletal muscles as the second heart. When the blood got out to the arteries, the skeletal muscles helped pump it. The heart didn't have any control of getting the blood back, but the skeletal muscles could press the arteries. As you walked and moved, it would push the blood back to the heart.

We were all there and we went to Dr. Tuttle's class the next day. He came in and he asked, "Did you strong-arm boys go to the physical education meeting?" No one responded, but I managed to blurt out, "Yes, sir."

He challenged us with, "Well, what did you guys learn? What did they talk about?" Now it is hard to believe that we had grown men in there. Nobody replied. Dr. Tuttle came back with, "You mean all of you guys went and none of you know what happened?"

I thought, *Eddie, you are a grown man; you've got children; you were over there; you heard what he said; and you've got to get up and say something.* Man, I grabbed myself, stood up, and he immediately said, "State your name." I said, "My name is Eddie Robinson." Dr. Tuttle went on, "Well, Eddie, what did they talk about?" I replied that Dr. Steinhauser talked about the second heart. Dr. Tuttle answered, "A second what?" He started laughing, saying, "What the hell do you mean?" Man, I thought he was a son of a gun when he said that. The guys in class didn't laugh at me because they all had heard Dr. Steinhauser say there was a second heart.

So I used my notes from the lecture to explain it. I had written down every last word Dr. Steinhauser used. Dr. Tuttle was a bit startled and declared, "I'll be damned; a second heart." The thing that delighted me most of all was that Dr. Steinhauser had decided to visit the physiology exercise class that day. He stood up and told Dr. Tuttle I was right. Dr. Steinhauser walked to the front of the room and took over and lectured the whole class hour.

Everyone was scared of what Dr. Tuttle's reaction was going to be when it was over. Me, too. I got up fast to leave when Dr. Tuttle yelled, "Eddie, come here." I was really nervous and then he said, "That was a damn good thing you did."

I told him I was lucky because I didn't know how I stood up in the first place. He laughed a long time when I said that.

I thought a lot about that. Here were grown men, back at school and confronted by a professor who may not have had much patience. They were scared and intimidated. There was no way they could listen, interact, and really learn.

I learned a lot about football from how Dr. Tuttle acted and how the other guys reacted. If you criticize someone for a mistake, you've got to praise him when he does something good.

Winning with Grace

I had another life lesson when I was in graduate school at Iowa. Their head coach was Dr. Eddie Anderson. That lesson was to pay a compliment when you win.

Bob Westfall was considered to be the nation's best fullback. He played in a spinning single wing for the University of Michigan from 1939–41. When I saw Coach Fritz Crisler demonstrate it, I just figured that was the best thing. Then I met Westfall and saw him demonstrate it. It was great. Frank Carideo was teaching advanced football. It was at that time that I met Charles Henry, who was black. I was able to help bring him to Grambling to head up our physical education program. Henry later became the assistant commissioner of the Big Ten. I believe he was the first black man to hold such a position.

Frank was teaching the class, and Henry was in it with me. They were discussing Minnesota's single wing. They did their spin on the spot where Westfall at Michigan would step and catch it. He would run to a spot and make the complete spin, moving in all the time.

Coach Carideo told the class that we were going to look at the Michigan spin, but I knew he was confused and said that in the class. The way he described it, I knew it was the Minnesota spin. I told him that in the Minnesota spin, they'll spin on the spot while Michigan will step and spin. He asked me why I was so sure and said that he really doubted me. I responded that I had seen Westfall at the all-star game in Chicago and personally spent time with him because I was doing the single wing. A debate among the students went on until we saw the film. Sure enough, the guy from

Minnesota was just spinning right on the spot. Then they put on the Michigan film, and Westfall took the step before spinning.

I said Bob Westfall was supposed to be the best single-wing spinner in the game of football. Yet another hot debate started. It got hotter when Dr. Eddie Anderson suddenly appeared. He was the head coach and Coach Carideo was his assistant. Dr. Anderson hardly ever spent time with the grad students or in the faculty offices.

Someone shouted, "The man is here . . . Dr. Eddie Anderson." We were talking about people playing end, and I was telling how we blocked the end. Dr. Eddie Anderson burst into the conversation and advised me that I couldn't block him. Just like that. Everyone was very silent. He repeated, "You couldn't block me like that." He asked if I had any film of our play and I said, "No, sir, I don't have film here, but I do have film at home." He asked how fast I could get the film to Iowa. Man, this was the first time he was with us and Dr. Anderson was slugging away. This thing was almost getting too heated. I said I didn't think I could get the films to Iowa very quickly. Dr. Anderson responded, "I'll get them here tomorrow. Just give me the address, talk to your secretary and I'll get my secretary to arrange everything."

Sure enough, the film was there for class the next day. There was so much excitement knowing Dr. Anderson would be in the class that you couldn't get in this room. The word was around that we had been in there discussing this heatedly. So boy, they were all there to see the films that I had. I had a lot of big guys at Grambling, including a big fullback spinning. There were guys coming out of the line so we put it on one of them and he just moved right down the field. As the film rolled, I pointed out how it was done.

The room was filled with sparks. Doc kept saying, "You couldn't block me like that," over and over. People in the room kept pointing to the film, showing how well it worked. Then Doc would jump back at them, "You couldn't block me like that."

I told them to cut the film off. Then I said, "Gentlemen, let me tell you something. I now agree. They blocked some guys, but they couldn't block Dr. Eddie Anderson." And the students shouted, "What do you mean?" I answered, "He was an all-American end— one of the best ends who ever played the game—so they couldn't block him. You don't block all-Americans." Boy, it got quiet in there. Then I said again, "We blocked those people, but blocking you, Doc, an all-American, is different thing than these guys who are not all-Americans."

Doc ate it up, leaving in a hurry but not before he promised to come back the next day to continue the discussion. We had a time. Coach Carideo told me this was the first time this had happened at Iowa. Usually the assistants went over to Doc when they had something new. For him to come over two or three days in a row—that had never happened. By the time he came back, I had learned about deferring to authority figures by almost blowing it.

So many good things took place at Iowa. The education was great, but I think I learned more about life and coaching from the people there. When you look for good people, you find good people. If you look for bad people, you just might find them. Just treat people the way you want to be treated. So simple yet so hard for some.

American Football Coaches Association

The teachers at Iowa and the coaches at the clinics had urged me to join the American Football Coaches Association (AFCA). I attended my first AFCA convention in 1951 after suffering through a bad 1950 season. We'd started the 1950 season with four wins and a tie. Then everything unraveled and we lost three of the last four by a combined score of 130–14 to Tennessee State, Bishop, and Prairie View. I went to the AFCA looking for new ideas or good advice.

I had a crazy reaction when I walked into the hall where AFCA president Ray Elliott, the head coach at the University of Illinois, was addressing the coaches. Ray was a great a speaker. I guess my mind was playing tricks with itself because the first thing I thought of was, "Eddie, how long would it take you to be the president of this organization?" Now that was some imagination for a guy walking into his first convention. Twenty-five years later I became AFCA president. Good things take time.

For me the AFCA was one of the first national organizations where race was not a factor. I was, of course, sensitive to the fact that I was among a handful of blacks in the AFCA at that time. When I joined, other black coaches in the AFCA were A. W. Mumford from Southern, Jake Gaither from Florida A&M, Fred Long from Wiley, and Alex Durley from Texas Southern. The word about what the AFCA could do for coaches didn't seem to be known at the black colleges. I don't think anyone tried to keep us away, but we sure didn't know about it. I started my own campaign to get more to join. Through the AFCA, I've heard and mingled with America's greatest coaches, the very men who helped to make this such a great game.

Amos Alonzo Stagg

I met Amos Alonzo Stagg at the 1951 convention in Los Angeles. He was eighty-nine years old at the time and was still coaching. Coach Stagg had won more games than any coach in history. Everyone wanted to shake his hand. All the coaches went wild, lining up side-by-side, fifty to sixty deep. It took a long time to get around to him.

I was on the tail end of the line and was so excited then to have the opportunity to talk to a man who was football's greatest innovator. Decades later, when Alabama and Grambling had won a lot of games, I remembered telling Coach Bryant that we could win, but Alonzo Stagg made all the innovations. I figured that since he had done all of this for football that he probably had three ears and maybe a third eye. As I got closer, I was looking for that third ear and that third eye—or whatever gave him the advantage over other people. When I finally got right in front of him on the dais, he extended his hand and I extended mine. I held his hand a little longer than usual, and the guy in back of me said, "Kiss him, Eddie, and move on. Let somebody else shake his hand."

I was really glad to meet him that day. Coach Stagg attended the AFCA conventions until he was 101 or 102 years old. We all have so many memories of the coach. One of the best was a letter he wrote to his then fourteen-month-old son, Amos Alonzo Jr., telling him the kind of man he wanted him to be, how he wanted him to treat other men with respect unless he found out that they didn't deserve to be respected, how he wanted him to feel about the country, how he wanted him to take care of his mother if he should happen to die early.

My copy of that letter got lost in my house for about ten years. I lose a lot of things in my house. That's one reason Doris and I cannot move. I mentioned the loss at a convention, and a coach from UCLA sent it to me. I ran so many copies as soon as I got it so I would be able to find one when I needed it.

He was mandatorily retired at age seventy by the University of Chicago in 1932. Coach Stagg then took the University of Pacific job until 1946 and "retired" at age eighty-four. He was "Coach of the Year" in 1943 at age eighty-one.

Like a lot of coaches, retirement didn't suit Coach Stagg. He simply couldn't stay away from the game after he retired from Pacific. He joined Amos Alonzo Jr. as the co-coach of Susquehanna

University in Pennsylvania from 1947–52. Coach Stagg Sr. really retired at age ninety-two, the year after I met him.

When I think of all the tributes I received in 1997 when I retired after fifty-six years at Grambling at age seventy-eight, I only had to reflect on Coach Stagg to gain a real perspective. Meeting Coach Stagg was surely the highlight of my first convention. I'd always go looking for him at future conventions to chat with him. Each time I tried to learn something new. Sometimes it was about football. More often, it was about life.

Rebuilding Toward a National Championship

No advice or new ideas from the convention helped with the 1951 season when we had our first losing season since my first year at Grambling.

That 1951 was a tough one. We had an omen on a bus trip in the Blue Bird, which was how we traveled in those days. Grambling traveled everywhere on the Blue Bird, which saved us a great deal of expense money.

We had the radio on in the bus during the 1951 National League playoff between the Dodgers and the Giants. There was tremendous tension among the guys listening so intently to the game. Most of our team was made up of war veterans, many of whom had seen action in the Korean War. When Bobby Thompson hit that game-winning home run, the announcer said, "It's going, going, going; its gone. Now whiskey will flow like wine, and bodies will float down the Harlem River."

As we got near our destination, a tire blew out, making an explosive sound. I looked around and there were only five guys sitting up in their seats. As I stared at this strange scene, I recognized these were my youngest five players and they hadn't gone to the war. All the veterans who had been fighting were down on the floor and under the seats. The blown tire sounded like a gunshot to them, and they all went down. So I realized on the day the Giants won the pennant that the war was not over for too many veterans. And that maybe wars never end in the minds of those who defended our country.

The season was a disaster. We had lost three in a row to Prairie View, Tennessee State, and Arkansas A&M. We weren't even in those games. We were 2–5–1 going into the last game against Bishop. Prospects were to end the season with four straight losses. That had never happened before or since. Bishop had beaten us 35–0 in 1950. But we managed to close the season on an upbeat note when we beat Bishop 52–0. One of the great things about college football is you really can never know who is going to win on any given Saturday. That was sweet, but sweeter still was knowing that Willie Davis would be joining us soon.

Willie Davis

Willie was from Texarkana and was highly recruited. I spoke to his cousin, who told me that Willie's Momma was a devout Christian. I could relate to Willie right away because, like me, he came from a broken home. When I had dinner with the Davis family on a recruiting visit, I told them about Grambling's campus, its great faculty and academics, and, of course, about Grambling football.

As I was leaving, I told Willie's Momma, "I've told you everything about Grambling, but there's one additional thing I must share. If your son comes to Grambling, he's going to have to go to church." Willie later repeated to me what his Momma said after I left. There was no doubt in her mind. "Oh, Lordy, you're going to Grambling!"

Whenever I see Willie today, he still teases me about that. He tells me that that "was hitting below the belt."

Willie Davis was a great football player. I'll always remember the time I was in George Steinbrenner's office. He had two volumes of books by Vince Lombardi, the legendary coach of the Green Bay Packers. Nobody knew the game better than Lombardi.

In one of the volumes, Lombardi wrote that Willie Davis was the best linebacker he had ever coached. He talked about his amazing feet, his intelligence, and his ability to deliver a blow. That underlined my experience with Willie.

We had a tradition at Grambling in which the great players would return to campus for spring practice. They would work with the other guys and pass on their techniques. Tank Younger started it. He was blown away when he came back in 1952 and looked at Willie Davis. After he saw him perform and witnessed Willie's foot speed and power to deliver a blow, he predicted that Willie Davis would be a great pro player in the NFL. When I read what Lombardi said, it brought back what Younger had said about Willie Davis.

Willie helped turn the program around between 1952 and 1955. We had two real good years (7–3–1 and 7–3) in 1952 and 1953. Bishop had humiliated us in 1953, 67–34. I don't know where our defense was that day, but they sure weren't at the stadium for our game. No one scored that many points against us in the next four decades.

Another loss was to Texas Southern by 22–7. Our offense, which averaged nearly twenty-seven points a game that year, must have found where the defense went for the Bishop game.

The Nation's Mood Changes

The mood in the nation was tense as we prepared for the 1954 season. The Supreme Court had rendered the decision to integrate public schools in the *Brown v. the Board of Education* case in May.

Resistance was mounting in the deep southern states. Blacks, of course, had a sense of optimism that real changes were now going to come quickly. The optimism was always side-by-side with apprehension about how whites might react. We heard about new activity by the Ku Klux Klan and the creation of White Citizens Councils, but Grambling itself seemed removed from the furor. It wasn't always easy to concentrate on football when history was happening around you and your own people were involved in the history making.

The 1954 season was a big disappointment because we went 4–3–2. But we achieved revenge for two of our losses in 1953 when we knocked out Bishop 45–7 and tied Texas Southern 19–19.

We needed a great season and 1955 proved to be it. We gave up only 27 points in our first seven games while we scored 264. We had never had such big margins, averaging 38–4. We were beating some pretty good teams in that stretch including Alcorn, Tennessee State, Bishop (85–0), and Jackson State.

But game eight was Prairie View. They are down on their luck now, but man, they could play football back then. Heck, they were the SWAC champions in the previous four years and had beaten us by scores like 40–7, 34–12, 25–13, 32–0. We only got close to them in 1954 when they won 26–19. We all knew Prairie View stood between us and greatness. But nothing could stop us that year, and we blew them off the field, 26–7.

Willie Davis went on to help us go unbeaten at 10–0 and win our first Black National Championship with a win over Florida A&M in the Orange Blossom Classic, which Tank came to see. Now that felt real good. We'd won our first nine games by a combined score of 328–40. Florida A&M sure wasn't like the rest of the season, but we walked away with a 28–21 victory.

Willie had big support on that team with a great runner named Edward Murray. I hadn't noticed Edward at first when he was in high school because he was only 140–145 pounds and about 5'7".

But he ran like Tank Younger and nobody ever caught him. The story of Edward Murray showed me you can't afford to pass people up without looking at them. He did things that were just hard to believe that a person that size could do. Edward and Willie helped get us to the Orange Blossom Classic. There were 45,000 people there to see that game in Miami against Florida A&M (FAMU). Jake Gaither, the legendary coach of FAMU, had created the Orange Blossom Classic and called it the Black National Championship. Jake was a real innovator and entrepreneur.

Because this team was so great, there were often arguments about whether this team was better than the 1942 team that went unscored on and was undefeated! Nonetheless, there were people who didn't think Grambling belonged in the same class with the other fine black college teams.

When we got to Miami we found out that FAMU's sport information director (SID) had been fired because he asked, "What is wrong with Coach Gaither?" in the papers. Why was Gaither bringing this little country team from Grambling to play in the Black National Championship game in the Orange Blossom Classic? These country boys can't be any football team. Well, we whipped FAMU. Coach Gaither knew who he was inviting. Maybe he didn't know we were that good.

They had great ball players. After they kicked the ball off to us, Murray faked it back to the fullback, turned back and threw a complete pass. When a FAMU guy forced him out of the pocket on the next play, a big end tackled him. Some of our guys told me that the end challenged Murray with, "Don't come around my end. You haven't been reading the papers. . . . I'm up for all-American. You can't come around here or I'll tear you up."

Edward showed his guts when we called that next play. He made that same motion and faked it. This big boy came through and Willie trapped him. While he was down on the ground, Willie told him, "Even if they've got you up for all-American, you're not going to make it now because they see you down there on the ground." You could have driven a car through that hole after Willie trapped him and Murray went eighty-nine yards.

FAMU had a great backfield led by Frazier and Gallimore. All the pro scouts were there to see them. Willie Gallimore became a great pro with the Bears. Everyone was talking about Cleveland's Paul Brown being in Miami to see these FAMU stars.

Willie was known for his quickness and how hard he hit. If he tackled someone one-on-one, you could often hear a sound like a thud on the field. Paul Brown heard more than one thud that day in Miami. Playing defensive end, no one went around Willie. He made great plays all night long, and Brown ended up signing Willie on the basis of what he saw.

Thus, Willie spent two years with the Cleveland Browns before destiny brought him together with Lombardi at Green Bay. Willie became a Packer legend when he helped lead them to win the first Super Bowl against Kansas City. He played hurt, just like he did at Grambling, and never missed a game in twelve NFL seasons. Willie Davis was really something. He was there for ten years, played in a bunch of pro bowls, and was chosen by Lombardi as team captain.

Willie was always a leader, on and off the field. Long after his playing career, I heard Bill Curry speak of Willie's impact on him. Curry was a rookie out of Georgia Tech with a deep Southern accent. Curry hadn't even expected to be drafted, let alone make the team. It was the first time he'd been around blacks, and he was sure they would single him out as a cracker because of the way he spoke.

One day Curry was walking alone and heard a voice call him from behind. "I thought it was God," recalled Curry. It was Willie, who took him under his wing and gave him the confidence to be a fine pro and go on to be a veteran NFL assistant and college head coach. That was Willie Davis, the man. To this day, Willie is the spokesman for that team when people look back at the Lombardi era.

While he was with the Browns I suggested that he come back in the off-season and take some additional courses at Grambling to help him with his postplaying career. I thought he could even help us coach some of the team members while he took the classes and inspire them in their own studies at the same time.

I realized that although he had graduated, I didn't know what Willie had majored in. I knew what almost everyone else was studying, but for some reason, I had not asked Willie. That was a lesson for me, not only because I should have known, but also because of his answer and how I could have helped him then if I had been aware of the circumstances. I never took a student–athlete's course of study for granted again.

I asked him what he had majored in at Grambling and what he wanted to study now. I was going to send the information to the registrar's office so Willie could get registered for his classes after his pro season ended.

Two days later Willie hadn't told me, and I went back to him and asked what was wrong. He disclosed, "I just don't know what I want to major in." When I responded, "Why?" Willie asserted, "Because when I first came to Grambling, I told my advisor that I wanted to major in business. However, my advisor told me I didn't have the mentality to major in business so I just picked another field."

Imagine, Willie Davis had wanted to major in business and this woman told him he would be wasting his time. It made me sick to think that this advisor discouraged a student as bright as Willie Davis. I wondered about all the others she had counseled. Or what high school students are told not to study.

I asserted, "Well, you're a scholar–athlete, and if you look at your own transcript, you could have majored in business. Why don't you take a couple of courses now, and when you come back next year then see what you think about it."

He did and when he came back the next semester he hadn't made anything lower than a *B*. The following off-season, Willie was working in Chicago and went to University of Chicago, where he earned a master's degree in business. That was a real lesson for me and all my coaches. We have to be active with all the academic people at the university. Of course, in most cases, the academic people are going to be right, but we can't let anyone discourage our student-athletes with what they want to do.

Now Willie Davis is an extremely successful businessman. He is the same person that this advisor contended didn't have the mentality to major in business. She had thrown him off quite a bit—it could have been completely devastating with anyone but Willie.

She probably had some opinion of athletes not being as smart as other students. I thought she probably had talked to some other athletes, and she was putting them all in the same class. As bad as that was, we used Willie's case as an example to help other guys, to show them what people can really do. Willie has come back to the university and helped the president. He has helped the program in many ways, so it's just been wonderful for us. But I was real happy that he didn't leave Grambling thinking that he didn't have the ability to do it.

Today he owns radio stations and is even into television, as well as some other business ventures. So I was real glad that we had a chance to talk about it and helped put him back on the right track by doing what he wanted to do.

Grambling's new president, Steve Favors, announced the Eddie Robinson Chair during Grambling's Founders' Day ceremony in 1998. Willie Davis had donated $100,000 and committed to raise another $500,000. The state of Louisiana will match everything. Willie Davis gave me one of the proudest moments of my life on that day.

He has done some outstanding work for our nation as well. I was honored to help present Willie the Lou Gehrig Award in March of 1999. To say I am proud of Willie Davis is a major understatement. Willie is in the Pro Football Hall of Fame, but if there was an "American Hall of Fame," he would be one of the first people inducted.

Our First Black National Championship Trophy

We went to Atlanta to receive our first Black National Championship trophy, which was being presented by the 100% Wrong Club. The club has been a major black organization doing good things in Atlanta for years. I think the men who organized the club were trying to poke fun at themselves with the name "100% Wrong," since they had become so influential. President Jones was coming to hand me the award during the ceremony. It was a huge thing for Grambling, and for me and Doris. I worked so hard on the acceptance speech. I felt it was the most important speech of my life at that time.

Branch Rickey, the owner of the Dodgers, was also there along with Dan Rooney, the owner of the Pittsburgh Steelers. The audience was almost all black besides these two men. Mr. Rickey spoke about Jackie Robinson and all he had gone through. At first you couldn't hear a pin drop. The 1,000 or so people in the room were on the edge of their seats, catching every word about their hero from the very man who had made the Jackie Robinson story possible.

Mr. Rickey was hitting everybody hard. I was thinking ahead to my speech. Doris had worked with me to prepare the acceptance speech. When Mr. Rickey got through talking, my president was up there in tears.

I was waiting for President Jones to make the presentation to me, when he told the audience while glancing at me. "I want you all to know that we're happy to be the recipient of this award. You don't know what it means to Grambling." I was ready. Now it was supposed to be my part to speak. The place was packed. The mood was incredible. I was there with my speech, which I had studied all the way from Grambling to Atlanta. I had worked it and I was ready to go.

Then President Jones put his arms around me and declared, "Eddie, this is Grambling's greatest night. You don't need to say anything. Mr. Rickey said everything. We just need to go on home and let the Lord take over from here."

He was something, so religious. With all due respect for the Lord, I proclaimed, "Hey, what about my speech? I studied that speech from Grambling to Atlanta and I didn't get a chance to say it." He should have let me say it.

Boy, oh boy, he was some kind of guy. There were many times I thought that if he hadn't come along to hire me that I might have gotten caught on the streets in Baton Rouge. I thank God that Dr. Jones just grabbed me and took me. Nevertheless, I surely did not want him to grab me off the stage that night. It took me some time to get over it, but I later recognized that having Mr. Rickey talk about what Jackie Robinson had gone through was far more important to those attending than anything I might have added. President Jones was my teacher, even when I did not realize it.

5.

FAMILY, FAME, AND CIVIL RIGHTS: 1955–69

Now things at Gambling were really rolling, but I always recognized that Doris and our children were everything to me. There were so many things I loved about Doris then, just like it is now. We always gave the children time, including starting the day together each and every morning at the breakfast table. We would always get up before they did, especially when they were school-age. We didn't want to be rushing around but wanted to place all our attention on them.

Working to Keep Things Straight

Things were almost always just perfect, and we'd talk nonstop at the table. If we were quiet, the children knew something wasn't right and they'd tell us to "go back in the bedroom and get whatever straight you got to get and then come back out here." They never saw us fight. Never will. Lillian and Eddie know how much we love each other and how much we love them and their families.

We wanted our marriage to be a good marriage. We never had

a violent moment. We never even had a strong argument. Neither of us ever told the other to shut up or called the other person a bad name. We knew couples who might push or strike each other or their kids, but this never happened in our house or with our kids.

Lillian and Eddie have never seen me raise my voice like some people do so often. Doris and I just wanted to make our marriage special. We always said that the key in marriage was always knowing what you were saying because you can't take it back. While you can be forgiven, you can't take it back once you have put it out there. Doris would tell me that some of her friends had their husbands or boyfriends say, in the heat of an argument, something like, "You're not worth a damn," or something like that. Doris would tell me those women would never forget those words even if they forgave their men. That was a great lesson for me with Doris.

So Doris and I came up with our own system for our marriage and our lives. We wanted to make it work, whether we were walking around in our little town, when we went to someone's house, had our own house parties, or were traveling out of town.

We invited other faculty to come to parties after our ball games. There wasn't too much entertainment for adults here. It gave them something to look forward to, and we sure enjoyed it also. The parties gave Doris the opportunity to prepare things and invite people to the house. My Momma was living with us then, and she'd just about cook enough food to feed two or three football teams. Momma was one great cook.

All the people who were not knowledgeable about football found out about the parties after the games, and most people were trying to come. This kept Doris involved. But just as important for us was the notion that it was important for me to let my team see that Doris and I were a team.

Doris couldn't go on the regular trips if her presence meant she would have to cut somebody out of the bus. We weren't able to get a car until about 1955 when we were going to our first important bowl game, the Orange Blossom Classic. President Jones got us a car. He made the down payment and fixed it so I could pick up the note.

After we got the car, we went to more places, but we mostly just brought the entertainment home where we could share it. We also went to church together each Sunday after we joined the New Rock Valley Baptist Church, and we have been there for fifty-six years!

Eddie Jr. and Lillian Rose

I always wanted our kids to know that I loved their mother, and she was always letting them know how we felt about each other. Lillian and Eddie Jr. sometimes joked that we didn't care enough about them because we spent so much time together. They both went to Grambling High School, where Eddie was quite a good quarterback. Lillian played high school basketball but was not a star. She did have a beautiful voice and was a very good singer. Lillian Rose was good academically, like her little brother.

When television came out, Eddie Jr. or Lillian would tell us, "If you're going to look at television, then look at television. If not, then get up and go to some other place in the house." The kids, who wanted to watch TV, noticed that we looked at each other more than the television and we were wasting their potential viewing time. Doris and I didn't need TV; we had each other and we could just sit around the house, talk, and learn to do new things. We were always really happy with each other, and Eddie Jr. and Lillian knew it.

The guys on the team would often come by. I encouraged that because I thought it was important that they know that the coach is a football coach, but he's also a Daddy and a husband. Eddie Jr.

and I might be playing basketball. Of course, Eddie was smaller than the college football players, so I would pull him aside to give him pointers. He was a good athlete but was so much younger. Doris told me I shouldn't help him in front of the other guys—that it looked unfair.

I'd coach Eddie and she was against that. Doris would tell me, "You can't show Eddie how to whip the other boys." I said, "But, baby, they're bigger than he is, and I have to tell him some things." She emphasized, "Well, you get him back in the house and tell him. Either that or show the other boys, too."

When Eddie was playing with them, I could look out of my bedroom window and see them. There were times when I saw that Eddie might need to go left to get around one of my guys and I just wanted to tell him how to do it. However, Doris was right. I could only tell him later so the guys would be reassured that I was not ignoring them.

The paperboy was a real good friend of Eddie's and he was regularly with him. There was many an afternoon when I'd be walking home from campus. The neighborhood ladies sometimes were looking all around their yards as I approached their homes. Then I'd hear from them, "Coach, have you seen that paperboy? He's late all the time." I would start laughing to myself because I guessed that the paperboy had stopped at my house to play a game of basketball with Eddie. I also knew that if he was late, Eddie was beating him and he was trying to win one back.

But if I came home and the ladies weren't out in their yards looking, and the papers had been delivered, then I realized the boy had whipped Eddie and was on his way. On those days, I would work with Eddie on his game because he didn't like to lose. We had a lot of fun.

Doris and I worked on how it would be best to discipline our children. Before I came home I'd call and ask Doris, "Darling, how did you and the children make out today?" At first, she'd answer,

"What do you mean?" I told her, "Baby, look now, if you know it's around the time that I'm coming home, call me and tell me that I have to discipline Eddie. I don't want to have been playing with him, having a great time coming in the house, and then have to discipline him." That didn't make any sense; Doris and I needed to show a united front with the children. That's why we started this practice of calling before I came home. We just tried to carry the family together and raise a good family. I wanted Doris to be part of everything.

I didn't want to arrive to hear Doris say I had to punish Eddie; he's done this or Lillian's done the other thing. I wanted to know before I got home. Because when Eddie saw me coming he'd run out in the yard to greet me. We might shoot a couple of baskets and I'd put him on my back. We would walk and tussle, playing all the way into the house. Then I would see Doris. I could always tell by the way she was standing if there had been a problem that day and she was waiting for me to take action. It didn't take us long to get our signals straight. I'd call, she would tell me what I needed to do when I got home, and I was ready to do whatever it took.

Surrogate Daddy

Lillian and Eddie both went to Grambling State for their college education. Nemiah Wilson was on the team when Eddie Jr. played at Grambling. Nemiah was out of my hometown of Baton Rouge and was a very good football player. He hung out with Eddie Jr. all the time; but I was having so much trouble with Nemiah, I told Doris I needed to talk to her about him. She looked at me and told me, "You might be a pretty good coach, but you aren't real smart where the guys are concerned. Right under your nose, the reason you're having trouble with this young man is you carry him every place you carry Eddie. He sees what you're doing for Eddie and how you and Eddie are getting along. Nemiah wants you to be his Daddy, too. The more time that you spend with him, the better you all are going to really get along."

Doris helped me to really find that out. I wasn't aware of the fact that it was happening. Ladies pay more attention to that kind of thing. Nemiah had come from a home where he didn't have a Daddy. I guess I became a father figure to Nemiah—a mentor before I really knew what the word *mentor* meant. I wanted to model my behavior for him to show Nemiah how to succeed. So I began to include him with Eddie Jr. We took him to church, had him over for meals. It got better and better for Nemiah.

Nemiah is still part of our family. After he graduated, he played for Denver, the Jets, the Raiders and the Bears in the NFL. He had a ten-year NFL career. Nemiah's daughter went to Grambling, and he and his family have remained good friends with Eddie Jr. He visits us pretty regularly. Looking back, this was another gift from Doris and helped me to learn to be better as a person and as a coach. I've tried to be a mentor to all my players ever since. Considering that I always considered my players as sons, it was easy to be a father figure for them if they needed one.

The Civil Rights Movement Begins in Montgomery

As the great rivalries among the black colleges grew, my fellow coaches and I had the pick of the best young black players in America. It was a curious position to be in for two reasons: first, we knew our fortune was based on the fact that in the late 1950s there were still not many black student-athletes attending white colleges in the North, and second, there were almost none in the solidly segregated schools in the South.

As our black leaders intensified the fight for rights with bolder challenges to power than ever, there was little doubt that the segregated universities of the South would be prime targets. I also knew that when that was successful, we would have more competition for recruiting the future star black student-athletes.

As we celebrated that first National Championship, we could not help but keep an eye on Montgomery, Alabama, where Rosa Parks had been arrested on December 1, 1955. Whites had been arresting blacks all across the South for generations, but the reaction to the arrest of Rosa Parks told me that we were entering a new time. The bus boycott that followed her arrest lasted for almost a year until the Supreme Court ruled against segregation of public buses, changing the course of history.

I had been preaching for years that you can change things if you were willing to pay the price and use the laws to challenge the inequalities. I know that seemed mostly like a thought as I told it to my student-athletes at Grambling, but Martin Luther King Jr. was making it a reality. He was willing to stand up and face the consequences and was bringing about changes. I had not heard of Dr. King before the bus boycott. I have never stopped thinking about him since then.

I didn't know if I could help lead people as a civil rights activist, but I knew that I could help to groom young black men as intelligent leaders at Grambling. The stereotype that blacks can't lead whites or that they aren't smart enough to do certain things had been trotted out so often that most whites—and sadly, some blacks—readily accepted it.

In 1956, there were no black head coaches at the big white colleges or in the NFL and no black quarterbacks at either level. If we could make a big enough impact with football at Grambling, if our plans worked and our goals were met, then the national stage would provide us the opportunity to smash the stereotypes that blacks couldn't be leaders, be they athletes, civil rights activists, corporate leaders, or politicians. That was something that I wanted to accomplish very badly. I wanted to help show the way, to tear down those brick walls so blacks could coach at the big, predominantly white, schools.

Coaching amid the National Tensions

So as our new leaders emerged on the national scene, as the battles heated up when Arkansas's Governor Faubus refused to let Little Rock's Central High School be integrated peacefully in the fall of 1957, as our hopes and fears grew at the same time, I continued to do what I knew best at Grambling State.

We had followed the National Championship season with a solid 8–1 record in 1956, when our average margin of victory was nearly twenty-four points. But in 1957, our program began to slip slightly with a 4–4 record. The four losses were not close games at all. Wiley punished us, 44–12; Prairie View beat us by 25–14; Texas Southern embarrassed us, 59–14; and Jackson State took us down by a score of 39–20. Our coaches and I knew we needed a boost. Something was missing and we decided to look at adapting our offense. The single-wing offense had served us well, but time may have caught up with it.

Wing-T

Therefore, I went back to Iowa in the summer of 1958 to study the Wing-T and bring it back to Grambling. I had gone back earlier—soon after I had done my masters—as I still wasn't one hundred percent positive regarding my future. I didn't know whether I was going to go into physical education or stay in coaching football. It was then that I saw the Wing-T.

I went up there to get the Wing-T and I got it. That's when I met Forest Evashevski and Willie Flemings. Oh, he was such a great back. Flemings was 5'11" and could stand flatfooted under the goal post, jump, and dunk the ball through in the goal. He was a tailback in the Wing-T.

I saw Flemings take the power test and saw what he could do. It was right after the University of Iowa won the Rose Bowl. When Flemings played basketball, this 5'11" boy would just be up in the air and hang out there. He wasn't tall enough to be up there, but he had so much power that he could do those incredible things.

I went to see Jerry Burns, who later went to the Vikings as a coach after great success at the University of Iowa. At that time, Jerry was an assistant coach to Evashevski, but he was a master of the Wing-T business. Jerry was also recruiting for Iowa, studying for a graduate degree, and teaching a course in advanced football.

He was trying to recruit a kid in Chicago but didn't want to miss teaching his class. I told Jerry to tell me what he was going to teach that day and that I would teach the class for him. When he looked quizzically at me, I said, "I've been in football a pretty long time and I could conduct that class while you go to Chicago, but on one condition." I asked for a key to the dark room, where I could watch films to get that Wing-T offense down. Jerry gave me that key, and I locked myself in the field house for an all-night session. It was so intriguing and I was finding the things that I needed to run the Wing-T. The wingback position was the key. Whoever held it had to have great hands, outstanding speed, and be a good blocker.

I saw what the great plays were and how they were run. That's how I brought the Wing-T to Grambling after the summer of 1958. I put it in in '59 and we've been using the Wing-T ever since!

I knew we couldn't rush installing it into our own offense, so we stayed with the single wing in 1958 and managed to go 6–3. It was frustrating because we were convinced that the Wing-T would have helped us right away. We had recruited some excellent players with running backs Jamie Caleb, Howard McGowan, and Ken Jackson. Curtis Cotton was a terrific halfback. Jerry Robinson would be one of our first wingbacks in the Wing-T offense. Ernie Ladd, one of our greatest players ever, was with us in the late 1950s. All of them eventually had shots in the NFL.

Junius "Buck" Buchanan and Willie Brown

We were ready in 1959. Not only did we have a new system and all the great players I just mentioned, but we had recruited Willie Brown and Buck Buchanan to our program. Both eventually made the Pro Football Hall of Fame.

I could tell that in both cases these were special men. And I knew, from that first season in 1941 on, that the most important thing in football is the guy who plays the game. I told that to Willie when he got here. You can't coach a person unless you love him. I loved these guys and looked at them as though they were the ones I wanted to marry my daughter. Willie was very smart. On the field, I never saw anyone who could pick off a pass as well as Willie. Heck, he did it for sixteen years in the NFL.

But right from the start, I could see he was coaching material himself, a leader. Not only was he a great pro player, but he became a college head coach at Long Beach State. That was quite a statement because in Division I football, outside of the historically black colleges, there have been a total of only fourteen black head coaches in the history of the game. Willie Brown became one of them. Of course, Willie has also been an NFL assistant coach and is now with the Raiders.

When Willie was here, I emphasized to him, "I want you to be a proud person, to work up to what you can be. I want you, like all my players, to be a good family man and a good citizen." Doris still remembers that whenever Willie came to our home for a meal he would always choose to end up in the kitchen washing dishes. He was constantly thinking of others.

I always told Willie he could really play any position because he was so fast. Finally, it got down to playing him at either split end or tight end. I settled on tight end because most defenses put their fastest defenders against the split end and their slower defensive backs on the tight end. It worked.

Willie Brown just ran away from everybody, even though he was really out of position as a tight end. Willie's speed and blocking ability made him impossible to beat. When we ran an end around with Willie, we would always get the first down or big yardage. Willie was a team leader, on and off the field, making big plays in the game and in life.

As I said earlier, Tank Younger knew greatness when he saw it. He felt the same way after he saw Junius "Buck" Buchanan play for the first time at Grambling. Buck was so big and had so much speed. Buck said the only reason that I was able to recruit him was because I told him Grambling was about ten miles from New Orleans. When he came here on the recruiting visit, he said, "Let's run down to New Orleans." One of my student-athletes responded, "Man, now you're talking about 300 miles." Buck insisted, "No, Coach told me it was ten miles." I didn't tell him that, but Buck always joked that I did.

I'll always remember Buck's first day of practice when he beat Ernie Ladd in the 40. You could see Ernie, who had been our fastest lineman, turn sad. I was trying to teach our team the Pro 4–3 defense. However, it turned out that I put tackles where the defensive ends should have been and the defensive ends where the tackles should have been. Buck and Ernie Ladd were our defensive ends, and nobody went outside on us successfully. Buck and Ernie helped turn every attempt to do so inside, where we always caught them. It was 1960 and it was our best defensive year ever. We held several teams to negative yardage.

When the pro scouts saw us play, they told me I had the defensive ends and tackles in the wrong place. I corrected it and we got whipped. We went right back to where we were when we were winning with our own version of the Pro 4–3 defense.

Buck was funny. When Willie Brown was inducted into the Pro Football Hall of Fame, Buck told people at the ceremony that "Coach Robinson didn't tell me that you had to be named Willie to come to Grambling and get into the Hall of Fame." Willie Davis went first and Willie Brown went second.

We were just so proud to have Buck and Willie here at the same time between 1959–62. We also had defensive tackle Ken Thomas, linebacker Leon Simmons, defensive back Charles Cook, offensive tackle Robert Burton, and wide receiver Stone Johnson in that same recruiting class. All had shots in the NFL.

However, it wasn't easy to adjust to the Wing-T and all the new players. We were a disappointing 4–6 in their first year. We lost five of those games by a total of fourteen points, but we still lost. They don't post total points at the end of the season, but they do put wins and losses out there for all to see and remember. But those close games assured me that we had some players ready to lead us, and Buck was at the head of that class with Willie.

In the next year, we went 9–1 and tied for the SWAC title. The Wing-T was our new offense, and it was clicking. Buck was growing in both skills and size. You could almost watch him grow. He was 6'6" and weighed 225 when he got here, but he was growing. By the time he finished a fourteen-year pro career, Buck was 6'7" and weighed 274 pounds.

In their junior year we were a solid 8–2, losing only to Jackson State by one and to Southern, 20–9. We felt optimistic about 1962 when we closed the 1961 season by defeating Texas Southern 23–19, and then blowing out Wiley 71–28, and Alcorn 49–0. Then we started the 1962 season by winning the first five games. With that beginning, we thought we were really going to have a great year. Then the roof collapsed. We lost the next two to Jackson State and Texas Southern; were tied by Arkansas A&M, and embarrassingly by Wiley College in a game in which we didn't score a single point for the first time since 1956. To worsen the result, we had beaten Wiley badly 71–28 the year before. How do two teams that scored one hundred points one year score zero the next? Like I said, you never know what will happen on any given day in football.

I'll always remember the morning when I broke my sleep at the beginning of the day to find Buck Buchanan was the first person drafted in the American Football League. With all the players we had and would send to the NFL, we really celebrated that milestone in 1963. That was a great feeling to know that one of Grambling's players was the first man drafted in the AFL. Wow, what a day that was.

After missing it in his rookie year, Buck was an all-star for six straight years and became the first person from Grambling not named Willie to be inducted into the Pro Hall of Fame. Buck worked for Kansas City after his playing days were over.

Buck had a great, great career, but I know he would have traded a few of those years for better health. It was a nightmare for all of us when he contracted lung cancer. He fought it hard but finally let go on July 16, 1992. That was a very sad day at Grambling and, especially, in the Robinson household.

The Early 1960s: America's Turbulent Times

The base of the civil rights movement was expanding during Grambling's Brown/Buchanan era. College campuses across the South were becoming alive politically. The lunch counter sit-in in Greensboro, North Carolina, in February of 1960 was led by several courageous students from North Carolina A&T. By the time our 1960 season opened, more than 1,500 high school and college students who staged sit-ins had been arrested. They paid the price, but lunch counters were being opened to all.

The Freedom Rides were crisscrossing the southern states, leading to violence against the riders and the arrest of many of them. But they were also leading to the end of segregation on interstate transportation.

Some big state universities, including Georgia and South Carolina, were quietly opening their doors to some blacks. But the bigger news regarding integration of colleges was when James Meredith, kept safe by 500 U.S. marshals, enrolled at the University of Mississippi in September of 1962. Meredith graduated a year later.

I wondered what Bear Bryant, the legendary football coach at Alabama, thought when Governor George Wallace, one of the biggest symbols of segregation and racial hate in America, unsuccessfully tried to personally block the enrollment of a black student at the University of Alabama. In all of these cases, it was good to know that President John Kennedy was using the federal government to protect the rights of those involved in standing up for their rights. By 1963, there weren't many black homes I visited that didn't have photos of Martin Luther King Jr. and John Kennedy prominently displayed.

As I thought about my role and that of my student-athletes, I had to measure the victories with the terrible prices that were being paid. One June night in 1963, I listened to President Kennedy say that America "will not be fully free until all its citizens are free," and the next night I learned that Medgar Evers, one of our brightest leaders in Mississippi, had been gunned down and killed in his own yard.

In August of 1963, we had what I think was one of America's greatest moments when Martin Luther King Jr. delivered his "I Have a Dream" speech before 200,000 marchers on the footsteps of the Lincoln Memorial in Washington. A month later we had one of the worst moments when four little girls died in the bombing of a Birmingham church.

The Civil Rights Movement and Grambling

We knew the places where blacks could go and we usually did. But as the movement heated up, so did our challenges. One time we decided that we would try to eat at a Holiday Inn on the way to Houston. We called and asked them if they would serve us a meal and were surprised that they said it wouldn't be any problem. We told the manager that we would have our players go through the buffet line, like they do at Grambling, eat, and leave. The manager admitted that the hotel was struggling for money so they would do what they had never done before—serve blacks.

Nonetheless, we were concerned because the manager might react a little differently when forty-five large, black men poured out of a bus and into his hotel lobby. We got off the bus with ties, slacks, and jackets. Our coaches had talked to the team about how to act and what to expect. We went through different possibilities, including what to do if someone offended one of us. We didn't want to take any chances that we would provoke anything.

After we finished eating, our student-athletes put everything back that was supposed to be put back, our business manager paid the bill, and we began to leave. Then the hotel manager stopped us and asked, "Can you look me up on the return trip? Tell us what time you're going to be passing through; we'll be here to serve you."

From then on we never had any problem with that kind of thing. There is too much competition out there. Heck, we are buying fifty to sixty meals at each stop. The dollar is all-American. It doesn't know from black and white. But it took until the late

1970s for some American businesses to recognize that the dollar was color-blind. We tested the waters early, but I know those young people tested a lot more at lunch counters in Greensboro and the Freedom Rides, which opened up interstate transportation throughout the South. They helped us get served that day at the Holiday Inn.

We had some student-athletes who were activists during these times when the civil rights movement was peaking. However, there were more activists among the regular student body who demonstrated for changes than on the team. I wasn't sure how to handle the protests. People were getting killed and hurt in the civil rights movement. I knew I didn't want that to happen to any of my guys. At the same time, I was grateful that some people had the courage to make a stand for all of us. But the parents of my student-athletes were expecting me to take care of their sons' education, safety, and well-being. Therefore, if I saw some danger coming, I headed my student-athletes away from it. I know that in the minds of some people, I shouldn't have done that.

But that's who I am. I believe if I'm the leader, then I am supposed to take some criticism when I tell my student-athletes what's right and what is wrong. It was expected by others—and by myself—that I would advise them on the options that they had. If I wasn't going out to demonstrate, then I didn't want them to go out to demonstrate. I could never have faced a mother or father if their son went out and got shot. What would I say? And student activists were getting killed. I shuddered when the bodies of James Chaney, Michael Schwerner, and Andrew Goodman were recovered. Those three brave young men were brutally killed in the summer of 1964—the price they and their families paid for their efforts to improve race relations in America.

I know there were people then who were giving me the Uncle Tom stigma, but I was doing what I believed was the right thing for my student-athletes. I wasn't going to go out and hurt somebody or let one of my own get hurt to disprove that I was an Uncle Tom.

Coming from my background, growing up in a society so completely segregated that I didn't even notice what I was missing until later in life, it must sound strange when I say I always tried to transcend race, to make it irrelevant. I admit I am a dreamer. I always tried to be a person who would stand up and talk. I am convinced that if you can have a dialogue that a lot of things can happen.

Blacks and whites in the civil rights movement were fighting for the right to equal opportunity because blacks didn't have that in so many areas. By the mid-1960s, the number of blacks in the NFL and NBA were increasing. I wanted all my players to graduate. I wanted some to become so good in football that they would make it to the NFL. I think our basketball and baseball coaches had the same double dreams for their student-athletes. We needed to break those barriers, whether it was in sports or in life. If you are black you might have to do more to make it, but you can make it. Our Grambling guys proved that over and over again. I don't know if it is different in other parts of the work world, but in sports we expect discipline and loyalty. If an NFL team saw a guy protesting, I am sure it would have been reluctant to draft him. I don't think that's right, but I am quite sure it is true.

In my profession I just wanted to be as good as the best, whoever that was. That was not as easy for a black coach to prove. Still, I wanted to be as fair to the white man as I wanted him to be to me. I needed to show him that I was going to treat him the way I wanted him to treat me. I know that was such a major lesson from my father. It was a gift that saved me from wasting my time with anger when I could use my mind to become a better person and coach.

I told my student-athletes then—and, sadly, thirty years later was still telling them—that every NFL owner is white. Nobody who looked like me has ever owned an NFL team. So if an owner thinks one of my student-athletes hates whites because he read about him protesting, he is not going to take him. Protesting doesn't mean hating others. It means just the opposite; but if it is misinterpreted, then one more door would be quickly shut. I just told them how I thought it would work. It was up to the player to use the advice or not. And that was for his future and would not affect how I would react to him as a player on our Grambling team.

Every night I go to bed I know who made the Eddie Robinson the public sees. Without my student-athletes, I know there's no me. I want them to know how I feel about them. I want them to experience success in life and go on to be good people. Yet I know that as the team's leader, I had to be a little tough. Sometimes the players probably saw the tough as mean. It's sad that a man has to have a little bit of toughness to be successful, to push his tail out of bed and make him get up and work hard to support his family. If they thought I was mean when I rang that bell in their dorms so early each morning, I was simply making sure they got up.

Our guys needed to see that if we were working at the same job and I'm black and the other guy is white, both of us are trying to feed our family. The white guy has no reason to give the job to me by doing a poor job so I can have his job. He's got a family, too. We will always be competing, and blacks can't give whites any excuse to let us go.

Reacting to Integration

Doris had always tried to do the same things with her students that I did with my student-athletes. She had been teaching English and speech at Lincoln High School when schools were still segregated.

Doris was then transferred to Ruston High after the schools were integrated. I don't remember any protests against integration in Ruston. I do remember that Doris came home and told me that Ruston High was a much better school. It had more books, equipment, and everything else to make it easier to teach and to learn.

She wasn't concerned about being at an integrated school. Doris just tried to do her work and show the kids that the education is there and they've got to get themselves prepared. Some black kids looked at her like she was crazy, believing they were trapped by their skin color. While we both believed being black didn't make life any easier, Doris tried to get her students to understand that if they weren't prepared, then they couldn't take advantage of the free enterprise system and use the best judicial system in the world if they needed it. You have to learn how to use these things. I know a lot of blacks think they can't get a fair shake from the system because they are black. I can understand that, but in too many cases we don't use or test the system.

For example, some blacks think we'll never get justice when a black man is killed. Some don't want to even bother with the police because they think the police will never help blacks. But how do they know for sure? I believe we've got to test it by insisting the authorities go in to investigate. We have to understand the system to use it. That's what education is all about. We've got to know where we are. We don't live in Germany or France. We've got to know what goes on in the U.S.A. and what goes on in Louisiana. We've got to know what it's going to take for us to live well wherever we are.

I have an inward battle all the time when people say "them and us." I pay my income taxes. I pay more than some people and less than others. I'm going to pay them because I want my piece of the pie. If you love something, you'll fight harder for it. You can't expect to get without giving. You can't expect to try to change something if you don't understand it. Life can be a battle. You can't win the battle without a game plan. Doris tried to give her students a game plan; I tried to give my student-athletes a game plan.

I relied on the civil rights messengers like Dr. Martin Luther King Jr. to carry our collective voices for change. Not only did we have great leaders, but the police were supposed to back them up. Now we know that did not always happen, but the Constitution made them liable. That's how President Kennedy sent troops into so many southern cities. The Constitution was there to protect the rights of the people, and we finally had a president who used it to help blacks in the South. It nearly broke our hearts when President Kennedy was murdered. What a loss for our country.

It hurt really badly when someone told me I couldn't do something because we didn't have the money or because I was black or I worked for a black college. The pain drove me to strive to prove them wrong. Never easy to fight the pain. It was painful for me the first time I learned that I couldn't go to LSU as a student or even watch a game there simply because of the color of my skin. I guess they were trying to tell me I was inferior when, as a boy, I was caught and beaten trying to sneak into an LSU game. I was literally clubbed because I wanted to watch a game. Yes, that was painful and hurtful. But I wanted to see those games to learn to prepare for what I knew my future would be. So when I discovered you could work at the stadium before the games and then you could watch, I began my ritual of waking up at 5:00 A.M. each Saturday to work until the game started so I could watch football. Maybe that was the first time I learned I could accomplish more by working for change within the system rather than openly fighting against it.

It was painful that Doris and I had to prepare sandwiches for Grambling's players in the 1940s because blacks were not allowed in the restaurants. It was painful when the Blue Bird, our team bus, broke down in the 1950s and a mechanic waved a wrench at us while shouting, "Don't bring that nigger bus in here." But I had to deal with the pain and go on. I knew the man who clubbed me and the mechanic hated me because I was black. But I also knew they were ignorant people, and I could never act as though all whites believed the same things about all blacks.

I never hated LSU. I looked at it and I dreamed. I'm a dreamer. I wanted to know why LSU could do some things and Grambling couldn't. I thought Grambling should get the same scholarships and grants as LSU. But that, of course, has never happened. It's not stopping us from trying. So we had to do more with what we did get.

It is a matter of pride and trying to compete. My job was to get my student-athletes to want to be as good as anybody else. To do that, they had to play the game, be intelligent, and be good people in our society. They needed to be intelligent enough to know about everyone's rights. If they are discriminated against, then it's time to use the system and take the violator to court. If we believe in our Constitution, then when something goes wrong it is our responsibility to take action.

It may not happen all the time, but you've got to go through the proper procedures. Are you willing to give the other person the same that you want them to give you? This is what you have to do. Sometimes it means speaking up for someone. It may not be as big as a court case, but it will be as important for the person you speak up for. I feel so strongly about this.

Hank Stramm and Goldie Sellers

A good case in point happened with Goldie Sellers, a former Grambling student-athlete, at the first Super Bowl in New Orleans. Hank Stramm was the coach and Sellers's days with Kansas City seemed over.

When the game was over and we were about to leave, I asked Sellers, "What are you going to do?" He said, "Coach, I don't really know what I'm gonna do as far as the team is concerned. They have given me an opportunity to play. They have been very fair to me. I wish they would let me come back next year; I would try to improve myself and be better. I don't feel I lived up to their expectations this year. I would do that if I got another chance next year."

I got on the telephone and called Hank Stramm at his hotel. "Hank, I got something that I think you need to hear." He said, "Why don't you come down here and tell me." So we took the bus to his hotel. I said, "The is the young man I'm talking about, Hank." Then I told Sellers to leave us alone for a few minutes.

After Goldie left, I said, "Hank, this guy played for me. I don't know what you ever said about him, but you need to know what he said about you. Sellers just told me that he would be grateful if the team would have him back. He said the team and you as a coach have been good to him. He didn't know whether he gave back as much as he had, but he feels if he gets another chance, he's going to do everything he possibly can do to be better than he was this year." I told Hank that the fact that Sellers said you had been fair to him was one heck of a comment. Most people don't do that. I thought this was the type of compliment that a coach should hear.

Goldie is doing real well in business now. If I hadn't told Coach Stramm, he never would have known that somebody said that kind of thing about him. You've got to be able to give to others in the same way that you want them to give to you. So that's part of it. When I start looking at myself, I wonder, "Now how does this sound coming out of a black man's mouth?"

But I think that you've got to try to be as much a part of this society as anybody else. Now that's my feeling that I've developed in seventy-eight years. So much has happened to me—so many fine things. I know bad things have happened to others, and I can't speak for them. I can't even speak for my kids because they haven't had the same experiences. So, this is how I see things. This is how I developed attitudes about things. This is how I feel about our way of life and what it stands for, and how you can be a good American.

I believe I am using common sense. This came from my Daddy, who hadn't gone to school but was sure intelligent in a different way. One thing he said over and over was that "you can't ever know what's in a man's house unless you go inside and look." I've applied that to so many people and so many situations.

It was sometimes harder for me to say these things in the sixties and seventies when there was so much protest. I would think that people in the black community are now looking at my philosophy as much more on target, and that it was on target all the time.

Father Kevin

While I went to church every Sunday and did everything to get my guys to do the same, religion was rarely brought into the locker room. However, we had a priest who became a fan of Grambling about this time. Father Kevin was the priest for the campus Catholic church and for the town of Grambling's Catholic church. He traveled everywhere with us and helped us lighten our moods with his sense of humor. Father Kevin was often the only white person traveling with us. Color meant nothing with Father Kevin. He became a member of the team. We all respected the cloth he wore.

We were about to play Tennessee State, which had beaten us the year before. We were in our locker room right before going onto the field when one of my players asked me, "Coach, I know you're Baptist, but we would like to have Father Kevin lead us in prayer."

I said, "Yes, indeed. And when he's finished we'll get the Methodist, then we'll get the Baptist. We'll get them all if it's going to make us play better." I had been there when Father would be praying the Lord's Prayer. When he'd get to the end, we would all say, "Amen." But on this day, it didn't come out like that. He opened it up for me.

The place was rocking. Tennessee State's old stadium was so noisy you couldn't hear much. I told the fellas that Father Kevin was going to lead us in prayer. To my great surprise, Father Kevin called upon the deity and told him to treat us well. Father told God that they hadn't treated us right last year, that they'd thrown rocks at our buses. Man, this priest was getting our boys up by praying like that. He told the Lord it really didn't matter to him who won the ball game, but he wanted the Lord to know that Tennessee didn't treat us right. He told the Lord that these were a bunch of good young men at Grambling. They went to church and did good deeds. But Father Kevin said again he didn't care who won as long as the Lord knew it was guys who didn't know how to treat people right versus good guys.

Then he began to switch, letting the Lord know that Grambling needed to win this game to have a chance as conference champs and at a national championship. I don't know if God heard Father, but our boys did. Instead of saying amen, he said, "Coach, will you say a few words now?" I said, "No, no. Open the door, man, they're ready. Let them go, man."

When they opened that door they were just snorting, trying to get out of there. Saying nothing was the best thing I could have said. They were going to tear the door down. We got down there and played well.

At halftime we were leading them 18 to 6, and we were coming back up the hill to the locker room. I was thinking about what I was going to say. Father had gotten us sky-high. We had really put it all together.

The door, of course, was locked, and we were madly calling for Doc Harvey, who had the keys, to open it. Now the boys were ready to tear down the door to get in instead of to get out. Doc finally got there, got his key, and opened the door. We couldn't believe our eyes when we saw Father Kevin. He'd gotten locked in when we went onto the field and missed the entire half. Our guys went back out in the second half with Father Kevin, who was happier watching us win the game than he had been locked up in the first half.

Father was quite a guy. We had many good times with him in the 1960s and 1970s. When he died, we lost a good man.

Quarterbacking in Black and White

Grambling had some great quarterback stories between 1965 and 1969. The first one was personal and was about Eddie Robinson, Jr. My son was Grambling's passing leader in 1965. I was filled with pride to have Eddie help lead the team to an 8–3 record while winning the Southwestern Athletic Conference (SWAC) Championship. We had been cochamps in 1960, but this was our first outright championship since we joined the SWAC in 1959. Henry Dyer rushed for 1,025 yards and scored thirteen touchdowns that year.

The loyalty of our former players always helped us to more fully develop our current players. They would bring NFL techniques to our spring practices. When I think about it now, I realize how fortunate we were. We had Willie Davis bringing us Lombardi's strategies and teaching our quarterbacks Bart Starr's controlled passing style. We had Tank Younger showing us how the great Rams quarterbacks ran their system. We even had Doug Jones, who played at Ruston High but didn't go to Grambling, practice with us in the spring. Doug was one of the great pass-pattern runners with the Cleveland Browns. Doug was teaching our guys how to run the patterns when I said, "Teach me, too." Doug told me I wasn't going to play, but I convinced him I might have to teach it to the next set of student-athletes who came to Grambling. So he taught all of us the sharp cuts and roll movements from the Browns' offense. We wanted to have a sophisticated passing game because I always hoped we would place the first black quarterback in the NFL.

We had a fine QB in the year before Eddie Jr. in Mike Howell, who passed for 1,032 yards and eleven touchdowns in 1964. But Mike really didn't want to play QB for us because he wanted to play in the NFL and knew there had never been a black NFL quarterback. He wanted to be a defensive back for us but agreed to play QB for Grambling. Doug Jones told the Browns about Mike, and he signed with Cleveland to start a seven-year NFL career as a DB.

It makes me sad when I think back about all the great black quarterbacks who changed their positions either to play in college or in the pros. I wonder now how that must have hurt all these guys because someone said, "Blacks can't make it as the quarterback!" Did they buy into the stereotype that Blacks couldn't lead whites? I worked hard with my guys to let them know it was only a stereotype and that we all could be leaders of people, no matter what their color was.

James Harris and Charlie Joiner

That was all about to change because for the next three years we were blessed with one of our greatest quarterbacks ever. James Harris was the original "Shack." I knew he was the one who would break the barrier every bit as much as I had known that Tank would be our first man in the NFL. James passed for a staggering 4,128 yards in his three years at the helm of Grambling. He threw for forty-three touchdowns while completing 249 passes. His target was often the incredible Charlie Joiner, who caught 112 passes in three years.

Gambling was the SWAC cochampion all three years and won the Black National Championship after going 9–1 in 1967. We lost only five games in those three years. Four teammates were drafted from the 1966 team: Norman Davis, Julian Gray, and Louis Jackson were all DBs and Richard Stebbins was a HB. The National Champs sent six: Wesley Bean and Henry Davis (both LBs); DBs Essex Johnson, Robert Atkins Jr., and Roger Williams; and DL Harold Jones. In James's and Charlie's senior year, they were joined by five others in the draft: Henry Jones (FB), DBs Hilton Crawford and George Muse, Edward Watson (LB), and DT Richard Lee. Now that was a group we were so proud of, top to bottom.

But the top two were world beaters. Charlie Joiner played eighteen years in the NFL, hauling down 750 passes, amassing more than 12,000 yards with those receptions, while averaging 16+ yards per catch. His sixty-five touchdowns alone could have made him Grambling's fourth Pro Hall of Fame inductee.

I had handpicked and prayed for James Harris to hurdle the color barrier as an NFL quarterback, just as I had hoped and prayed that in 1949 Tank Younger could shoulder the burden of being the first player from an historically black school to seek a spot on an NFL roster. I wouldn't let James Harris ever give up the idea that he would be an NFL quarterback. Ernie Ladd and Buck Buchanan had an off week with Kansas City when James was about to start his last game for us against Southern. By then we knew he was headed for the NFL as a QB.

Southern was on top, 32–27 with two minutes left when we got possession. We were moving the ball well but then stalled and had a big third-down play. Ernie came over to me and said, "Coach, we need to have James pass the ball. We've got to throw it to Charlie (Joiner)." I told him it was up to James. I called time out and asked James what he thought. Being the leader he was, James insisted that we mix up the plays between a run and passing. Ernie was going crazy, "Just throw it." Now Ernie was a seasoned pro, but the pros weren't paying me to help Grambling win so I told James to call the plays. I had taught my men how to execute plays. I wasn't going to make the plays. My job was to teach. It was James's job to execute.

He hit Charlie on a down and out to get the first down. We needed eight yards and picked up thirteen. On the next play, James stepped back and Charlie ran down toward the end zone and then cut. James faked the pass and tossed it to our fullback, who ran twenty yards for the touchdown. We won 34–32 in one of our most exciting games ever against Southern.

Charlie was a great pattern runner, maybe our best ever. President Jones was nervous when he first saw James and Charlie play together. James would seem to throw the ball in a direction where there were no receivers in sight. It was our down and out. James was throwing to a spot, and Charlie knew where the ball was going to be and his blinding speed almost always got him there. These were two very intelligent men. Both graduated and had distinguished careers in the front office and in coaching in the NFL after their brilliant playing careers.

Charlie Joiner played for eighteen years with the Oilers, Bengals, and Chargers. It was no surprise to me that he became an NFL receivers coach, most recently with the Buffalo Bills. I was very proud to be there when he was inducted into the Pro Football Hall of Fame in 1996.

I intensively recruited James, who was a star at a high school in Monroe, Louisiana. Four years later, James was the Buffalo Bills's eighth pick in 1969 and started the season opener against Detroit over Jack Kemp and Tom Flores. These were the days when OJ Simpson was with the Bills.

James's beginning was better than his ending in Buffalo. Shack really had a tough time and was cut. He was just hanging around in the city after he was let go. When I found he was still in Buffalo, I called Tank Younger, who was then a scout for the Rams. He didn't hesitate to try to get James a real shot with the Rams. James later played for the Chargers after the Rams in what became a stellar thirteen-year playing career and an even longer tenure in various NFL front offices.

We were lucky to have Tank in Los Angeles when Buffalo turned him loose. James was back in football. I had told him he was young enough and strong enough that another team would pick him. James and I had talked about the racial overtones of him being the first full-time black quarterback in the NFL. If he had been openly talking about a racial factor in Buffalo's decision, he might as well have hung up his spikes after he was cut.

The Rams had three good quarterbacks. One was Pat Hayden, who was a Rhodes scholar. The Rams also had Ron Jaworski, who was quite a player himself. The other was our own James Harris. People were asking if the Rams could win with James Harris as the quarterback. What they meant, of course, was could they win with a black quarterback?

There was a whole lot of talk about who ought to be playing. I was very close to James. He was calling me every night and we'd talk for hours. I wrote him a letter telling him what he needed to do. He needed to be the first one at practice and be the last one to leave. He had to practice hard and run all the plays with fire. I told him to study all the other quarterbacks, and that he needed to pay close attention to everything that the coach was telling Pat Hayden. Whatever he told Pat might help James. James had to stop worrying that he was not going to be the starter and just practice like he was the starter.

I told James to be careful with what he said, and he always should say good things about the team. I impressed on him he should not make his not playing into a racial issue, even if he thought it was. I insisted that, even if it was sometimes difficult, that he needed to be gracious about the team and his teammates.

Then I called Carol Rosenbloom, the owner of the Rams, and told him that we needed to talk about James Harris. I emphasized that James was a youngster out of the South who hadn't been around whites very much. I asserted that I thought that he could win the Super Bowl for him if he was given the chance. I was calling to ask Carol if he could bring himself to put his arms around James Harris to give him more confidence.

I shared the advice I had given to James with Carol. He was pleased with what I had told him. Carol had heard I was advising James and felt good about it. So you know what he told me? He said, "Eddie, that's what he's doing." I told Carol that I was especially happy to hear that because of the difficult experience James had had in Buffalo.

In 1976, James became the NFC's leading passer. The Rams won twenty of the twenty-four games he started for them, and he was named MVP in the Pro Bowl. It took a while until he was able to show his talent, but it once again showed that having the type of support given by Tank and Carol Rosenbloom was invaluable in a person's career.

Like Tank, James has gone on to have a distinguished career in the front offices of several NFL teams, most recently as head of pro player personnel for the Baltimore Ravens. Like Tank, James both broke restraints on the field as a player and then in proving blacks could be leaders in the team's front office.

James Gregory: Grambling's First White Player

With everything going on in our nation, it was inevitable that I would decide that we needed to integrate our own team. I didn't need a star player like James Harris, but I did need a guy the other student-athletes would respect and someone who could take being a very real minority both on the team and on the campus. James Gregory was the person who filled the bill.

The way James Gregory got here is an interesting story. Ed Stevens, his coach at Cocoran High School, had "Convincer" Calloway as his assistant. Convincer had played for me at Grambling. Eventually, Ed Stevens came to work for me at Grambling as linebacker coach and as the women's track coach.

I went out to speak at a Cocoran awards banquet for coaches Stevens and Calloway. It was there that I met their player, James Gregory. He was talking to me about going to college and I asked him about Grambling. Then he said, "Mr. Robinson, are you telling me that I could come to your school?" I said, "Yeah, you can come to our school." His coach said James didn't have that much experience but was sure he could help us.

Greg knew how to mix, how to get along with people, and the players liked him. The players put a protective ring around him so certain things never happened to him. The media came to me and told me, "Eddie, we understand that before Greg came you talked with the team about how you wanted them to treat him." I said, "Yes, I did that."

I learned that in graduate school. The chairman of physical education at Iowa, Dr. Charles McCloy, paid special attention to the black students who had come to Iowa. He knew it could be lonely for people who were in a small minority. He was the advisor to all of the blacks who had been at Iowa and paid close attention to all our schedules. "I want to work with you and your schedule. I want you to graduate." And then he said, "When you want somebody to talk to, when you get lonesome, come on over to the office and talk to me. We can take time and talk." He was always that kind of person, and I wanted to be like that.

So I told my players they had to see that nothing happened to

Greg. I said, "We're an American university and a lot of you'll probably end up going to a white school someday. You're going to have to get along there. Since James is a football player here, this is what you really need to do."

I remember a game with Wiley when they hurt James Harris. Then they hurt his backup. I went over and got Greg up to get ready to play. Henry Davis, our captain, called time-out. Davis was nicknamed "hatchet man." Gregory was snapping to get in this game. But it looked like Wiley thought they couldn't win, so they were playing the game real rough. Henry Davis came over to me and said, "Coach, do you know what you're doing?" I said, "Do I know what I'm doing? Yes, I know what I'm doing. I'm getting ready to send Greg into the game."

He said, "Coach, you can't put him in now." When I asked why, he responded, "You know how the game is being played. Wiley is trying to hurt us. If Greg comes in the ball game, I don't know if we're going to be able to protect him. But we will try, even if it causes a war." He asked me to talk to the Wiley coach. Our guys said it simply, "He's the Tiger, and we are not going to let them deliberately take shots at him."

So I told the official, "Tell the Wiley coach right now or when we have another time-out that we need to talk." After two more players got hurt, I called the ref and said I was coming out on the field to talk to the Wiley coach. "I want to talk to you. Our players are not pleased with the rough way you all are playing now. I'm putting in a new quarterback and he's white. If we have any problems, my team will aggressively protect him. They want you to know that it will be a war, and they're going to do what anybody should do to help protect people on the team. They want me to tell you to talk to your players. I'm going to tell the remainder of the guys on our bench that we don't want anything to happen." I went back and got my bench together and Wiley got its bench together. We finished that game without any trouble.

When Greg first came, the guys carried him around. He only ate at the table with the football players. We didn't have any incident. We talked about it among ourselves. We talked to him. He was the right person. I don't know anyone who could have handled it the way that he did. And Gregory came through between two of the greatest quarterbacks that we had had: James Harris was on his first team and Matt Reed was on his last team.

Gregory didn't get a chance to play as much as he would like to have played. And he didn't play as much I had wanted him to play. He wanted me to let him be a receiver. For one thing, Greg didn't have great speed. But even if he did, imagine changing a white QB into a receiver. This was at a time when most of the black coaches were upset because so many coaches in the NFL were taking the black quarterbacks and making them receivers.

I told Greg, "Look, I know you want to play receiver, but I'm not going to let you. I'm going to work with you as a quarterback. Many of us are criticizing the people in the NFL for taking every black player who played quarterback, bringing him in, and making a receiver out of him." Therefore, I told him he was going to have to really be satisfied playing quarterback because I was not going to put him in as a receiver. It probably was selfish on my part. He might have played more if he changed, but I just couldn't move him to a receiver because I thought some people might say, "Eddie is trying to pay back the NFL for what they've been doing to us." I didn't want it to be like that.

James Gregory was a fine young man. He worked hard on the football field and to get along on a campus where he could have been ostracized. Greg also did well in the classroom. Nonetheless, after four years he hadn't graduated. Then he went home for vacation in the summer after the spring semester of his senior year. He called me to say he wasn't coming back to Grambling. I told him to put his Daddy and his Momma on the phone. I told them all that he had to come back.

Mrs. Gregory asked, "What do you mean? He's used up his eligibility. I don't think we really can afford the costs at Grambling." I told Mrs. Gregory, "He's used up his eligibility, but we can help him until he has completed his education. He can stay here, complete his courses, and work with us in athletics. He can help us coach." Like with all our student-athletes, I said, "When James leaves here, I want Grambling stamped on his back: that he has his degree from here and he's played here." They were thinking that he could finish for free or nearly free at a California state college. That would have been easy, but it wouldn't have finished the job we'd started at Grambling.

James Gregory came back to Grambling and stayed here until he had those things stamped on his back. It was a proud moment for his folks and for me when he marched in the graduation ceremony.

James Gregory became a high school football coach in California, where he had some real good teams. Some of his players came to Grambling. I have seen him at the AFCA conventions. I sold him on the conventions, so he went whenever he could. And I love to see him there. He will always have a special place for us at Grambling. Of course, I took some heat for bringing a white player to Grambling. I got a lot of letters saying that Grambling should not have done so, that we didn't need a white quarterback. But on our campus, things were quiet because everyone got to know Greg. He made that part easy.

Ironically, I had another white quarterback, Mike Kornblau, as my career came to an end in 1997. In fact, in the 1996 Bayou Classic, Grambling and Southern both had white quarterbacks. That got a great deal of national media attention and a storm of criticism. I couldn't understand that. Heck, this was near the new millennium. I guess some people have not moved as far down the racial equality path as we had hoped.

By the end of the 1960s, we had a new Civil Rights Act, a Voting Rights Act, and black officials were being elected even in the Deep South. In sports, Althea Gibson had won at Wimbledon a decade earlier and Arthur Ashe had won the 1968 U.S. Open. Charlie Sifford had won the Long Beach Open in 1957 and the Alameda Open in 1960. Bill Russell had gotten the coaching job with the Celtics in 1966. The all-black Texas Western basketball team beat Adolph Rupp's all-white team at the University of Kentucky for the national championship in 1965. Muhammad Ali had won a victory in the Supreme Court in spite of raising a storm of protest by becoming a Black Muslim and, later, challenging the Vietnam War. We seemed to be on the move toward equality.

However, the waters were hardly still. Malcolm X, Martin Luther King Jr., and Robert Kennedy were all assassinated between 1965 and 1968. City after city, including Watts, Detroit, and Newark, burned during riots. Many blacks, especially our youth, were leaving Martin Luther King Jr.'s message of nonviolence behind in favor of Stokley Charmichael's message of Black Power and the emerging Black Panther Party under Huey Newton and Eldridge Cleaver.

The world of sports had its own dramatic racial trauma at the Mexico City Olympics as our black athletes protested in unprecedented ways, drawing global attention to their anger as it reflected the anger of many young blacks.

But I tend to look at such complicated issues like race relations in basic terms. I had just seen my team of all black men embrace an outsider as a teammate and treat him like a brother. I knew that we had learned something from Greg and he from us. We all taught others some things in the process. It was important enough that a movie, *The White Tiger,* was made about it. Now I wish more of our nation had seen us or the movie then so that more of our citizens could have absorbed what happened at Grambling State in those troubled times.

6.

THE INTEGRATION
OF WHITE SCHOOLS

The integration of the predominately white schools had a profound impact on Grambling. Without a doubt, the effect was not only on football but also on the students, faculty, and administration. People at the white colleges couldn't know. Maybe they didn't care or want to know. It was not for many years that educators from white schools sought input from the black colleges on the effects of integration on them.

For me, the first sign that it would dramatically change our program came when we recruited Bobby Mitchell, who went on to be a great player for the Cleveland Browns. We had talked to him about coming to Grambling and had him pretty much convinced. Then he ended up at Illinois, which would have been unheard of shortly before then when blacks simply did not go to Illinois.

When I saw this type of thing happening and realized how things were really changing, I became aware that we had to worry about how we would fight back against the schools from the North who were recruiting blacks. We were ready to compete with them but hadn't fully prepared for what happened when the southern schools opened up.

Here I am around 1949 or 1950.
(*Author collection*)

Me and Doris.
(*Author collection*)

My two children—
Lillian and Eddie, Jr.
(*Author collection*)

On the sidelines,
1969. (*Photo by
O.K. Davis*)

On the sidelines, 1971.
(*Photo by O.K. Davis*)

On the sidelines, 1982.
(*Photo by O.K. Davis*)

I'm wearily waving to fans after another tough battle during that long last season.
(*Author collection*)

Here I am with Doug Williams, former Grambling State president, Dr. Joseph Johnson, and Sugar Ray Leonard, 1988. (*Photo by O.K. Davis*)

Me with "Tank" Younger (left) and Charlie Joiner (right), a pair of ex-Grambling State stars who went on to pro stardom, in 1985. (*Photo by O.K. Davis*)

Talking with Ted Marchibroda and the late "Buck" Buchanan, 1984. (*Photo by O.K. Davis*)

Me and four-time Super Bowl champion Terry Bradshaw, at a Louisiana Tech/Nebraksa game, 1998. (*Photo by O.K. Davis*)

Me with Vernon Cheek (former S.I.D.) and Silas Payne (player) during a final season post-game interview. (*Author collection*)

I am receiving a call from President Clinton after my last game. (*Author collection*)

Me and Doris. (*Author collection*)

My grandson Michael Watkins and my great-grandson. (*Author collection*)

Here I am at
the College
Football Hall
of Fame.
(*Author
collection*)

I am being prepared to receive my honorary degree from Yale in 1997. (*Author collection*)

Me and the late Paul "Bear" Bryant in 1979. (*Photo by O.K. Davis*)

We had to find better ways to compete both for the great student-athletes and for national attention so Grambling itself could continue to grow in size and academic stature. Our football program had made so much progress in those regards in the first twenty-five or so years. But it was obvious that we were losing athletes to the northern schools in the early and mid-1960s, and it was only a matter of time that the walls of segregation would crash down in the big southern schools.

Grambling Players in the NFL

Football, of course, had a huge impact on the college environment. I always recognized that the public would get to know Grambling's name if Grambling had players running with the Bears, the Eagles, or the Saints on Sunday. We were getting our share of student-athletes graduating and going to the NFL. Collie Nicholson's writing had already helped us achieve that. That was doing good things for the athletic program but even more for the school itself.

When the scouts came, we knew they were very interested because getting to Grambling is not so easy. Therefore, we always took good care of the scouts on our campus. I'd give them what they wanted, but they had to give me what I wanted. I'd tell 'em, "I want you to hang around and come by my house for sandwiches. There are some things I want to ask you." I pumped them for information about the game in the NFL and what new things they might have seen in college football. I was still learning.

Louisiana Tech produced a lot of pro players right down the street in Ruston. I always watched what they were doing. It was hard to compete with them with the kind of budget that we had. However, instead of crying and using "poor" as an excuse, we just found out how to do it. And when you're at an NFL stadium and see the name of one of our graduates flashing across the screen, that's a great statement about Grambling State University.

I told our players in the NFL that they had to play every play like it was the last one. And don't feel that a coach or general manager didn't like them if they were not playing. The coach and GM are trying to win as best they can. They've got to eat and pay house and car bills and bring food to their family. I tell my guys if they can produce, they've got to show the attitude that they *can* produce. Play like you deserve the job, that you own the position.

If you don't have success, don't look for an excuse. Look for a way to get the success. It would almost be like our losing a ball game and me blaming our coaches. Well, I've been working with these coaches for a long time. They are also looking to keep their jobs so they can take care of those in their lives. I've got to believe that my coaches want to win as much as I do. So we don't cry about it. We just try to get better.

I knew we couldn't keep our program at the higher levels if we simply kept playing on our own campus. I had seen what Jake Gaither had achieved with the Orange Blossom Classic and how college basketball teams had thrived for decades by traveling to New York City to play in Madison Square Garden.

I will talk about the development of our own "classics" later. Now I want to look more closely at the impact of integration of higher education and on me as a coach.

Bear Bryant and the Integration of the Southern Universities

When I started at Grambling I never thought that schools like LSU and Alabama would integrate. I just wasn't thinking that something like that could happen. I realized that I was coaching some fine athletes, and I just figured that each year would bring more.

Most football fans have heard the story about Sam Cunningham going to play at Alabama for the University of Southern California in 1970. In a single day, Cunningham helped humiliate Paul "Bear" Bryant, one of the football's greatest coaches, and the University of Alabama, one of the most important football programs in America. He scored three touchdowns against Alabama—in Birmingham. USC doubled Alabama's score, 42–21.

Sam just ran all over and around the University of Alabama. When the game was over, some football fans in Alabama were saying, "Get us some of them." Alabama and Coach Bryant seemed like the last line. When Bryant decided to recruit blacks, that opened the gates for the other coaches to go on and convince their school administrators that black athletes could help them win, too.

I remember meeting the Alabama coaches at the American Football Coaches Association convention in 1971. I was in line to get my meal from a buffet and they asked me to come sit with them. One of them said to me, "We don't want to embarrass you, Eddie, but we want to tell you something. Please don't take this as criticism. You know what has been going on in the country?" and I assumed he meant integration. He said, "We want to tell you that we know you have a lot of great people fighting this business of segregation and fighting for civil rights. But you need to know that compared with all those guys doing this in Alabama, Sam Cunningham made more progress in integrating the races than anybody else. More than any of your leaders have ever done. Because when he left, the fans were ready for Alabama to get some black ball players." I wondered how Bear Bryant was taking all of this. I knew him but not well at this time. I got to know him very well much later.

Later that afternoon I thought back about a decade when I had seen George Wallace stand in the door to block the admission of black students to the University of Alabama. I knew there were many whites who'd supported him. Heck, he ran for president and got a lot of votes. I was so disappointed that a governor would do such a thing, but I didn't openly go to the media to do anything about it. I didn't raise my voice when this happened. I didn't see this as my opportunity to do something so I didn't make any public statement, but I was really disappointed when it happened.

I was old enough to know what had been going on and knew it wasn't going to change overnight. I was sure that was really going to stall chances of the football teams getting integrated at those schools. But I didn't think that was the end of the story at a place like Alabama because of what was happening in professional football, the emphasis the schools were putting on winning, and the increasing amounts of money colleges were making from football. I never lost track that this could possibly happen because schools watch other schools, but even more importantly, the alumni watch the other schools and they all want to be number one. Sooner or later, even racism can be overcome by the desire to be number one!

There are so many stories about Bear Bryant. It's like an epic: Things just keep building and building on the things that he did. You never know what was legend and what was real. Most of it seems real.

I knew that Bear Bryant was a nice guy. Coaches don't have control of what will happen at the university, of who will and who won't attend. But I know how he acted when Alabama would come up against teams with black players. Cunningham was one. Johnny Rodgers at Nebraska helped bury Alabama on national television. It was one more event that would lead to recruiting black athletes at Alabama.

I went to Nebraska to speak at an athletic banquet. I had a chance to tell Johnny Rodgers that he had done something that was very important through that televised game. The American public had opened their arms for him after they saw what he could do. During my speech I nodded to him and said to the audience,

"There were no excuses. The potential that he had and what he had shown America could happen was wonderful." I told the gathering that I knew that day that Johnny Rodgers had had a great impact on the future of athletics in America. And this game surely did have a great effect on the future of football because of the way he played against Alabama.

So those games with Sam Cunningham and Johnny Rodgers hastened integration in the South. Coach Bryant was the right guy to be involved because he was strong enough to make this move. More people would be ready to follow him if he would do it. When he signed Wilbur Jackson as his first black player in 1971, it was good for football. It was even better for America.

There were certainly some coaches whom I worked with or against who integrated their teams just to try to get better teams. Some did it because they thought it was the right thing to do. They all wanted to improve their team and wanted to hold their job, to feed their families. They would do whatever they could do to win. The alumni could be harder to judge. While they wanted to be number one, there were surely some staunch segregationists among the alums, especially the older ones.

I think there were coaches at that time who wanted to integrate because it was right. There were people like that. But I think most coaches, especially at big southern state schools, integrated out of necessity. They realized there were many black players who were future all-pros with great speed, size, quickness, and intelligence. If they couldn't get them at Alabama or Mississippi, then those guys could end up playing against them and beating them, just like Nebraska and USC beat Alabama.

So it wasn't so much a matter of what they felt about integration; it was mostly about wanting to win. If they could convince the alumni that their school could win with this black student-athlete, then the alumni might understand what it would mean to their program for this person to play.

At the big state universities, it was the program and who was be-hind it—that's what ultimately made the difference. The whole state—the alumni, administrators, students—they all wanted their university to be number one. And then there was the growing tele-vision money out there. Each school wanted to be showcased on national TV. If they had a real good showing and an exciting game, then they got the open slots on television for the next season. That's the way it was.

The Impact of Television: Howard Cosell and "100 Yards to Glory"

A man who really seemed to understand all those things and who tried to help us was Howard Cosell. Meeting Howard led to a pro-found friendship. He was a classy man, who became an enormous help to our program when he had the courage to battle the net-works to get a documentary produced about Grambling State football. Sports columnist Jerry Izenberg from the *Newark Star Ledger* gave Howard the idea. They ended up working together on the project. Izenberg wrote the script, and Howard was the producer.

They didn't tell me until after it was done, but it was not an easy show to sell. It was actually sold to ABC's New York affiliate in 1968. There was even controversy right before it went on, with some TV people thinking a show about a black college was too small a story. I thought back on that when *Nightline,* ABC's top news show, did a full show on me and Grambling the night before my last game in 1997.

The show, which Howard called "Grambling College: 100 Yards to Glory," got great reviews and even won an award after it was shown on ABC's affiliate in New York City. ABC finally put it on the national network. I believe that was the night that white

Americans began to know where Grambling was located and how it was serving our nation by providing a quality education for blacks. We were now on the national stage and had bought some time to act to keep our momentum in the face of losing out on the recruits we usually would get.

Grambling's Playback

Howard Cosell's "100 Yards to Glory" showed me what TV could to for us. I knew then I would work toward our own TV broadcasts. Television was also important for the black schools at that time. The black schools could share in the television money. We would get "x" number of dollars per appearance. The NCAA was real fair with us. When they made that television money available, it did a whole lot for the school's athletic program. Grambling got quite a few appearances around that time, but that, of course, changed after all the schools' teams became so integrated.

Although it was in 1971, I remember our first televised game like it was last week. Grambling beat Morgan State 31–3 in the opening game of the season. It was the first college game that was nationally telecast that didn't involve two Division IA schools. The ratings for our game beat out Stanford–Arkansas and Ole Miss–Alabama that weekend.

We had a two-hour Sunday morning television show. The show was called *Grambling's Playback*. They would have to edit the game film into this time span. Our entire schedule was on TV that season from the opening game to the last game. We were very visible on television, and a lot of people got to know us while we made money for the program.

We weren't getting the kind of money that the other teams were getting, but we had worked out a program with the TV people so that people saw *Grambling's Playback* and came to know about

Grambling. When we played in a city and the fans came to see us, they liked the fact that "their game" could be seen on TV the next day. Heck, they might just see themselves on *Grambling's Playback*. And local white folks in the Grambling-Ruston area got to know me, our coaches, and our student-athletes from the TV show. I think that helped us make other kinds of breakthroughs in rural Louisiana. The Sunday telecasts carried beyond Louisiana across the country. They were sponsored by Oldsmobile and Budweiser and were syndicated on various affiliates by Jim Hunter Productions.

You know how some say football is like religion. Well, Grambling football on TV put that to the test. Quite a few ministers called me to complain, but I told them the timing was not under Grambling's control. Many of them had to juggle their Sunday morning church programs to avoid being in conflict or competition with the Sunday morning Grambling football. By midseason of the first year, no one was complaining and most were cheering. We were becoming the national black team, just like President Jones and Collie Nicholson had envisioned.

Even now people come up to me and tell how they used to look at the Sunday morning shows. People who were out of town would extend stays in hotels on Sunday to be sure they didn't miss *Grambling's Playback*. It didn't hurt that we played some great football in those years. In the four years the show carried, we won or shared four SWAC championships, won forty-one games, only lost eight and won two more National Black Championships! There were forty-three Grambling players in NFL training camps in 1971.

We sent up thirteen more draftees and a bunch of free agents in those next four years, including Gary "Big Hands" Johnson from the 1974 team. Big Hands played for eleven seasons in the NFL. Sammie White and Dwight Scales, star wide receivers in the NFL for eleven and nine years, respectively, were snaring passes for

Grambling in the last years of the TV run. Two of our three quarterbacks in those years got drafted into the league. Matt Reed had great years in 1971 and 1972. Of course, Doug Williams started his spectacular career with us in 1974 when he threw for 1,150 yards, a figure he would triple by his senior year in 1977. I will talk much more about Doug later.

Origins of Grambling's Playback

The way the show came about was interesting. I was active in the SWAC Conference and was at the meeting when the TV producers came in to make an offer to SWAC. The TV people were very blunt. They said that they were apprehensive that many SWAC coaches had no experience with TV and wouldn't make such good subjects. They made us the offer and suggested how it would help us. Frankly, the dollars in their cash bin didn't match the expectations of the SWAC schools. SWAC had so many star student-athletes that our people thought we would get a better offer. The coaches from the stronger teams told the producers that we wanted more money. The reality was that by rejecting it, we were about to get nothing.

The head of the TV team responded that he was very disappointed because of how hard his TV team had worked to put this offer together. He emphasized what TV would mean for SWAC by showing off the kind of football players and coaches we had to the whole nation.

When he left, I followed him and we walked together to his car. I told him that Grambling would accept the same package that SWAC had just rejected. I talked to him about Grambling being the network's team and how we could make a great program together. He listened to me and said that we would get back in touch. The deal was made soon thereafter. When Grambling fi-

nally started putting things together, some of the guys in SWAC
wanted to know what the TV deal was going to pay us, but I didn't
tell them.

They said, "You've got to tell us what you're getting and then
you're going to have to give some to us or we're not going to play
Grambling." Well, that created a problem, but it was easy to fix. I
told them how much Grambling would share with each school we
played against on TV. Each team that appeared on the program received a certain amount. We got it going and *Grambling's Playback*
was a real success.

I did Oldsmobile commercials in exchange for a fee. They had
it set up so I'd always have an Oldsmobile by giving me a big dis-
count on my own car. No black coach had done commercials before Olds came to me, so this was a gigantic breakthrough. Now
when I do commercials for Burger King, I think back on the fore-
sight of the people at Oldsmobile and General Motors.

When you think of the money black athletes and coaches make
today from endorsements and commercials, it makes me feel so
good to know I was part of the changes happening in America.
Even though the commercials were centered around this particular show and I didn't make a fortune from them, I was one proud
American when I became the first black coach to have this happen
to him. People would talk to me about the Oldsmobile commercials as much as the games. They knew we were making history.

Grambling's Playback swept the country. People would be up early
because it came on at 10:00 A.M. The game would be about an
hour, and the rest was conversations about the game and the commercials. It was also a great opportunity for Grambling's players to
become known across the nation. A national audience saw the
guys each weekend. That really pushed Grambling's program. The
show went from 1971 through 1974, when ABC TV finally signed
a contract with SWAC as a conference.

The TV program forced us to make physical improvements at

Grambling. At first we had no lights in our stadium. When we put them in, they weren't bright enough for TV. Therefore, I began to point out how many night games were being televised. We added more lights. We did a whole lot of things to be able to continue to have the program. We paid attention to the needs in a press box. Then we had to build a cooldown room for the players. We had to create things to accommodate TV trucks.

I tried to get a lot of the things that I saw at LSU for Grambling. One time I went there and the LSU grounds manager took me to see something new they had installed. He walked out onto the field and turned a valve and forty sprinklers jumped up. Back at Grambling we didn't even have a groundskeeper, let alone a manager. When the field was dry, I'd go out there with our old hose to water our whole field.

After seeing it at LSU, I knew Grambling was going to work to get a sponsor who would install those sprinklers for our field. At Grambling, we went to find out how they got it and what it would take for us to get it. Then we'd plot the strategy to do it. We had to get ahead. That's how it was and still is. I was always proud Grambling was on the cutting edge for the black colleges.

Ironically, I think *Grambling's Playback* also had a lot to do with some of the white schools deciding to go ahead and recruit black players. They had a chance to see how great SWAC players were. All the colleges around the country saw our guys every Sunday morning, and it increased their interest in taking future black student-athletes away from the black colleges.

Prior to the TV shows, people were always asking me how were we able to get our players into the NFL. I didn't have the answer other than coaching, having good techniques, Collie Nicholson's "golden pen," and the players' God-given talents, combined with their hard work.

But on TV everyone could see the players. They'd see we had an abundance of talent who could be going to the other schools. Although it also showcased talented black players to coaches at the white schools, while it lasted *Grambling's Playback* did help us keep many of the great black athletes interested in Grambling. Their parents also saw us play and saw how we carried ourselves off the field. Parents knew that if their sons came to Grambling, then they could see them each week on TV. That was a very big draw for us.

I think quite a few of the SWAC leaders who voted against the original conference TV program were pretty upset about Grambling going it alone. But Grambling always listened to people if it meant something for our university.

Sometimes you just have to tell people the truth. Their response almost always was, "Well, Eddie, Grambling gets more games than the other schools." That was true and some other black schools resented it as being unfair. I told my coaching colleagues that they had to be aggressive, but also they had to know how to get the TV stations interested in their teams. I always offered to help them because I knew that having strong opponents with national reputations was good for Grambling football. The other coaches rarely asked for or accepted the help.

I don't know how I developed a business sense, but it was becoming clear to me in the late 1960s that TV people were not going to come to small campuses in rural America. If we wanted to be on TV, we had to go to bigger cities like New York, Los Angeles, and Dallas. In the beginning it was hard to get other black colleges to want to play there. But then they recognized who the TV people were going to cover. A game in a big city with a sell-out huge crowd was simply more appealing to TV than one on a black college campus where there were only a few thousand people in the stands.

Today most schools are lucky to get one appearance. Now we have to fight with the TV people to get games of black schools on TV. That's why those annual national games have been so important to the black colleges. This is why the Bayou Classic is so important for Grambling and the schools we play. It guarantees us a spot on national TV. That has kept us known as a national university.

Fellow Coaches

I know how much I learned from my fellow coaches at the clinics. They took me under their wings and taught me so many things. Therefore, I recognized that I needed to share my experiences with upcoming young coaches. Regarding the lack of TV coverage, I would tell some of them, "Don't be mad at the TV people if you don't get a television appearance. Look at your facilities. If you don't have the right facilities, then the TV people will go to a school that has them. They're trying to do a show and there are certain things they need." I told them to try to allocate their school's resources, so, if TV was important for their program, then they would need to improve their facilities. Now I knew, of course, that many schools couldn't afford to do these things, but I wanted the young coaches to know what to be ready for if the money became available.

The new coaches wanted to be buddies with the veterans, but what they needed was for us to teach them. When I came along as a young coach, no one told me about the American Football Coaches Association and what I could do with it to help myself. When I joined, I learned so much. They accepted me. Being black didn't seem to mean much of anything to the other coaches.

Eventually I became an officer with the AFCA. When a young coach joined, I'd tell him what he needed to do to effectively run the ship in his organization. People mentored me, and I was always going to pass that on. As I thought back to my first AFCA meeting, I had achieved my seemingly unattainable dream when I became AFCA president. Then I reached even farther back by trying to encourage all the high school coaches in Louisiana to become associate members. We needed each other.

So this is how it was. We would talk about every aspect of running a football program, from game plays to the facilities we played in. The AFCA did so much for me at all stages of my career. I want the young guys to take advantage of it from their first day on the job.

Needless to say, I wanted Grambling's own athletic department staff to grow even more. There was no athletic director when I got there, and I kind of evolved into the position. I accepted the job of AD because of my love for the university and my desire to assist with the growth of Grambling.

Whatever it took to help Grambling grow, we did it. We are just so proud of this university. There was a general at West Point who used to say that everything in his life was the Corps, the Corps, the Corps. Since 1941, when I got off the train in Grambling, it's been Grambling, Grambling, Grambling!

When our staff went to the national professional meetings, we wanted to bring back information to share with colleagues who hadn't gone. Finally, I got Grambling's president to promise that my football coaches could go to the American Football Coaches Association Convention every year. Grambling's athletic business manager went to his national meeting, the basketball coaches went to theirs, etc. Eventually we raised the money for all of this. We wanted them to know what was going on in their professional worlds. I was trying to get them interested enough to want to keep up with what was happening nationally.

I know a few coaches at other schools misinterpreted my advice as a way of letting them know how great Grambling was. They didn't all understand that I was trying to help them.

Some looked upon Grambling as the haves versus the have-nots. We were always ready to go to the next level. Most admired what we were trying to do, but there were always those who seemed unwilling to rise to the challenges and became envious.

Along with the use of TV to counter the effects of the integration of the white schools, we also emphasized other things. The core element of everything else was that Grambling quite simply was a great university to attend for any student.

Graduations Versus Emphasis on the NFL

I'm most proud of several things. The first was our graduation rate. If a student-athlete came to play football at Grambling, all of my coaches knew it was our job to be sure he left with a degree. It was our job to be sure he developed as a person and not just as a football player. We knew that most of our guys would never see an NFL game live, let alone play in one. Heck, if he did make the NFL, that was for a matter of years, not a lifetime. They needed to leave here ready for life. Those are the promises we made to a young man we were recruiting.

Recruiting Better: Selling Grambling's Entire Package

I never, never told a kid not to go to a certain school. I never bad-mouthed another school or another coach. That would be so unfair and unethical to play with the mind of a seventeen-year-old boy. When I recruited a guy, I wanted to find out if he was interested in Grambling. And if he was interested in Grambling, we wanted to talk about what he had to do to be at Grambling. If he was interested in another school, I wished him well and also told him, "Wherever you go, whatever else you try to do, try to graduate. If you don't graduate, you're going to be the loser. And America will also lose because you can make a difference."

You will not be able to find anyone who would say, "When I talked to Coach Robinson, he told me I'm making a mistake if I go to a predominantly white school." I would never have said that because integration is what we've been fighting for all these years. So many marched and demonstrated for the right to go to whatever school you want to go, to live where you choose, to sit where you want on the buses. So I couldn't tell a potential recruit not to go to certain schools in Louisiana because they were predominantly white. I know the other coaches. Many are my friends. If a young man chose to go to another school, I didn't ever want him to be able to say, "Coach Robinson told me I'd be making a mistake coming here." I didn't want that.

Integration really made a better recruiter out of me, and I think it made better recruiters out of all of us by making us more aware of what Grambling had to offer the student. Sometimes people in athletics don't really know about their own school's academic program. Our staff learned how many student–athletes graduated with degrees in physics and other majors. We learned about what the job opportunities were for graduates within each degree program. We found out where our former student–athletes were working and had them help our current student–athletes. We all could have been regular admissions recruiters for Grambling because we believed in our university. We became more of the heart and soul of this great institution that has educated and nurtured so many young women and men.

It was easy for our football staff to be completely positive recruiters. We never had to say, "Don't go to that school." When I was making a first phone call to a potential recruit's home, I had to say something to get the parents' attention to help them think about why their son should attend Grambling State University. I didn't start by discussing a victory over Southern or Tennessee State. Straight off I told the parent and their son, "If you come to Grambling and work hard, I guarantee you will graduate and get a good job. I can't guarantee you'll be a star football player or get drafted by an NFL team. But if you work hard, we will help you and you will be prepared for a great life."

Of course there were parents who lived to see their kids play on television and make it to the NFL. They often didn't realize that the life of a professional football player is relatively short. On average, it's less than four years. When the parents pressed on this side of being at Grambling, I always asked them that if their son was lucky enough to play in the NFL but did not get an education, what did they think he would do for the rest of his life? How would he support his family? What would he have to fall back on? It was really about telling him the truth and trying to coach with integrity. I just had to be like that. I couldn't have lived with myself if I had been any other way.

I want everyone to recognize that Grambling is a great American university. When Grambling's graduates step out in the world, I want them to be respected in the job market. As integration slowly progressed, some of our graduates became "the first" black in this or that company. We tried to make them understand that as the "first," he had to set the standard. He had to do his job so that the other guys who followed would have a clear path. People would say, "Oh, he's from Grambling. He must be a smart guy. Hard working." That's what I wanted to hear about our guys. That's what I *do* hear after all these years.

I know I was old for a coach when I retired, but I frequently thought of the story about the old man who was a bridge builder. One day a man told him, "Oh, man, you're too old to build that bridge. By the time you get through with it, you'll be on your way out and won't be able to use it." The bridge builder responded, "Yeah, I know that, but the younger generation is coming and they're going to need this bridge to cross the river." He wanted to set a good example for as long as he could. This is how I feel. Young people are looking for somebody who'll tell them the truth, and I wanted to give it to them. I really wanted them to see me do and say the right thing.

I don't use profanity myself, although I have occasionally slipped with "hell" or "damn." I have caught myself saying, "Hell, don't dis him again," or, "Damn, stop that behavior on the field." I think when you're in school, you should have learned additional vocabulary. My guys were all in college. They knew better words. They heard me using them and not reinforcing bad language. Too many people expect bad language from black youth. Not me—I wanted them to set an example and break such ugly stereotypes. It's not only white people who expect bad language but blacks also. If we want to be leaders, then we have to lead.

Black Athletes at White Schools

I know that when I look at the statistics of some of the predominantly white schools, I see so many black athletes on football and basketball teams. But I also see so few in the student body itself. That makes me realize that integration had the biggest impact on athletes at the historically black schools. We lost recruits to the predominantly white schools. It didn't have such a big effect on the student body in general. That's partially true because of the place that athletics holds in our society.

We were still learning what we could do in the future. We weren't perfect then, and we knew it would get even better. But we always knew no matter where we played, no matter who we played, we told our guys that the right thing to do was to give the people a good show. The fans paid their money so we had to give them a show. We also always knew how the media could help. Some coaches thought of the media as an adversary. I saw them as allies. If we were honest and accessible to the press, they would be fair to Grambling football. We were and they were. It helped us to get that good media attention wherever we went to play.

This is what we were mainly trying to achieve at that time. It was not a matter of this poor black college couldn't achieve anything. We wanted to show America that we could do whatever the other schools could do. In some cases, we tried to do it better and did. No one associated with Grambling football, Grambling itself, or black colleges in general will ever forget the first Bayou Classic in the Superdome. They brought the television cameras to Louisiana and we put 76,000 people in the Superdome! The Bayou Classic was the crown jewel in a series of classic games we started. By then the television world and football fans everywhere knew that Grambling and black college football were not going to die because so many black players were going to formerly segregated schools. We knew it was up to us to make it work. We could not let it die, just like we couldn't let the black colleges themselves die. If black college football was important to football, then the education available at black colleges was one hundred times more important to higher education in America.

7.

THE BIRTH OF THE CLASSICS

So we had this formula to balance the tides of history in Grambling's favor. We wanted integration. Our people fought for it. We wanted integration to propel Grambling State even further into the national consciousness. If whites were paying more attention to black Americans, maybe they would do the same for black universities and football teams. We could hope, anyway.

Our goal was to keep the name of our great university in front of the public by expanding our national platform. We had our guys in the NFL. We had the weekly TV show after the airing of Howard Cosell's "100 Yards to Glory." We had massive exposure in the black press thanks to Collie's writings. What I had not yet been able to work out was how to play in front of the big crowds. I knew what I wanted to do but not how. The "what" was clear ever since we played in that 1955 Orange Blossom Classic against Florida A&M before 48,000 fans. We wanted our own classics.

With so many great black athletes going to the white colleges, we had to get to America's cities. Our alums there could come out, and we would build that national university that our visionary President Ralph Waldo Emerson Jones had set as our target in the late 1940s right after our soldiers came home from World War II.

The Sugar Cup Unclassic

I have always wanted to do what others have done well. The Orange Blossom Classic was our first opportunity to play in a big stadium. When I came back I was so excited that I wrote to the Sugar Bowl committee and told them I had a proposition that they couldn't refuse. They gave me a date for an appointment, which couldn't come fast enough because I was sure they would buy the idea.

I told them about our game against Florida A&M in the Orange Blossom Classic: 48,000 people, a great game, something really spectacular. The fans loved it. I said, for me this game seemed like a prelude to an ever bigger game. I had done my homework and suggested to the committee that we would call it the Sugar Cup Classic. This was 1956. I assured the committee that this would get the people of New Orleans warmed up for the Sugar Bowl.

They asked us for time to consider it. They finally made up their minds. I'll always remember what the chairman said. "Eddie, this is a great idea and if someone could execute or make that idea a reality, it could be a great game." But he said, "We have problems right now simply trying to produce the Sugar Bowl successfully." They wouldn't support us.

I thanked the committee for giving me time to talk to them, but I was so upset with their response I didn't know which way to turn. Then I recalled Frank Sinatra's song in which he sings that when he finds himself down on the floor, he gets back up, and gets back in the race. I knew it was time to get up and go to somebody else. I felt like I was flat on my face, but I left the Sugar Bowl committee and went to meet some of the black businessmen in New Orleans.

They were very interested. They couldn't picture how black teams would look in the Sugar Bowl, playing in the Tulane Stadium. It had not dawned on me when I was talking to the Sugar

Bowl committee that a remnant of segregation might be part of the factor keeping Grambling out!

It took many years but we finally got the black businessmen to put an organization together and went to the city, which gave them what turned out to be a dilapidated high school football field called City Park Stadium. It was a far cry from the 76,000-seat Tulane Stadium. Accepting that site was a huge mistake because it took away from the big-time aura I'd envisioned. On top of that, our opponent was a weak Bishop College team unlikely to draw fans. The day itself mirrored the poorly conceived effort. We had the type of a downpour that is famous in New Orleans. The parking lot was so muddy that cars couldn't get in or out of it.

Needless to say, you could hardly play on what remained of the grass on the field. Rain fell throughout the game, further drenching the fans. Instead of 70,000 at the Tulane Stadium, we might have had 2,000 at the 1964 Sugar Cup Classic. Nobody came because nobody even knew they had a City Park Stadium. We had an 8–1 record going in and won 42–6 over outmanned Bishop. But the failure demoralized us all, and we lost the Orange Blossom Classic to FAMU by a score of 42–15. Financially we had lost our shirts. As the Blue Bird made its way north afterward, I knew the Sugar Cup Classic was dead. But I never lost sight of my dream.

I got back to campus and speculated what it would be like to be at a Nebraska, Alabama, or Ohio State. At those schools, I wouldn't have been trying to build a dream game that might bring 50,000 people to a stadium in a city far away from my home and our campus. But I couldn't afford such speculation because I was at Grambling. I was close to my 150th victory, and no white school had ever talked to me about, let alone offered me, a job. Upon retirement, more than 250 victories later, it remained true that no white school had made me an offer. I don't think I would have ever left Grambling, but sometimes I thought it would have been nice if someone wanted to give me a shot at a big white school.

Unhindered by such mental drifting, I always focused on the job at hand. That was in 1965, and I was ready to try a game in another city when I was approached by the Urban League about playing in New York City. Our first big success with a game of this nature was the Whitney Young Classic in Yankee Stadium.

Whitney Young Classic

We had been holding talks with the leaders of the Urban League about using a football game to help them raise money for the "street academies" they were trying to establish. There were so many adults in New York and around the nation who didn't have the basic educational skills necessary to earn a living. We were told how bad things were in neighborhoods in Harlem and Bedford Stuyvesant.

The street academies were for men who had approximately a third-grade–level education. They weren't about to go to class with eight-year-olds, so the Urban League began raising money to open the street academies. They would buy store fronts on corners in New York, fix them up, and make them into these "street academies."

Adults then went to school there to prepare for the General Equivalency Diploma (GED) exams. Their early successes made such great stories. We went to Harlem to see the conditions of the city and to visit the academies. We had certainly been told the truth about the ghetto in New York. Things were bad there. Poverty in a city had a whole different feel than poverty in a rural town like Grambling.

The Yankees' Michael Burke joined the discussions. The Yankees were very interested in having the benefit game at Yankee Stadium. Man, I had only dreamt about Yankee Stadium up to that point. We couldn't quite get the details set. We were getting impatient and some were ready to give up the whole idea. Then Dr. King was murdered on April 4, 1968, and I went to his funeral in Atlanta.

I cannot remember a sadder day for America than the day Martin Luther King Jr. was killed. I watched the televised images on the balcony of the Lorraine Motel in Memphis where the bullet killed our prince of nonviolence. What would he have thought if he saw that cities burned as an almost ironic tribute to the loss of this giant? What had he thought since riots had taken place in the last three years of his life in more than fifty cities across our nation in spite of his pleading for nonviolence? I wondered if he died despairing. I soon learned of his sermon on April 3 when Dr. King preached, "I don't know what will happen now. We've got some difficult days ahead. But it doesn't really matter with me now. Because I've been to the mountaintop. I won't mind."

Everyone was concerned about what would happen next. Who would lead the civil rights movement? The funeral was both sad and so inspiring. I left Atlanta that day knowing that I had to go back and help the Urban League to reclaim lives in New York, doing things as I always did—through football.

Before we left Atlanta, I got together with Morgan State's Coach Banks and Jake Gaither of Florida A&M. We talked about a game in New York. Bill Curtis from Balantine Beer met with us and suggested an all-star game in Philadelphia. A Philadelphia newspaper wrote about the possibility. By the time I got home, Michael Burke was calling. He said, "I thought we were friends. You've been talking with the Yankees. Whatever you do in this area, it has to be done in Yankee Stadium. We want to help in this effort." That's how we started the Whitney Young Classic.

Jake didn't want to play. He had a good team at FAMU. Banks had won twenty-five or twenty-six straight games with Morgan State. We were pretty good, too. I thought among the three of us we could get two teams. Then I told them what Michael Burke had said about playing in New York at Yankee Stadium. I prodded my rival coaches, telling Earl Banks, "I guess you are protecting a great record, but Jake and I are not protecting anything." Earl knew it could be a big success and grabbed it when Jake didn't bite. So we agreed and played Morgan State in the first classic in New York.

We got all the logistics straight for the inaugural game in 1968. Collie Nicholson and I were in New York preparing for the first game. It was summer and, boy, it was really hot. There was steam coming off the pavement. We were down around 8th Avenue and 48th Street and noticed there was a fight that night at Madison Square Garden.

I used to listen to fights from the Garden for years. As I looked at the Garden's marquis, I heard the voice of announcer Johnny Addie in my head. Collie and I got tickets. Man, I was in Madison Square Garden. It was a real sports capital. At the start of each fight Johnny came out. He had on his After-Six suit. He looked good standing there in the middle of the ring. As he stood there, seemingly without any purpose but looking good, the microphone floated down into his outstretched right hand. Then I closed my eyes as if I was home listening and heard his voice come alive. But I opened my eyes and I was there and so was Johnny Addie. That was a dream come true for me.

We were at ringside when they got ready to go for the main attraction. Johnny got in the ring, still looking great. He stood there, stretched out that right arm, swept the microphone to his face, and began with his familiar, "Ladies and Gentlemen"—the crowd was pumped for his introduction, but then he want on—"the manager of this establishment has asked that I inform you that the temperature here in New York today is 104°!" The people collectively went "Wow, wow, wow!" and he said, "They asked me to inform you that the temperature in the Garden is only 78 degrees."

Nevertheless, I could see that Johnny was soaking wet. Then a drunk fan shouted out, "I don't care. Tell it all. I paid $100 to be here in this fights. It doesn't cost nothing outside." The Garden broke out into laughter. Boy, some of those guys.

As a young man I never missed the Friday night fights on radio and later on TV. Collie and I were melting down inside the Garden but would never have traded the experience. It was like we were lost in a dream, not even thinking for a moment why we were in New York.

Morgan won the first game, 9–7, and the schools made good money, even after most of the profits went directly to the Urban League. The success made Jake Gaither bite, and he was finally ready to bring FAMU to New York for the next classic in 1969. A decision had been agreed to, without our knowing, to have game two between Morgan and FAMU. They were ready to put Grambling out since we lost.

I got a call from Howard Cosell at about the time this was happening. I told him that Florida A&M and Morgan were going to play and that this was a bad blow to me. Mr. Wingate, the head of the Urban League, walked by me in the room right at that moment.

Howard got hot and said, "What the hell do they mean that Grambling is not going to play in this? No way Grambling can be out." I told Howard, "Well, this is what he said." So Howard told me to tell the man who was running the show to come to the telephone. When he got back from the telephone, Grambling was back in the game, and we've been in the game ever since. It was always Grambling, but other teams came to play us, including North Carolina A&T, Norfolk State, and Bethune-Cookman. Florida A&M finally came in 1981.

George Steinbrenner

The game was a great success every year with at least 60,000 fans at each game. I was shocked when Collie and I came to New York to negotiate for the game in 1976. The Urban League informed us that this was going to be the last game as their finances made them unable to underwrite or guarantee the game. Collie and I were stunned and didn't know what to do. It was late in the morning and we were scheduled to be on a 2:30 P.M. flight back home.

We were sitting in our hotel lobby, about to go to our rooms to get our bags and head for the airport. As I headed for the elevator I saw a copy of the *New York Daily News* on a table. The cover was a full face photo of George Steinbrenner, the owner of the Yankees. It was almost noon. I went to the room to call Howard Cosell. His wife, Emmy, answered and informed me that Howard was on the West Coast. Thank goodness she trusted me and gave me his phone number.

I told Howard what was going on and asked him about George Steinbrenner. "George might help. I'll call George now. You call him in ten minutes." Howard gave me George's personal phone number. It was 12:20 and we had to catch a cab by 1:00 P.M. for our flight.

I called and got right through. I explained what the Urban League had decided. He told me to come right to his office. It was 12:40. I said, "Mr. Steinbrenner, we have a flight with nonrefundable tickets. I'm afraid we don't have time to visit with you now." He replied, "Don't worry. We'll take care of the tickets so you can leave later today."

We walked in and George Steinbrenner quickly assured us that the tickets were not the only thing he would help with on that afternoon. In the face of the loss of our first big national game, one that by 1976 had led to the successful launches of other classics, George Steinbrenner quite simply agreed to guarantee the Whitney Young Classic. He did so in 1976 and in every year since that day. I fell in love with George Steinbrenner in 1976 and love him even more today. He has become a close personal friend over the years. My grandson, Eddie III, works for the Yankees in Tampa.

George Steinbrenner has ruined Doris. In the summer he'll call to ask if we would like to come to see the Yankees play. Next thing I hear Doris telling her friends how we go to New York, stay at the Hyatt Regency Hotel, eat at the best restaurants, and get driven around in a limousine. She tells her friends that if we want a vacation, the Yankee's owner does it right when he brings us to New York from Thursday until about Tuesday.

Doris is George's number-one fan. She thinks George owns New York! I must be his second biggest fan.

His generosity to Grambling has been remarkable. He has given Grambling a great deal of support and has brought the Yankees to Grambling to play on our campus three times. Grambling has promoted big exhibition games in New Orleans for the Yankees. No one really knows these things about him. Telling about our relationship is one of the reasons I wanted to write this book in the first place. The TV people said they were so surprised when he cried in the locker room after the Yankees won the 1998 World Series. His reputation as a hard-nosed man is misplaced as far as the Robinsons and Grambling are concerned. He wants to win the baseball games. Yet George Steinbrenner is a great American who cares about this country. He has a huge heart and a great deal of compassion for his fellow man. Doris and I are so lucky that he is our friend.

Shreveport: Prelude to the Real Bayou Classic

The early successes of the game in New York made us rethink how to get a game in New Orleans again in spite of the Sugar Cup disaster. Ever since we left the mud field known as City Park

Stadium, I knew the Sugar Cup didn't go right because we were missing something. Whenever Southern University came to Grambling to play in what we now call the old stadium, there would be four or five people for every person who got in. In one game more than 10,000 people just walked over the fence until it collapsed. It wasn't anger but enthusiasm for the game. We needed to harness that enthusiasm for the good of our schools and for the good of football.

It really became a personal thing. Most of the other people never dreamed about their work, couldn't imagine being the best in their profession. Whenever I listened to the radio and heard an announcer talk about the coach who was doing great things, I wanted to be in that coach's shoes.

I knew we had big potential for this game. There was a stadium in Shreveport. In those days there was no *NFL Monday Night Football*. I recalled Monday night college and high school games at this stadium when I was going into high school. At that time, Southern University was the big school that had played there. The game usually took place right after the closing of the Louisiana State Fair. The fair was dismantled on Sunday night. The organizers would have Southern and another black school play Monday night.

I went to my president, Ralph Waldo Emerson Jones, in 1973, right after that game when our fans knocked the fence down. We had made some money, but we could have made so much more if we had had the facilities and a way to seat everyone. The president and I were, of course, good friends. I went to him and said, "Mr. President, what would you rather do? Would you rather bring 3,000 people [the size of our student body at that time] to 40,000 people or bring the 40,000 to the 3,000 and pay the tab?"

He said, "Eddie, don't play around with me by asking me a question like that. Anybody would tell you that if they are footing the bill they would want to carry the 3,000 to the 40,000." I kept on, "Is that actually what you think?" He said, "Sure, that's what I think," and we laughed about it.

Then I asked if we could take the Southern University game off our calendar in Grambling and move it to Shreveport, where we could seat between 40,000 to 42,000 people. He inquired if I thought it would work. I responded, "Mr. President, you've seen what happens on our campus. Its a great rivalry and if we put our home game with Southern in Shreveport, we will make a lot of money." President Jones agreed.

Southern refused when they heard the plan. I asked why? There was no reason, even though it was our game. I had to go back to the president and ask him if he would go to the Louisiana Board of Education or if he would let me go the board. I had already spoken to some board members. I told them we could possibly make enough money to cover our scholarships and pay off our athletic bills in Grambling.

A board member inquired about how we were going to divide the profits. He liked it when I said 50–50 after all expenses were paid to both teams. I told him it's better to split everything and let the other school know exactly what's going on so they will work harder and sell more tickets. He couldn't understand what was holding things up. This board member, who represented the view of most of the members, said it was "a go" since it was our home game and we were splitting everything.

Everyone, including the fans, thought the deal was done and the contract had been signed. I knew Southern was not happy about having to come, and they still had not signed. But they knew the board was behind Grambling's decision.

All during the week before the game my guys kept asking me if I thought Southern was coming to Shreveport, and I always said yes! I told the Southern people that I was not going to push anymore, but someone better go and talk to our board or somebody is not going to have a job.

Man, after that they told me what I could do, and it was not about going to smell the roses. They were furious. However, some of their ex-ballplayers told them to play, so they brought the team to Shreveport. We were all there but we hadn't signed the contract. It came right down to 3:30 A.M. on the morning of game day when Southern finally signed.

Leonard Barnes was a great athlete for Southern. He was one of the best backs I have ever seen in his playing days. Leonard called me in my room and said he was in the hotel lobby with Ulysses Jones, who was the Southern athletic director. Leonard had convinced Ulysses to sign and simply told me, "The game is tomorrow; we ought to sign the contract." As if I hadn't spent months trying to get it signed. The situation was so ridiculous that it was funny. We all laughed about it for half an hour and had fun over the fact that we hadn't signed it. Looking back, I guess it was the great rivalry with Southern that made them seem like they wanted to block things instead of cooperate. I'm sure that Ulysses thought it was Grambling doing the blocking. It is fun to look back on it all now. We may have been laughing that night, but the games themselves were very serious. No one was smiling on game day.

All of the hoopla made some fans forget that we needed to win that game. We were 8–2 and hoping for a bowl bid. We needed to beat Southern to make up for losses to Tennessee State and Texas Southern. That day 41,000 people came to see us play a barn burner in a 19–14 victory for Grambling. It was incredible and a new stadium record that fell the next year when LSU came to Shreveport and drew 42,000 against Arkansas. The game put us into the Divisional Playoffs, where we beat Delaware in the Boardwalk Bowl and lost to Western Kentucky in the Grantland Rice Bowl. But this game in Shreveport had a meaning far greater than who won or who went on to a bowl game. This day was a piece of football history.

Although they lost the game, Southern went home smiling, we

got our money, and everyone who went had a great time. So now I was thinking Sugar Bowl again, but then, in the middle of the night, something came to me and I realized that it didn't have to be the Sugar Bowl committee and another bowl game.

Collie, Ulysses Jones, and I went to the stadium committee for a regularly scheduled game with Southern in New Orleans. The committee saw that between Southern and Grambling we put 41,000 fans in Shreveport. We could only imagine what we could put in New Orleans. Then we were in a position to get national corporate sponsors for a game between black schools in Louisiana. It was another dream coming true.

The first Bayou Classic was in 1974. I remember the feeling walking out on that field. This was a field Grambling could not even play on when I stared coaching. It could have brought back bitter memories of racial strife in sports, but for me it was a sign of how far America had come.

My memory flashed back to 1941 when I was on an independent all-star team after my final game for Leland. I was playing for the Baton Rouge Patriots and we were playing the New Orleans Brutes in New Orleans in an independent league championship. A black college star was not being allowed to play in the Sugar Bowl game that year, which was scheduled for Monday. He had agreed to play in our game on Sunday. He drew a huge crowd, which loved every minute of his contribution to our game.

That's why I went to the Stadium committee and not the Sugar Bowl committee in 1974. This was the birth of the biggest game between black colleges ever. I was a proud man—a proud American. We had changed things.

It was Doug Williams's freshman year. It wasn't one or two guys playing in the Sugar Bowl but twenty-two on the same field at the same time in a stadium where blacks couldn't play at all when I was young. We were moving things forward in our own way. We weren't demonstrating in the streets, but we sure were demonstrating on the fields.

We hired Pace Management, an outside firm, to manage the game for us. They had helped us earlier and we gave it to them. Pace helped us to get this game organized. They were doing all of the media work. At game time we broke out of the dressing room with our team to warm-up. I was stopped by the sight of it all, and all I could do was just stand there and cry. I could hear the announcer above the noise of the crowd. I'll always remember his words, "Ladies and gentlemen, the attendance at this time is 76,000 paid!" I had always wondered how we would feel with 20,000 to 30,000 people in the stadium and there we were, playing on a field with 76,000. I was crying on the field because I remembered what it was like when blacks couldn't play in that stadium. For the players, it was a big game. For me, it was walls falling down.

It was also a huge recognition of Grambling. I thought back to one of my first coaching clinics in the 1940s. I had introduced myself as "Eddie Robinson, the coach of Grambling College." One of the other coaches attending the clinic came back with, "Gambling? Gumbling? what's really the name of your school?" That brought laughter from the coaches. I knew they weren't trying to be mean, but I vowed to myself that someday everyone was going to know what and where Grambling was. That day had come with the launching of the Bayou Classic.

We beat Southern again. This time it wasn't so close and we won 21–0 to complete the regular season at 10–1. It was still a great, competitive game. We won our fourth Black National Championship and finished at 11–1 after we easily beat South Carolina State 28–7 in the Pelican Bowl.

While I knew the committee probably didn't care whether we ever won a game, let alone the Black National Championship, I knew that with the 76,000 paid we wouldn't have any more trouble with them because the dollar is all-American, every day and every week. This was the beginning of one of the greatest classics in Louisiana and in all of America. Almost everyone now knows about the Bayou Classic. We have had 70,000+ ever since, and eventually it became a regularly televised game on NBC and other networks.

When I look around I have to think this is one heck of a country. It makes me feel it could only happen in America. You are talking about a feeling—standing down on the floor of the Superdome with 76,000 people screaming and celebrating.

I thought back to even before 1941 to when I used to go down to LSU to help out before the games at 6 A.M. on game day. By then I had realized that if we studied a situation and worked full out toward the goal, we could do almost anything. We had the Urban League or Whitney Young Classic. Collie Nicholson was using his golden pen to tell the world about us. And Pace was helping us to meet our larger goals.

What a dream. The Bayou Classic is our Rose Bowl, our Sugar Bowl, and our Orange Bowl wrapped into one. It's one of the largest football events in the country, and it's played in one of the finest football facilities in the world. The Bayou Classic is more than a football game. It's a real happening, with all the pageantry of a bowl game. I am so proud of the part Grambling has played in the Bayou Classic. It's the epitome of the best in college football.

The Space Classic in the Astrodome with Texas Southern

The classic in Houston was another game that got a lot of resistance. We wanted to play Texas Southern, but they wanted more than a 50–50 split since it was "their game." Plain and simple, their athletics director, Dr. David Raines, thought we were making too much money in our other games. He also didn't believe we could ever draw enough people to play in the Astrodome. Therefore, we went to Judge Roy Hofheinz and asked him if we could play in the Astrodome. He responded, "Eddie, what makes you think we'd let you play your game here?"

I told the judge that I had read about him and I knew he was intelligent. Therefore, he had to realize that if we had a game there and he got the money from the concessions, it was better than letting the dome sit empty. The judge started laughing. I kept on at him, noting again that if he got the money from the concessions, it would be better than the building being there, looking pretty but with nobody playing.

Now he was listening and we were laughing. The judge asked me how many people I thought we could get to come. Collie said, "It's just a matter of time before we sell it out." I added that we might draw 15,000 to 20,000 in the first year; we'd have 30,000 to 40,000 by the third or fourth year, and, after that, capacity.

Judge Hofheinz looked at Collie and me like we were crazy. "Don't you know the capacity is more than 50,000?" I could tell he didn't believe we could do this. So I went straight to the chase. "Judge, let's not worry about the speculation. What is the price for the use of the Astrodome?" Judge Hofheinz said it would be $12,000. I guaranteed to put the money down to claim the date. He asked if we could come up with that. Collie said, "Yeah, yeah, we can have that to you, whenever you require it." Of course, Collie didn't have a penny and I had less.

The people from Texas Southern didn't go with us. Dr. Raines said he wasn't interested, so it was Grambling there negotiating it all. Collie and I went into one of the offices in the Astrodome and called President Jones. I said, "Mr. President, we are in the Astrodome." He jabbed me with, "I had to sign that travel record; I know where you are." I told him we had something he couldn't refuse but we needed $6,000 to get the Astrodome and then Texas

Southern would put up $6,000 so we would have the necessary $12,000.

President Jones asked us what we thought about it. I said it had real growth possibilities and might turn out to be a Yankee Stadium situation. He agreed to put up the $6,000. We told him we might need the cash soon and that we were on our way to Texas Southern to see if they would match the money. Dr. Jones told me to keep him informed and "hurry back."

We went to Texas Southern and explained everything to Dr. Raines, emphasizing that the key thing now was that we needed $12,000. We sat there in amazement as he said, "I'm not gonna get involved in that. I'm not interested in playing there." I tried to use humor and suggested the Astrodome could become Texas Southern's stadium. He didn't laugh. I knew this game would be a big winner for Grambling, but that we needed Texas Southern to sell out a stadium in Houston. So I went on, "Dr. Raines, if we get somebody else to put the money up, would you play." Ever the cautious man, he answered, "Well, I might but I might not."

Collie and I left to talk to Jack O'Conner, who was the president of the Houston Touchdown Club. They had given me a beautiful plaque and a good time at one of their affairs. We had a lot of fun down there. I remembered that Jack was connected with the Astrodome.

I got Jack on the phone, told him the situation, and asked if the Houston Touchdown Club would put up the $6,000 and make it an even three-way partnership. I informed Jack that, if he agreed, I would go back and get something in writing that Texas Southern would play, and we would divide it in three equal parts.

Jack asserted, "Eddie, this sounds like a winner. We will put up the $6,000." I didn't think Dr. Raines would refuse the initial offer, but I knew he couldn't refuse this risk-free offer.

The writers called it the Space Classic. We played the first game before 18,000; in the following year we brought in 28,000 or so.

By the fifth year you couldn't find a ticket on game day. Once again, Grambling had delivered, this time with Texas Southern and the Houston Touchdown Club as partners.

While black people in Houston were certainly free to go to the Astrodome, they had never had an opportunity like this before. They were there to see two black colleges go head-to-head. It was really something. Texas Southern had a fine marching band, and Grambling had the best one ever assembled. Those two bands put on a show the likes of which folks in Houston had never seen before. The crowd was a style show unto itself. People saved their best clothes. Man, you are talking about dressed up. We had never seen so many minis and micro-minis. The suits that the guys had— they were dressed up and having fun. It was the biggest party of mostly blacks that Houston had ever witnessed.

Realistically, Texas Southern wasn't going to be able to beat us often in that era. They won in 1965 and in 1973. We played to a 17–17 tie in 1981. They didn't beat us between 1973 and 1996, when they shocked us, 52–7. But there were some great games in between. From their win in 1965 until their win in 1973, we won six of the seven games by a total of twenty-eight points.

When the games weren't so close, the atmosphere and the entertainment took over. And the crowds kept the revenues flowing to the three partners. Soon after the success was proven, Texas Southern wanted to renegotiate the deal. After their victory in 1973, Dr. Raines proposed giving us the SWAC conference guarantee of $3,000. He said we didn't deserve half of the money since Houston was their city and this was their crowd. There was no way I would or could do this. We had to bring all the players and the Grambling Band. He said there was no way he would pay for the Grambling Band.

I declared that there would be no game under these circumstances. I couldn't believe it when I discovered that Dr. Raines had gone to Rice University to secure their stadium on his own. Here we were, making all this money for our schools, and Dr. Raines was about to kill the deal. It was so ridiculous that I only told a few people because most would have thought I was crazy or lying.

I called my president and informed him of Texas Southern's position. I appealed to him to let me make an entirely new deal and he agreed. I never wanted to let my president down because he placed such trust in me.

I went back to Dr. Raines with, "OK, you can have the game at Rice Stadium when it is your home game. We'll take the $3,000 SWAC guarantee for that game. But when it is our home game, we will play you in Houston at the Astrodome and divide the money with you 50–50."

I could see that Dr. Raines really did not want to do this, but I think he was at least a little stuck by the logic of it all. How could he refuse? He called the SWAC conference office and they told Dr. Raines that as long as Grambling had a place to play in Grambling, he didn't have to agree to the Astrodome deal. That was the out he needed. The game was over for all practical purposes.

We did get back to the Astrodome one year and drew 50,000 plus. I remember Jesse Jackson was there. But this whole episode with Dr. Raines baffled me. The Astrodome was perfect. The climate was controlled; rain couldn't affect a game. We were drawing big crowds, making money, and winning over new fans and potential future students to attend our schools. I don't know what Dr. Raines's Ph.D. was in, but I guess it wasn't in sports management!

People look at these big games today and they don't know the history and how difficult the games were to start back then or what went on since. That's what we faced. In my last year coaching, Texas Southern wanted to talk about starting it up again. Dr. Raines is, of course, deceased now.

Again, I never wanted to lose great opportunities because I was that boy at McKinley High who had dreamt of playing before 10,000 people! I had seen the great rivalry between LSU and Tulane. So I wanted my school to have the same chances for excitement and pride. I was always willing to pay the price to make it happen. I was convinced that you can do anything you want to do if you have an imagination and are willing to pay that price.

I realized that stadium owners would rather use the stadium, even if it first seemed odd to have two black schools playing, than keep it empty. Now the people at the 'Dome send me Christmas cards saying they haven't seen us in a long time and would be glad to have us back.

Tokyo: 1976–77

We were on a roll regarding innovative games when we were invited to Tokyo. I found out that we could get everything we wanted by being patient and waiting for the right moment. The organizers in Japan would only agree to bring part of the team because of the expenses. Frankly, I didn't think it was right, but I didn't argue with the organizers. Instead I questioned how they would break up a team that made you good enough to be invited to Tokyo. I figured that we could all sit together and get it done. Heck, we had sold out the Superdome and the Astrodome. We could do this. I knew it. We did!

The people from Pace Management were excellent at understanding these things. The lead man was named Allan Pace. He did a lot of other attractions all over the country and even the Tokyo game for us. He got the band to Tokyo and booked the Grambling Band in all kinds of places. I hated to lose the team when we stopped working with Pace.

We had to overcome the language barrier in Tokyo, and Pace Management sure helped with that. It was interesting to see how much the Japanese wanted to emulate Americans while maintaining their own culture. They were imitating our architecture with

some buildings. Their main stadium reminded me of Yankee Stadium. In spite of the fact that I couldn't understand what they were
broadcasting, the Japanese sports announcers *sounded* like ours. I
saw many Japanese who were trying to dress the way the Americans
were dressing. It was a great experience for our family and our team
to be in Japan, where we spent a full week each time. The fact that
we were the first American college team to play in Japan made it all
the more special. One year we stopped on the way in Hawaii and
played the University of Hawaii in their old stadium.

We played against Morgan in 1976 and Temple in 1977. Both
games were sold out. We beat Morgan and were in a tough game
with Temple. Temple had beaten us in Philadelphia in 1976. I
couldn't exactly tell why my guys were not themselves against
Temple. Then I called a time-out and asked them, "What's happening out there . . . we can still win this game." Then they told
me the Temple players were calling them "nigger" when they
lined up to try to draw us offside. I asked them if they had ever
heard "nigger" before? Of course they had. So I challenged them
to not let it bother them and to go play. I kept going at my guys.
Temple's got black players out there. You know they're not going
to call you that. Then my guys cracked me up and said it was Temple's black players who were shouting "nigger."

That was some kind of game. God, when I looked up at the
clock there were two minutes left and they kicked it into the end
zone. Doug Williams was ready. He would usually go into the
game and I'd send him the play or tell him the play during the
kickoff. This time Doug told me to send it to him. It was third
down and sixteen. He came out of the huddle without getting my
play, pulled a draw, and picked up eighteen yards. Then it was third
and eleven to go. Again, I didn't get the play to him in time. I think
Doug threw a screen and got fifteen yards for another first down.
So I just stood there and rocked with him while he was getting
closer. I didn't even try to send the play. We were down at the

eight-yard line and Doug called a final time out. Doug questioned me, "What's the matter, Coach? You are so slow now." I replied that I didn't get any play to him because I figured if he got us down there that far, then he could get us in.

Doug came back with a big, "No! Let's do it the way we've been doing it all these years." He said it helped him when I sent it in, knowing that I had given him the opportunity to change the play if he didn't like it. Doug asked what did I want to call. I appealed to his intelligence. "Doug, you brought us from our twenty to their eight. What should we call for? I was just standing on the sidelines watching you make a series of great calls."

Doug insisted that I had to make the call and let him react. I said, "Well, we've got Garraty, the second-string running back in there. Do you want me to put the first-string running back in?" Doug said Garraty was playing too well to come out now.

He asked me what I wanted. I said throw it into the end zone four times . . . I know you will get one in there. He said we couldn't do that because we needed to play like we had played all year.

I said, "OK, let's go with the sweep." Well, Doug called the sweep, and we went into the end zone standing up. We won, 35–32, ending a National Championship year with an incredible thriller. Doug came over to me and said, "You almost went back on something you told me when you recruited me. You told me if a man didn't believe in himself and what he was doing, he wasn't worth a damn. That has been my motto. You told me that when you lose, don't look back and second guess yourself because most times you will second guess yourself into a hole."

After the game, the entire team waited in the bus for ninety minutes for Doug to come out. The guys were hungry, tired, and mad at Doug. I sent a team member in to see if Doug was OK. The player came with his report: Doug had showered and was surrounded by seventy-five young Japanese kids waiting for an autograph. He told us to go back to the hotel and he would meet us there, but I held the bus. Doug finally walked on the bus, put his bags down, and sensed the anger and frustration.

Doug reminded his teammates that he didn't make the rules on this team. Eddie Robinson made the rules and he told all of us that we couldn't be part of this team if we didn't sign autographs, especially for the kids. "I'm hungry just like you are, and I stayed there until I signed them all." Doug was a real leader at Grambling. That never stopped when he went to the NFL or when he started coaching.

I was proud of how our student-athletes adjusted to the Japanese culture and how respectful they were of the people. The Japanese were fascinated by us. The Japanese organizers had a parade for the teams. I don't know if they had ever seen so many black Americans in one place, but I was confident that they had not seen so many big Black Americans.

We were all in Toyota trucks, which weren't really big enough for some of our players. One of our guys—we called him "Big Charlie" for obvious reasons—was 6'11" and over three hundred pounds. He was crammed in this little truck but never complained. The parade, which was almost a mile long, was moving at a walking pace. The Japanese kids followed Big Charlie everywhere. They all went up and touched him. His size and color made him unique in Japan, that's for sure.

Both cultures learned from each other. That's the best kind of experience for young people. The games in Japan, although we only went twice, represented real highlights in my career.

Concluding Thoughts on the Classics

I always wanted Grambling to be viewed as the equal of any school in Louisiana. That was never easy. When I was a child I used to dream about playing in the Sugar Bowl. I was too young to understand that blacks weren't allowed to play there. I just saw LSU there and I wanted to go.

I never played against them or coached against them, but I guess I competed against LSU all my life. LSU cast a long shadow in Louisiana. I felt we were always under that shadow. For many years I wondered whether Southern University or Grambling could ever play before the crowds LSU drew. Now I see that drove my dream for the Whitney Young and Bayou Classics.

I never thought I'd play in Tulane's stadium. I didn't know that we would rival the Sugar Bowl, and I didn't know that we would hold a record for attendance for a single game. I was so proud that my last game, the Bayou Classic in 1997, left $61 million in the economy in New Orleans. See there, no hate; that's pure American money. We're not always looking for something. We bring in two predominantly black schools to a Louisiana facility and contribute a lot to the economy. We are giving back to my state. I knew I could do anything that the other guys from the white schools in my profession could do. At Grambling, even in my last year, I was trying to do it better.

I remember when they first built the Superdome. People were complaining about the acoustics and how it was hard to hear. I was in one of those meetings and I got up to tell them that it appeared to me that Texas seemed to me a little bit prouder of their facilities than we were in Louisiana. I said that in the Astrodome they sell excursions even when there is no game. But in New Orleans, all I can hear is that the acoustics are not good and you can't hear well. I said maybe that's right, but last Saturday before 72,000 people in the Superdome, I hollered from the sidelines to Graves to get back. Unless I'm good at mental telepathy, Graves got back. He heard me.

We need to be proud of what we actually have. I told the governor one day that I wanted to bring more good news to this state than any coach. I told him that I say good things about my state, my school, my church, and about my nation. I can talk about Grambling; I believe in Grambling. I told him I feel whatever we need to have at Grambling the state is going to see that we get it because the state does it for everybody. I was being truthful about how I felt but was also giving the governor a message about Grambling's needs.

When I stared talking about playing in Tokyo and then in the Superdome in New Orleans, some thought I was really way out there. Then, when we started to be more and more successful with the various classics around the country, the schools that at first didn't want to join us started asking, "Whose game is it?" Then the politicking and disputes began in earnest. But Grambling's policy was always to share 50–50.

We knew that when you do that everybody will work harder to make the game a success and try to make it a better game. But there were always doubters. Once the 50–50 split was established, opponents would say, "But we have to travel farther; 50–50 isn't fair because we have more expenses than Grambling." We quieted them down when they finally read the contract and saw the way it actually worked. The 50–50 split came after all travel and all game expenses. Sometimes it is so hard to establish and keep trust. But once that trust is there, anything becomes possible.

In my final season I told the team that this was the greatest of times in the history of the United States for young Black Americans. I've never seen it like this. There are kids without degrees who can be millionaires because they can play ball. Well, that's great for a few, but not for everyone who is playing and certainly not for most students who will never pick up a ball. They need that education and then some.

I believe there isn't anything wrong with our society that some common-sense thinking can't fix. But there are some people who don't want to use that common sense. I always have tried to use it.

There are some things that I'm real proud of; I'm not brilliant and I'm not a Phi Beta Kappa, but I'm not dumb either.

I'm proud of the fact that we could leave our little town of Grambling and go to New York and play for thirty years since 1968 before nearly 1.5 million fans. Grambling only missed two years. I'm proud that we could take a Louisiana facility in New Orleans and create the Bayou Classic, running for twenty-five years. I guess another 1.5 million people have been there for that celebration.

I don't know how to thank the State Fair Association in Dallas, Texas, for putting their arms around us and letting us be the host team at the Cotton Bowl next to the Texas State Fair so we all could go to the bank smiling.

Dallas means a lot to me. I sometimes wake up at night and remember that scoreboard flashing in the Cotton Bowl. I'll never forget that night there when we beat Prairie View in the 1985 State Fair Classic. That was the night I broke Bear Bryant's record for most wins by a college football coach.

While Prairie View, our traditional opponent in the game, has had its ups and downs, the game never lost its glimmer as the city of Dallas got more and more involved. The State Fair game has truly been a classic. The Cotton Bowl has almost always been filled to its 59,000 capacity. Dallas showed commitment. The job they do has been first class in putting on this game. I have been to all the big games, and this is what you would expect from the Rose Bowl.

Now they know us in Texas. They look at Grambling as a school with good people who can make the Texas State Fair Association some real money. Some weren't sure how to treat us before we proved ourselves. They probably had never dealt with blacks as equal partners before. We had to deal with the aftereffects of segregated Texas when we started, but now we stay in the best hotels in town.

I tried to stop and look at what was going on. I tried to tell my student-athletes what was out there for them if they were willing to pay a price to reach their goals. I know it is unfair that they have to pay an extra price because they are black. We all paid it to be able to prove ourselves. That was and is the reality of life.

Rams Interview

I had apparently paid the price long enough to have proven myself capable of being a head coach in big-time football. Our successes were mounting in the mid- to late-1970s, and Howard Cosell was out there telling people I should get a shot at the NFL.

I will always recall my only interview for an NFL head coaching job. It was quite an experience and was with the Los Angeles Rams in 1977. That was Doug Williams's last year with us at Grambling. I didn't pay much attention to it when they first asked because I knew I wasn't going to take the job if it was offered. But I knew I had to go for the interview when Howard Cosell found out. He was going to blast somebody—it could have been me—for not trying or a team for not ever asking.

So I decided to go rather than face Howard. When it was time, I had all my guys meet down in the stadium. I told them I was going to Los Angeles, but that I wasn't going to take the job. I said "I'm going out there to find out what goes on and come back and tell you about it." I thought some of my guys might be ready to use some of the information. I thought I needed to go to find out what it was like.

The owner of the Rams, Carrol Rosenbloom, was a fine fellow. When I got there, he and his team officials had a lot of questions they wanted to ask. They'd ask me things and I'd go to the board to show them. They kept on asking me how were we able to do this and how were we able to do all that.

I said, "Mr. Rosenbloom," and he immediately stopped me

with, "Eddie, my friends call me Carrol." I said, "Well, Carrol, I want to be your friend, but I want to tell you one thing. If you offer me this job I can't take it. There are so many people that I'm close to who I've got to talk with about it, and I'd have think over it awhile. I know you want somebody who's going to tell you 'yes' or 'no' today, but I can't do that. I want to be fair with you."

Carrol responded, "Is that the only thing keeping you from taking this job if I offer it?" I told him this was my greatest problem with the job.

He quickly noted that his problems far outweighed mine. Carrol continued, "Look, as long as you've been at Grambling, if I hire you from Grambling they will have people writing me, hating me for taking you from Grambling to coach here. But that is not as bad as if I don't hire you after I brought you out here. They're going to call me a racist."

Carrol Rosenbloom never quite made the offer, and I don't think I would have taken it if he did. I just had a championship team and it was mostly coming back. In fact, we won three straight SWAC titles (outright or shared) and the Black National Championship in 1980 to begin the new decade. But that interview in 1977 was my one shot at the NFL.

I am sure that the Doug Williams era at Grambling was one of the reasons that made the Rams want to interview me at this particular time in my coaching career. In the years Doug was at Grambling, we went 11–1, 10–2, 8–4, and 10–2. We won the Black National Championship in three of the four years. No less than thirteen players from those teams were drafted, including three number-one picks. But our victory on October 23, 1976, against Jackson State, 28–6 showed that it was not only a Doug Williams era, but a long tradition at Grambling. That day against Jackson State marked my 250th victory!

While I was there for the job interview, Carrol and I spent time talking about James Harris and what he had done for the Rams.

Doris was with me. Of course, by then she almost always was. We went out to dinner with Carrol Rosenbloom; Hugh Culverhouse, the owner of Tampa; his wife; and other people from the Rams. We spent more than three hours talking, mostly about football. They wanted to know how our quarterbacks escaped the blitz so successfully.

The draft was coming up and I was telling them about Doug Williams—about what kind of guy he was, his style of play, and his incredible talents. I told them Doug was cut off the same piece of timber as the best we'd ever had. And, of course, he was.

They just kept asking about him. I was unaware about what was nearly ready to happen. Within a couple of days of my getting back to Grambling, I got a call from Mr. Culverhouse in Tampa. He said, "Eddie, I got you on the box and I got the media here. We have just drafted Doug Williams as our first-round pick, and I want you to talk to the media. They can hear you on the box, and I want you to say the things that you told us in California last week about all the things that he could really do on the football field." Apparently, the conversation that night in Los Angeles influenced them in selecting Doug with a number-one pick in the draft.

I never had a shot at a Division IA head-coaching position, but I probably would have turned that down, too. After forty-one years, Grambling had a new president who I wanted to work with. Dr. Joseph B. Johnson took over the reins in April of 1977 from Ralph Waldo Emerson Jones, my mentor and leader for the first thirty-six years of my career. There is no way to express how much I missed Dr. Jones. However, I liked Dr. Johnson and wanted to be there for him.

Grambling was a part of me, a big part of my life. I had a unique role to play there with young men who sought our help as players and as men. That's where I wanted to be. That's where I had been for thirty-five years by the time Carrol called. That's where I stayed for another twenty years.

8.

THE 1980s: RECORDS FALL

The 1980s began with one of our best wingbacks ever leading Grambling's offense. Trumaine Johnson was beautiful to watch. Trumaine caught 130 passes in the 1980, 1981, and 1982 seasons for almost 2,700 yards. He caught sixteen touchdown passes in 1980 alone!

I was inducted into Grambling's new Hall of Fame in 1981. I never doubted that it was players like Trumaine who, over my first forty years of coaching, helped me be inducted in the very same year as my mentor, former President Ralph Waldo Emerson Jones. The only previous inductee was our founding president, Dr. Charles P. Adams, in 1980. I couldn't describe how proud I was. The pride was matched a year later when my dear friend, Collie Nicholson, and our first great players, Tank Younger and Willie Davis, were placed in the Grambling Hall. This was not only a hall for athletics but for all of Grambling. That made it even more significant.

300 and Counting

There was so much talk about me potentially winning my 300th game as a coach when the 1982 season began. There had even been talk about me getting it in 1981, but the team went 6–4–1, including two losses and a tie in our final three games that year. Looking back, I recognize how hard approaching all these milestones had to be on our players. They were not just playing game-by-game like most teams. The press kept asking our student-athletes how they felt about potentially helping me win game 300. It was a real distraction for our guys.

We won our first two games against Morgan State and Alcorn. Next up was Florida A&M on September 25 in Tallahassee. There was more press there than usual, and our guys were anxious to take the field and make their mark. We hadn't played FAMU after losing the 1969 Orange Blossom Classic until 1978, when we closed what had been an unbeaten season with a 37–7 loss to them. They beat us again in 1979, 25–7. We finally tagged FAMU 27–10 in 1980 and again in 1981, 21–10. The FAMU series was a heated rivalry, but our Grambling men took care of business on that Saturday afternoon and we had number 300 under our belts. We finished the year with an 8–3 record. I had 305 victories.

Only three other coaches had ever eclipsed 300 and they were all legends: Pop Warner, Amos Alonzo Stagg, and Bear Bryant, who was still coaching in 1982. I couldn't imagine that people would ever mention the name of Eddie Robinson in the same sentence with them. There were so many fans celebrating in the stands and on the field. My guys were very happy. I could see the pride on Doris' face as she made her way toward me. The camera flashed away as we hugged. They caught the tears running down my face. In the locker room I told my guys how proud they had made me, and that the number 300 belonged to them and all those who had played for me at Grambling before them.

When Grambling threw a big party to celebrate my 300th victory, Collie Nicholson and I insisted that the sports editors of all the black weekly newspapers be flown there at our expense as Grambling's way of saying thanks for all their years of coverage and support before the white press knew about Grambling. They had made us into the national university that President Jones wanted. We were extremely grateful and wanted to share this moment with them.

Next up, the media began to talk about me catching Pop Warner at 313, Coach Stagg at 315, and Bear Bryant, who retired after the 1982 season, with an incredible 323 victories! There was little chance for my coaches and team members to get relief from the record book and concentrate on their own games and seasons. However, they were always great about it.

The Opening of Eddie Robinson Stadium

I certainly thought of Coach Bryant as the accolades for me mounted in 1983. The season opened with the dedication of the new Eddie Robinson Stadium on Grambling's campus on September 3, 1983.

The stadium sits toward the rear of the campus. It seats 19,600 and would have solved all the problems when the students trampled the fence for the Southern game before the Bayou Classic started. The stadium is shaped like a bowl and is set deep in the ground. You have to get pretty close to see the field from above. In 1983, it was so beautiful and was yet another reason I was so very proud to be a Grambling Tiger. We beat Alcorn to celebrate the opening.

However, it was hard to coach against Alcorn that day in the stadium that was named Eddie Robinson. The dedication ceremony was filled with so much wonderful emotion. We had gone through so many stages to get to that new facility. In 1941, we'd played on fields that didn't even have bleachers and still felt great. Once we got the program going, it was Grambling football, wherever it was being played.

I remember the first time when we got bleachers; I remember when they put lights in the old stadium at Grambling. The pride was really swelling on those days, too! It was hard to hold my heart in my chest when we opened our first real stadium at Grambling. The Eddie Robinson Stadium was actually the second stadium that we played in at Grambling.

But the honor conveyed by naming the stadium after me was overwhelming. The decision was made in the state capital in Baton Rouge. The state of Louisiana had been wonderful about naming stadiums after coaches. The stadium at Tech is named after its coach, Joe Aillet. And the one in Baton Rouge is named after the legendary coach A. W. Mumford.

I was so emotional for the opening that I could not adequately express myself. I'll never be able to tell Grambling how much I appreciated it because it was such a great thrill. I'm still excited about it when I go by it now! I'm just really proud that they saw fit to do it.

To see Grambling go from where it was when I started to where it is now! And all the great men who played on the fields, in the first stadium and now in the Eddie Robinson Stadium. They are the ones who made the program. The fields and the stadiums were only their stage.

We built some dreams here. When I came I could never have imagined what would be created. It is another "only in America" story. That is why I say over and over again, this is a great country—and nobody else can tell me otherwise because I've experienced it.

We only lost one game to Southern Methodist University in 1983 and won the Black National Championship and the SWAC conference by positing an 8–1–2 record. That last victory against Southern brought me even with Pop Warner with win number 313!

Whatever we were doing as a team, people kept honoring me. The boy whose parents never completed grade school received an honorary doctorate from Louisiana Tech University. How do you think Doris and I felt about that? One last honor in 1993 was being inducted into the Louisiana Hall of Fame. Louisiana was the state where I could not attend the white state university and where we could not play in the Sugar Bowl.

A Farewell to Bear Bryant

But I will not remember 1983 for our championship season, the opening of the stadium, or these other great honors as much as for the loss of the "Bear." Paul "Bear" Bryant died in January of 1983, a matter of weeks after coaching his final game at Alabama.

When Bear Bryant got ready to sign blacks in 1970, he didn't need to talk to anybody. He didn't call me and I didn't expect him to; I did not know him that well then. Coach understandably had a lot of confidence in himself and he could recognize guys who could help him win. He had a special feeling for what kind of people he was getting.

Coach Bryant impressed me as being fair to the people on his team. He played to win. Coach often told me, "Winning beats anything coming in second."

In my dealings with him, he was really a nice person. I was going to receive the Distinguished American Award from the Walter Camp Foundation in 1982. We were eating dinner with the people who had organized the awards on the night before the presentation. One of them told me, "Don't pay any attention to what's going to happen tomorrow at the luncheon, Eddie. When Coach

Bryant heard that you were getting the award, he told them that he was going to give it to you. He was quickly told that someone else was going to present the award to me. And then Coach told them, "Well, if I don't do it, nobody's going to do it." I asked what was going to happen and if they were still going to give me the award.

They said I was going to get it, but they didn't know who was going to make the presentation. Heck, this was Bear Bryant, the winningest coach of all time. I figured they had to let him do it. I was right and was honored that he made the presentation to me. Coach Bryant said wonderful things about me. Coming from such a giant, I was doubly honored yet felt undeserving.

I used to call him often in his last years at Alabama. We'd talk about the game itself. When he was getting ready to break Stagg's record, Coach Bryant offered me lots of good advice. He told how he'd be nice to people in the media who hadn't been nice to him. He learned that being critical of the media only hurt you in the end.

After we got to know each other better, Coach was always willing to help me. Buddy Young was scheduled to be Grambling's banquet speaker. He had been a great running back at the University of Illinois and also had starred in the NFL. The banquet was on Saturday, but on Thursday night Buddy called to cancel. Now we had no speaker, so just for the heck of it, I called Coach Bryant. He asked, "Well, what is Buddy going to speak about?" I told him he ran into a problem and he couldn't come so I was calling him to pinch-hit. Imagine calling the most famous coach in America to ask him to pinch-hit. Thinking about it, that was pretty audacious.

He said, "Well, just give me about five or ten minutes to get back to you and let me see how I'm going to get there. I'll get right back to you." Coach Bryant checked to see if his plane was available and it was, so he came to Grambling! After that he always joked about how small Grambling and Ruston were . . . so small he couldn't land the plane there. Coach thought that was pretty funny, but I knew he must have gone recruiting in towns a lot smaller than Grambling.

Then he extended an invitation to me to come to speak at his clinic! It was respect between coaches, like doctors or college presidents or writers. There was a camaraderie.

He wasn't the first white person who spoke at our athletic banquet. I'm not sure if I was the first black to speak at his clinic. His retirement meant that I would never be able to fulfill one of my dreams. I always wanted to coach against him, to have our Grambling team go up against Coach Bryant's Alabama team. We had come close once in his last few years, but never were quite able to schedule it.

At that time, somebody said to me, "Coach, he might beat you." I responded that he'd beaten everybody. We had nothing to lose. Win or lose, it would have been a great privilege for Grambling to have played against Coach Bryant's team.

I was honored when I was asked to present an award to Coach Bryant at a luncheon before a bowl game in Memphis in 1983. I realized that this was the first time—and may have been my last chance—to be up close with him and tell him about his contributions to football and America.

I always knew that he was the kind of guy who didn't want people to say much about him. If you'd be saying good things about him, he'd be saying, "You don't have to say that." I didn't care on this day because some things had to be said. I used to call him "Lord," but on this day I was going to simply call him what he was, "Coach."

On the way into the banquet hall I told him some of the things I was feeling. We were laughing, but I said, "get ready for me to go on about you." Of course, Coach Bryant protested, but I was determined and he saw it in me.

Therefore he looked relieved when we got to the dais and there were time cards in front of us. Mine said three minutes. Coach liked that but I was upset because there was no way I could say it all in three minutes. So I told the master of ceremonies that I couldn't live with the three minutes he'd given me. I told him that Coach Bryant had just retired from football and this was our chance to really give him a great tribute.

He retorted, "Coach, you just have to cut it down and keep it to three because we can't extend this for Paul and not do it for the other guys." He added, "We're not going to have a memorial to Paul."

I was frustrated. We exchanged more words but made no progress. My wife, Doris, caught my arm and told me, "Be quiet, just be quiet." So I slowed down and didn't say anymore. The emcee finally left to speak to someone else. Then Doris told me that "nobody's going to make you sit down once you're up. Eddie, you can't get up there and not say the things you need to say about Coach Bryant. He is retired. You have to talk about the contributions he has made to football. So when you get up there, say what you've got to say." Ever since that day, whenever I think about what she told me, I tell her, "Darling, you know, I fell in love with you all over again!"

She proved so right. So when I got up to speak, I talked about all those years of excellence, about breaking the unbreakable record of Alonzo Stagg, about all the young men Coach helped—not only his players but also his fellow coaches. Of course, Coach tried to stop me several times with, "You don't have to say that, Eddie."

I went on that he was the man who had led our profession, and how I thought that coaching football was one of the greatest and most rewarding professions in the world.

When I started, Coach thought I was going to have to stick to the three minutes so he didn't really expect too much from me.

But that week I had read a story about Mary Raymond Shipman, who had written about the loneliness of Abraham Lincoln at Gettysburg. I had never told this man how much we appreciated what he had done and how the profession loved him for making us all go on further than we would have gone. He had coached for thirty-seven years at the universities of Maryland, Kentucky, Texas A&M, and, of course, Alabama. Alabama finished number one six times. He won 323 games. We all thought that was a record that was out of reach. So when I went over to him to make the presentation, I told the audience about Mary Richmond Shipman. She realized how Lincoln felt at Gettysburg when the speaker of the day spoke about an hour and a half. When he stopped, he received thunderous applause. Then Lincoln spoke for five minutes and stunned everyone into silence. No applause!

Now we know that people have remembered his words forever, and that schools make their students memorize the Gettysburg Address. But as Lincoln stepped down, he didn't know how the crowd reacted since they were silent. I will always remember that the writer noted, "How could he know since nobody told him?"

The people at Gettysburg received Lincoln's speech in complete silence because they thought it would be sacrilegious to applaud after what he had said. I was cranking and Bear asked me to cut it short. "You don't have to take that long; you don't have to say that." And I could see the expression on his face. He didn't know what to do. So I went on and said that Lincoln had started walking through the crowd, which was still silent. Everyone stepped back to let him through until a frail woman plucked at his sleeve. "Mr. Lincoln, I lost a son in this war, but your words helped to heal the hurt in my heart." She helped Abraham Lincoln understand the power of what he had said.

Then I told Coach Bryant, "Today we are here to tell you that we love you; we appreciate what you've done for the American youth; that your rise from Moro Bottom to the pinnacle of success in American football will always be an inspiration for every red-blooded American youth."

I announced that "today we are plucking your sleeve" and I went over to him and plucked his sleeve. The crowd was silent. Now they knew what I was doing. I don't know how long I had been talking, but I know it wasn't three minutes. "We are telling you that we love you, we appreciate you, and we want you to know all this now!" I presented the award to him and went back to my seat. There was no more silence as a thunderous ovation started. Everyone was on their feet. It was something!

I just don't know how I held my tears back while I was speaking. I was looking at the water in his eyes. He wanted to be tough and didn't want anybody to see him cry. It was one of my proudest moments because the response of the crowd to Coach Bryant was exactly what I'd hoped for him. He was still saying, "You don't have to do that; you don't have to do all that." I did it partially because I thought I'd never live with myself if I had had that opportunity of telling him what he had meant to this game and I had let it slip through my fingers.

Coach never got out of the first paragraph when he got up to talk—he cried. Heck, no one had ever seen Coach Bryant cry, so it just tore the whole place up. The men were crying; the ladies were crying. Boy, when Coach Bryant broke down and cried, it was a heck of a time. He didn't want people to see him crying. The entire audience just stood up and wept openly while applauding forever. They were all plucking at his sleeve. Coach just couldn't get though his remarks, and he took his seat. Three weeks later, Bear Bryant was dead.

I'm grateful that I had that opportunity to tell him when he was living. If I had listened to that emcee when he said "hold that three minutes," I never would have had another chance to tell him in person. I told Doris, "Baby, you don't know what you did when you told me to go on and do it. You gave me something to remember." That was really a good day for me when I plucked his sleeve.

When Coach Bryant died, it was as if part a of me did, too. I recalled all the times I'd sat by him, learning about football at clinics and at the conventions. If Doris saw me with him, she'd turn around and leave. She knew I was not going to get up until Coach did. Doris would go shopping. My reverence for Coach Bryant cost me a lot of money because Doris really did like to shop.

More Records

Breaking Coach Bryant's record was on everyone's horizon for me as the 1984 season progressed. We lost our first two games of the season to Alcorn, 27–13, and Boston University, 16–9. We weren't focused on the individual games, and we had to have several team meetings to get things straight. Defeating Bethune-Cookman was number 314 and took me past Pop Warner. Number 315 witnessed me surpassing Coach Stagg. We toppled Prairie View, 42–0 on September 25, 1984, to achieve that milestone. That left only Coach Bryant in front of me.

The press made it hard for me not to think about Coach Bryant and the record. However, it meant more distractions for the team as we lost two in a row to Tennessee State and Mississippi Valley State. More team meetings and we got the focus back, winning our final five games of the 1984 season to finish at 7–4. That left us only four victories from breaking Coach Bryant's record for most career wins by a college football coach.

I emphasized that what we needed in 1985 was not to break Coach Bryant's record, but to win the SWAC by playing each game as if it meant winning the conference title. We looked good in the opening games, beating Alcorn and Central State. We had a tough match-up versus Oregon State in game three. A win would tie me with Coach's record. Our guys put on a clinic and we won 23–6. That left only Prairie View in our path.

Breaking the Record

The date was October 5 in the Cotton Bowl at the Texas State Fair Classic. It was so fitting that it happened in one of our special games. Coach and I had talked about the record at the awards luncheon just before he died. He told me that I'd have to prepare for all the things that would happen off the field: the interviews, the commercial and promotional aspects, and everything else.

We took the opening kickoff and went almost eighty yards in ten plays. Terrell Landry's pass to Arthur Wells gave us a 7–0 lead. We got the ball right back and scored on a short run. One of our guys made it 20–0 with an interception he returned for a touchdown. That's the way it stood at the half. We were 4–0 going into the game and Prairie View was 1–4. We knew we had them by the half. The interception was one of seven turnovers Prairie View made that night in the Cotton Bowl.

I pulled most of our regulars as soon as we scored again in the third quarter. By the fourth quarter, our third team was in the game. I didn't want to embarrass Prairie View. I was about to beat them for the record. I had already beaten Prairie View for my 50th, 150th, and 315th wins, passing Coach Stagg. They finally scored on a long pass with about ten minutes left in the game, making it 27–7.

While the clock ticked down to 0:00, I looked up at the Cotton Bowl scoreboard, which flashed, "TO EDDIE! THANKS FOR THE MEMORY!" The crowd of about 36,000 started chanting, and it grew louder and louder, "EDDIE! EDDIE! EDDIE! 324! 324! 324!"

As I stood there I remember thinking this team is very good, and I never wanted my going for the record to overshadow the hard work these young men and the coaching staff put in to be so good. I was a little frustrated because the live national TV coverage kept me away from my team right after the game. But I got to them pretty soon thereafter.

In the locker room I told the team that this didn't belong just to Eddie Robinson. I told them how proud I was of the way they'd played for Grambling that night. I'll never forget how they responded, "We're GRAMBLING! We're GRAMBLING! We're GRAMBLING!" That made me as proud as the record. We were really a team. We were one. That was football at its best, teaching life to us all.

Governor Edwin Edwards called to congratulate me, and he declared Saturday and Sunday "Eddie Robinson Days" in the state. President Ronald Reagan called me on Sunday morning. The president told me that he and Mrs. Reagan were happy for me and proud not only of the wins but of the men I had helped to develop. Ultimately, Doris and I visited the Reagans at the White House where we gave the president a Grambling T-shirt.

There were four generations of my family in the Cotton Bowl that night to share the moment. My Momma was there. Eddie Junior was more involved in this win than the first, as my assistant coach. Our grandson, Eddie III, was also there.

They were calling me the winningest coach in the history of college football! I was elated and a little bit sad all at once. Yes, I had the record, but I'd never believed anyone could surpass Coach Bryant. In my mind, he is still football's greatest coach. Quite simply, he was in a class by himself; that's all there is to it! I wasn't going to catch him even if I did get more wins. I still appreciate what he did for the game as well as the other great coaches who came before him . . . Coach Pop Warner, Coach Stagg, and all those who never set records but set standards. When my name started being called out with these legends, I had to shake myself to see if I was dreaming. I really didn't believe that it was happening.

I thought about Coach Kraft from McKinley, Coach Turner at Leland, and Pappy Waldorf at my first clinic. Much more than even the coaches, I thought of all my players. This team and the others. I wished more attention was being directed at them because they made it possible for me to get to 324 victories. From the standpoint of me as the coach, I didn't like it when the spotlight was on me. Football is the greatest team sport there is; no player and certainly no coach stands alone. The players' response in the locker room showed that so well.

The media kept asking if I was getting hate mail. They were making comparisons of my breaking Bear Bryant's record to Hank Aaron's breaking Babe Ruth's career home run record. Hank had been threatened and received so much hate mail that he eventually said that breaking the record was one of his worst moments in baseball. That is so sad. I think of Sammy Sosa and Mark McGwire in 1998 and how wonderful their record-breaking season was. It is terrible that Hank Aaron did not receive the same affection.

I was very pleased for Grambling and our program when *Sports Illustrated* put me on their October 14, 1985, cover. That was the only cover the magazine ever devoted to a program at a black college.

But I honestly got only positive mail. Maybe I was too old for hate mail. There were so many wonderful stories written by the media. Wonderful letters and phone calls. I received so many emotional letters. They really moved me. I got dozens of letters from Alabama, including one from one of Coach Bryant's former players. I think they may have all been so positive because it was clear that I was never going to use the record to diminish the heroes of other people. Heck, these coaches whose records I broke were *my* heroes! Especially Coach Bryant.

Much later when I went to Arkansas to speak, I asked someone to take me to Moro Bottom, which was the village Bear Bryant was raised in. It was a few miles from Fordyce in rural Arkansas. Coming from rural Louisiana, I felt at home. The man asked "What?" I said, "Man, I've got to see where Bear roamed." Paul "Bear" Bryant had gotten his nickname by wrestling a bear in a theater! And so they took me to Moro Bottom, where I visited the place where he had lived and I paid my respects.

Doris and Football

Before we were married Doris declared that she wanted to travel with me and the team. It had gotten easier to arrange for that in the 1970s, and by the 1980s she was a fixture. I always tried to accommodate Doris when there was a seat on the bus or the plane. She went with me to a lot of great places.

We went to Germany for the Air Force; of course, she went to Japan when we played in Tokyo, to New York, New Orleans, and Dallas every year. Doris was on all those trips. She came to almost all of my speeches as well, but I'll discuss that later.

Not only did we enjoy being together, but I also thought it was something that was good for the team to see us together so much. It created a pretty good scenario for them to see how a husband and wife could treat each other. I wanted them to see how important a wife was in the family picture.

Doris and I had discussed retirement for about twenty-five years. We talked about what we'd do when we retired. We never really settled on anything, but we knew we would need some income and decided we'd start a small business. We helped build a housing project with about forty apartments in Grambling in the 1960s. It is near campus and mostly occupied by students. We didn't make a lot of money from them, but what we did make helped. I was a man whose family never had anything in the family to pass on. With these apartments, Doris and I thought we would be able to pass them on in our family.

We were aware that the children wouldn't be with us forever, so that's what we planned for. We wanted to plan our future together, to make our life path clear. Too many people don't take the time to talk about these things and plan for them. But Doris and I always talked about our future because we were one in each other's eyes.

I'd tell Doris everything, even football stories. At first I didn't know if the football stories bored her. I thought they might bore quite a few wives, but I knew Doris had grown to love the game. Still I didn't know until one day I came home unexpectedly. Doris was in the living room with some of her women friends, retelling the football stories. It turned out she was writing my stories down so she could share them.

Doris eventually began to request that I tell her certain stories over and over. "Darling, tell me that story about Coach Long, or tell me the story about the man at Alabama State." Doris loves a good laugh. The stories also gave her more material for her friends.

Boy, she tried to tell them the same way I did. When the other coaches came to the house and were telling stories, she'd be there with her pencil writing their stories down. Then Doris would tell them to the other wives or to the people on the faculty.

We shared everything. We loved to just hang around the house together. We were each other's entertainment. I think the husband and wife should be able to stay in the same room for hours on end without having to run out. Being home is something you need to feel good about. We do, that's for sure!

We talk football, but we talk a lot of other things, everything, really. Doris has been so dear to me. She reads and finds new things for my speeches. She clips things for me out of the newspapers. Doris would get me to have my secretary type it and then make a file, which I could go through when I needed to.

We have had such a good relationship. I just pure love her as much as you could possibly love a wife. The fact that she shared my love for football was only the cream in the coffee. The brew was already so rich.

Hero of Destiny

The moments for Doris and me were very sweet in Baton Rouge when I was honored with a "Hero of Destiny: A Tribute to EDDIE ROBINSON" dinner in May of 1986. Howard Cosell, retired boxing champion Sugar Ray Leonard, and so many other celebrities were there that night. It was a real homecoming. I reflected on our past in Baton Rouge—moving there, my parents' divorce, grammar school, meeting Coach Kraft, McKinley High, and, of course, most importantly, meeting my sweetheart, Doris. It was actually an entire weekend named for me and was sponsored by the Grambling University Athletic Foundation and the Alumni Association.

It was a far different feeling than when I went to Baton Rouge for football. I always liked going there for football, but that weekend had added meaning for me because I was literally coming home. I always thought of Baton Rouge as our town, too. The event really was not so much for me as it was for Grambling. The way the economy was, we needed special events to help out. It was really a fund-raiser for scholarships for Grambling and for the Athletic Foundation.

Saturday's dinner was, in Sugar Ray's words, "the main event." Louisiana's senior U.S. senator, Russell Long, served as the honorary chairman of the event, and Howard was the master of ceremonies for the dinner. I kept the newspaper stories so I could remember what was said that night.

Senator Long cited me and Grambling for making great

progress. "It has been more than forty-five years since Ralph Waldo Emerson Jones drew Eddie Robinson away from a feed mill job to the campus of Grambling. Eddie and Grambling have come a long way since those early days.

"There were many things going against Eddie Robinson in those years, but he never gave up. In the process what Robinson taught is that winning does not have to be at any cost, that football games can be won honestly, that boys can be shaped into men.

"We're not here to pay honor to a record number of victories; what we're here to honor is Robinson's integrity. We're here to honor a man who for forty-five years has dedicated himself to an institution. He helped his student-athletes develop their bodies, but he didn't leave them until they had developed their brains and their characters." Needless to say, I was in tears when the senator spoke.

My friend, Howard Cosell, called me a "distinguished friend who is part of American history."

Sugar Ray Leonard also pulled my heart. "With a staff too small, appropriations too skimpy, facilities inadequate, Coach Robinson asked, like President Kennedy, not what Grambling could do for him, but what he could do for Grambling. What he did for Grambling State University is history.

"I'm here to help make this a true celebration for Eddie Robinson, a man who has dedicated his time, his life, his talent, and his philosophy to a great university. For a man to have accomplished so much with so little is truly a remarkable accomplishment."

The big names got people's attention. I was happy because Senator Long, Sugar Ray, and Howard were all people I admired and respected. But the next two people, who were not well known, were very special to me. George Mencer was my lifelong friend. We were seatmates together in Baton Rouge and had played football together at McKinley and at Leland. George praised me for my contributions to coaching. He also recalled the times when we "sold ice, shoveled coal, and sold strawberries and peaches to get $1.75 in a brown envelope at the end of the week." Mencer also noted the effect of Leland's Rubin Turner on me. He taught me to be a student of the game . . . never to stop looking for innovations.

As if that wasn't emotional enough, Catherine Kraft came to the podium. Man, I have already said what her husband had meant to me. There would not have been an affair that night if Julius Kraft had not stepped into my life in the third grade.

"My husband was privileged to coach Eddie Robinson. He always had the utmost confidence in Eddie. He said if he had five other players in the game as fine as Eddie, he'd never have to worry. He also said Eddie was destined to go places and do great things."

It was a great weekend. Our entire family was in Baton Rouge for the festivities, which began with a reception on Friday and included golf and tennis tournaments and a fashion show. Grambling and the city of Baton Rouge really did this one up. We loved being back home. Grambling knew how to embrace us. As we had for forty-five years, we embraced Grambling right back.

NFL Help for Black Coaches

The 1980s were not without incidents that made me reflect on race and sport. I had considered what to do with the Rams' job if it had been offered in the late 1970s. Frank Robinson had been named as Major League Baseball's first black manager in 1974 with Cleveland. Bill Russell had taken the helm of the Celtics almost ten years earlier in 1966. John McClendon had the head job in the American Basketball Association in 1961 with the Cleveland team.

Suddenly we had Al Campanis, then a senior vice president of the Dodgers, talking on ABC's *Nightline* about blacks not having the necessities to be big league managers or general managers. All the leagues started to respond. It seemed as though the NBA was far out in front. Baseball was caught up in the Campanis story. In the NFL, Art Shell became the first black head coach in 1989 with the Oakland Raiders. If it had been offered and I had taken the job with the Rams ten years earlier, would it have taken this long to hire an Art Shell? You could speculate that the NFL, the last league to hire a black in a top position—more than fifteen years later than the NBA or Major League Baseball—might have moved faster if I had. However, I never was really offered that position.

The NFL needed to seek other ways to integrate at the top. I never had any doubt that Paul Tagliabue had all the right values in this area. I am sure the program for coaches from historically black schools was the result. I know it helped our program.

About ten years ago we visited the Vikings as part of an NFL program to help coaches from the predominantly black schools. The NFL would bring the whole staff in for a week. You could go to all their meetings and hear what they had to say. It was a great opportunity.

We would write in advance of our arrival to set up film and projectors so we could see their system before we started to meet the coaches. We'd go to meet all the teams we could. We finally got down to the Cowboys.

I told our coaches they couldn't miss any meetings. They had to be there with their corresponding NFL position coach. Our coaches paid attention to this, but it was a holiday. We were up in the room looking at films and talking when Tom Landry, the Cowboys' coach, came up and knocked on the door. I said, "Yeah?" I didn't know it was him on the other side. He opened the door and said, "Eddie, I'm going to let the Cowboys off today since it's a holiday. Are you going to let your staff off? We have courtesy cars for your guys to use to go out on the town or to go visit Mexico." A few of my coaches might have wanted a break, but they knew we were there to learn football. I told Coach

Landry that Grambling wouldn't use the courtesy cars. There was so much we could learn. We kept them working. We were there trying to see the films.

The Cowboys' coaches told our guys to relax, to get out. My guys knew better. Man, we had come to try and see what they were doing, getting everything down. We were students of the game of football. My coaches could really learn this stuff quickly and well. Every time a Cowboy would crack the door, we were right in there, trying. They kept an account of our time and always kidded us about not going out. They just couldn't understand that we were a school without great resources and this was such an opportunity for our guys. We were always in the meetings with them trying to find new keys to winning. Our coaches wanted to go and do that. We didn't want the courtesy cars. We wanted to be better.

9.

THE FINAL CALL

Talk of Retirement

It is interesting that as I reached each milestone in my career, people kept asking me if I was going to retire. They wondered in 1985, when I broke Coach Bryant's record. They wondered before I turned 65, 70, and 75. They seemed sure as I approached victory number 400 that I would stop then. But retirement was a subject I didn't talk about unless someone else mentioned it first. I saw so many people on our faculty happy about retiring. In that sense, I think coaches are pretty unique. Right up to the end, I still liked to watch my guys develop and make the plays. My feeling for the game hadn't changed.

I was sure that after I had been out of coaching for three months, I would have been asking for something to do. I was paid all those years for having all that fun doing something I loved to do. I always knew that when I finally got out of coaching that I would find another job, maybe something to help youth. People say they want to rest when they retire. I never wanted to rest. But the simple fact was that I was in love with my work. I always said that if I couldn't win, then I didn't want to be a part of the game anymore. But how do you know? Grambling had a losing season in 1987 at 5–6. I was nearly seventy then and people said, "It's time to sit down!" But then we went 8–3 in 1988, 9–3 and won the SWAC in 1989. No one was talking.

As Dickens would have said, the 1990 season was "the best of times and the worst of times." It ended up being one of the most difficult and complex seasons I had in all my years at Grambling up to that point.

The media dared to compare this team with the best teams ever in Grambling history. When Mississippi Valley beat us, our kids went down. The media has been great to us, but that team was not ready to be compared with our best teams ever. We had won our first five and should have beaten Mississippi Valley, but they upset us, 38–20. That began a slide in which we lost two of our next three games to Jackson State and Alabama State. Fortunately, we came together to get back on track and won our final two games, including the big one in the Bayou Classic against Southern, 25–13. Nonetheless, the pressure from the media really hurt our guys in ways I had never seen before. Without the predictions, we would have been a satisfied 8–3 team. With the predictions, not many were happy.

The retirement talk came up again when we had a losing record (5–6) in 1991 for only the fifth time in fifty years! Some of our supporters went to our college president and said, "Eddie is too old. The game is passing him by." Fortunately, the president didn't listen, and we went 10–2 and won the Black National Championship in 1992. Some of those same people who said the game was passing me by went back to the president and asked, "We hope you have Eddie under a multiyear contract." I never even had a contract. Each year the president sent me a letter, telling me what my salary would be.

The 1992 Bayou Classic exemplified all the best of what I loved about coaching this game and why I wanted to stay. It was Marino

Casem's last game. His team was 5–5 and we were 8–2 going into the game. There were more than 73,000 fans in the Superdome and a national TV audience. The entire city was in a partylike atmosphere in anticipation.

Marino's boys were fired up. You could tell they wanted to win this one for their coach. The Southern Jaguars jumped all over us in the first half. We were down by fourteen points in the third quarter, but began to fight back hard. Still, it took a three-yard sweep by Eric Perkins, our quarterback, to give us our first lead with thirty-six seconds left! We won 30–27 in a real thriller.

Coach Casem taught me about class that afternoon. I know how much he wanted to win. He had been a head coach for twenty-six years, mainly at Alcorn and Southern, and had a great record. In a postgame press conference, he said, "I wanted to go out in a blaze of glory. But it's good to be going out against Eddie, going out before this many people, and going out as the head coach of the largest historically black school in the world." I saved the newspaper that day to be able to remember Coach Casem's dignity.

I still loved to go to practice. I couldn't wait for spring practice to get out there! I might have been a little slower in the end, but the passion was still in my gut.

I watched too many of my coaching friends retire and die within two or three years. Bear Bryant went in a few months. I didn't want to test that, so I stayed as long as I felt I could make a contribution.

There were young men left to help. As long as I thought there were teenagers willing to listen to real Grambling values, then I wanted to stay right there on the field.

Somewhere in the back of my mind, I was trying to make a contribution to our society. I got frustrated and worked up at people who just talked but didn't take the time to put their arms around kids when they needed them. We've had kids at Grambling who have had nobody in their family come to see them play, not once in four years.

My primary goal at Grambling was always to encourage young men. I constantly tried to take away the lie that you can't do something because you are black. Until the day I stepped away from the field in New Orleans in 1997, I kept telling my guys they could do anything they wanted to do, if they were willing to pay the price.

I know there have not been many coaches in the business who stayed more than twenty years at one school. Thirty years was quite unusual. Back in 1974, when I was fifty-five and into my thirty-fourth season, I told Doug Porter, who was then my forty-two-year-old chief assistant, that he should stay at Grambling because he would probably succeed me in a few years. Decades later, Doug joked with me because he was smart enough to take the head coaching job at Howard. He later moved to Fort Valley State. We remained good friends even when we became coaches of rival teams.

Grambling was a respectable 7–4 in the 1993 season. Three of the losses to Alcorn, Hampton, and Alabama State were by a total of eight points. But when we lost the Bayou Classic in the last game of the season, the whispers started again. Too old! I was determined to prove them wrong.

In 1994, at age seventy-five, we finally got Steve McNair's number in the opener, beating the Alcorn Braves, 62–56! Our own Kendrick Nord put on an incredible show, clicking on seventeen of thirty-three passes for 485 yards and seven touchdowns! We didn't stop Steve McNair by any means. He passed for five TDs and 534 yards. It was tight all the way. We broke a 56–56 tie with nine minutes left when Kendrick drilled a twenty-five yard pass to Curtis Ceaser in the end zone. We did not convert for the extra point. Alcorn got the ball with about a minute remaining, deep in their territory. McNair ran a brilliant series, and the Braves called a time-out when they reached our sixteen-yard line with time for one more play. McNair had proven over and over that one play was all he needed in such a situation.

I have never prayed to win a football game. But McNair had beaten us three straight years. And he was about to do it again. So this once I went upstairs to talk to the Big Tiger. I told him, "This is Eddie. This boy has whipped me every year. You know I don't have much time left. And you know I always contribute to the church. I think it's about time you step in." Sure enough, Chris Simon deflected McNair's pass and we won, 62–56.

Four Hundred: A Club Apart

I kept on praying and we started with a 9–0 record. Our average score was something like 50–20 after nine games. We had a shot at reaching 400 that year if we went undefeated and won the Heritage Bowl.

Kendrick Nord and Curtis Ceaser were having great seasons. Kendrick ended up setting the junior passing mark with more than 3,000 yards. Curtis caught a lot of Nord's passes, breaking Grambling's record with fourteen TD receptions. He averaged more than twenty-two yards a catch. Norman Bradford would pile up over 900 yards rushing and another 500 on passes from Kendrick. We were strong and no one was saying, "You've got to quit."

Next up was the Florida A&M Rattlers in Joe Robbie Stadium. It was a dreary, rainy day in Miami. The dream of that team to win the 400th game for me was washed away as Grambling lost 13–0. We had more yards than FAMU but never got inside their twenty-yard line.

I think it hurt us for the rest of the season because our guys were so focused on 400. I know they wanted to be the team that won it for me. I felt badly because I know the loss to FAMU shook their confidence, knowing that they could no longer get number 400 for me.

Then we lost the next two to Southern and South Carolina State's Bulldogs. The last game in the Heritage Bowl was very hard to take since we had a 27–16 lead in the fourth quarter and lost 31–27. The questions about retirement began to come fast and furious. But I was more concerned that this great group of student-athletes felt they were the team that didn't win the 400th game for me. They were a fine team, and their record was a really good one. Our coaches met with them several times in the postseason to let them know how proud we were of them.

If 1994 had been an undefeated season, one that ended with my 400th win, Doris thought it would be a good time to get out. But that wasn't my thought. If I thought I was blocking someone else from coaching, or if I had been losing, then I would leave. I still just loved it. The key thing was football still fascinated me. My health had been good. I never drank, never smoked. Maybe my long career was a reward for the way I had taken care of my body. I was still confident but the criticisms certainly stung me and made me think about things more. Times were changing.

It was obvious that my 400th win would come in the 1995 season. We started off with a 39–17 win over the McNair-less Alcorn State Braves. Hampton's Pirates then won the Whitney Young Classic, 16–7, at the Meadowlands before more than 61,000 people. It was beginning to look like the game against Prairie View, our fourth of the season, would be number 400 as we had all but beaten Central State in our third game. That would have been win number 399, setting up Prairie View for yet another footnote in the history of GSU football. As mentioned earlier, I had won my 50th, 150th, 315th (passing Coach Stagg), and 324th (passing Bear Bryant) against Prairie View. That scenario blew up when Central scored on a fourth-down pass as the clock showed 0:00 to win 16–13.

Prairie View was off the record hook. The game was a blowout before 63,000 at the State Fair Classic in Dallas. The Prairie View Panthers went 0–11 in 1995 and showed why in the Cotton Bowl, losing 64–0 to our guys. It was the fifty-first consecutive loss for the once proud Panthers.

That brought our team home to Robinson Stadium where 11,500 fans gathered to see us face the Mississippi Valley State Delta Devils. They had only beaten us three times in thirty-nine previous matchups, and they hadn't won a game in 1995. Ironically, someone pointed out that my 200th win came against the Delta Devils in 1971.

I didn't sleep real well on the night before the game and was sort of scared when I got up that morning. I had been up late with our offensive coordinator, Melvin Lee. He knew me so well. The 1995 season was his thirty-seventh year with me as an assistant coach. Coach Lee had been the center on our 1955 unbeaten, which won our first Black National Championship. It would be almost impossible to describe how much Melvin Lee meant to me over all these years. It was his genius that helped make our Wing-T offense so effective for so long. But in 1995, our offense had some problems to work out. Coach always was ready to work with me on it, no matter what the day or hour.

The game was nationally televised on ESPN-2, and our team itself looked nervous in the first quarter. Our offense picked up, especially our running game, in the second quarter, when we scored three touchdowns to take a 21–0 lead at the half.

Led by Jason Bratton and Jeff Nichols, we got over 300 yards on the ground. Kendrick kept Mississippi Valley's defense off balance with ten completed passes for another one hundred or so yards and we won, 42–6. It had been almost ten years to the day since we beat Prairie View to break Bear Bryant's all-time record.

Once again, all the praise was going to me instead of the guys who made the plays. I told them that I wished I could cut up all of the victories into 400 pieces and give them to all of the players and assistant coaches I've had. They were the ones who truly deserved the credit.

As the game ended, there were balloons, fireworks, and people dancing on the field. The fireworks spelled out, "Congratulations, COACH ROBINSON 400 Wins!" The Grambling band formed the number 400 on the field as fans and players stayed in the stands and on the field cheering. My coaches, photographers, fans, and players had surrounded me on the sideline. Fans and players, even some Mississippi Valley players, hugged me.

Before we left the field, there were calls from President Clinton and Louisiana Governor Edwards to congratulate me on reaching the 400-victory mark. President Clinton said, "I'm so proud of you. What's even more amazing is never missing a game. The American people are proud of you."

I cry more than most people, and I was sure crying that day. For a person like me, it was a great moment. And what an honor it was for our commander-in-chief to call me on the phone.

To show you what kind of guys I had playing for me, they brought back the goal post after an enthusiastic group of fans tore down part of it before the stadium announcer was able to ask fans not to destroy it. What was a tradition at the big football schools and in the NFL was an expense we couldn't afford at Grambling. Our guys understood that, even after number 400! We needed to repair that post because a new one would have eaten too deep into our budget.

Two days later, Doris and I flew to Disney World to ride in a motorcade in our honor. They had me place my handprints in cement. Imagine, Eddie Robinson and Mickey Mouse. The next day, I was inducted into the Blue-Gray Hall of Fame in Birmingham, Alabama. Bear Country!

Like other milestones, there was an emotional letdown, and we lost our next two games by a total of four points. More than 12,000 came to Shreveport and saw the Golden Lions from Arkansas–Pine Bluff win in the last minute, 17–14. It was the first time they'd beaten us since 1959. We were tied and locked in a thriller with Jackson State when they sacked Kendrick Nord for a safety and then ran back an interception of one of Kendrick's passes. Both scores took place in less than two minutes. But Kendrick didn't give up. He passed for the TD and converted a two-point play to make it 29–28. However, Jackson State recovered our on-side kick and ran out the clock.

We evened our record at 4–4 with an easy win at home over the Tigers of Texas Southern before 13,500. Kendrick threw three TD passes to Broderick Fobbs, whose father, Lee, had been an assistant for Grambling after playing for us in the 1970s. We split the next two against Alabama State, losing 37–16, and Elizabeth City, who we beat 48–8. There were only 3,500 fans at our home game to see Kendrick connect for three more TD passes.

That brought everything down to the Bayou Classic. We had to beat Southern to avoid a sixth losing season. Unfortunately, the Jaguars were ready for the challenge. They beat us, 30–14 and then won the Heritage Bowl over FAMU for an 11–1 record.

We have a closely knit profession in college sports so we didn't really bad mouth anyone. There would be no real point to it. But it definitely felt good to beat certain coaches. With some schools we simply had great rivalries. Southern was one of them.

Most football coaches really respect each other. We shake hands before and after the game, and we say a lot of good things about each other. We can stay in the room a little longer talking and telling stories than most people in other professions. We get along really well.

It is very hard to say which coach I admired most throughout my career. I would have to say it was Coach Mumford at Southern. As I said earlier, I wanted to play for him. He was a classy gentleman who knew the game of football so well and motivated his players to execute the plays as well as anyone in the game. He was a football genius and a great person.

Playing against Southern was always special. That became even more true after we started the Bayou Classic.

I think the coach I admire most right now is Joe Paterno. He's a great man. Joe has been so loyal to Penn State and has been a consistent winner. Now there are quite a few great ones coaching, but Joe is extraordinary! I would have liked to have played against Penn State.

There were a few other legendary coaches whom Grambling did go up against. There was Billie Knicks from Prairie View, Morgan State's Edward Hunt and Earl Banks, FAMU's Jake Gaither, Texas Southern's Alexander Durley and "Big John" Merritt and Henry Kean at Tennessee State. Of course, Marino Casem did an incredible job at Alcorn for more than twenty years and then at Southern.

Casem used to tell people that Grambling didn't just regroup from year to year, but that we reloaded. I would respond that if we reloaded, he had somehow always been able to take the bullets out of our gun. An awful lot of Grambling's alums assumed that our gun wasn't loaded with me at the helm anymore. But the losing season in 1995 was hardly our only problem.

The NCAA and Grambling

Even the excitement and national attention over win number 400 didn't silence those seeking a coaching change. The critics gained a weapon when the NCAA began an investigation of our program in 1995. What killed me about the NCAA investigation was that suddenly there were people who were saying that no matter what we had done for 56 years, these problems meant Eddie Robinson was not a good person. I couldn't imagine how people could say that but I know that at least a few did. There were stories in the media that hurt because they were not true.

I had figured we had done everything we could possibly do to follow the NCAA's guidelines. This was the first NCAA investigation of Grambling football in the fifty-six years I was there.

Most of the big schools have one or two "compliance" specialists, who make sure their schools know and follow all NCAA rules. Like all colleges, we needed them at Grambling but had not been able to afford them. It did turn out that several Grambling teams, including our football program, had some minor violations. We should have known, but we didn't.

Grambling accepted the NCAA's sanctions. There were some minor findings against other parts of Grambling's programs, including some in women's sports. None were big infractions. None were attributed to me as the coach. Several assistants, including Eddie Jr., were cited for minor violations. They had watched players practice during a noncoaching period and had made improper recruiting contacts with prospective transfers. But I had to take responsibility for the entire program. That was my job as head coach.

I was upset by how the entire investigation started. As I understand, it all began with one guy who didn't get a job in Grambling athletics. He got mad because he thought I should have given him the job. But I was no longer the athletics director, and I couldn't hire him. The NCAA team listened to him and, I guess, must have believed him because the news of the investigation was on the sports pages of newspapers across America.

I understood that they had to investigate it when somebody reported something. The NCAA had to do the same thing to us that they did to other schools that have been found to have violated the rules. But I was confident that my role would come out the way it was—clear. Yet I know that some people read about accusations and assumed we were guilty. There are people who are going to believe whatever they read, no matter how ridiculous. That's why I have been blessed that ninety-nine percent of the writers covering Grambling have been fair and objective. Many people read the articles and thought, if it's in the paper, it's the truth.

Most writers who covered the story ended with the NCAA's findings. But there was one writer who never stopped. I figured he wanted me fired and this was his way to seal my fate.

But I never really questioned the NCAA. If they didn't have the NCAA around to police the games, to change the playing rules, and to eliminate the cheating, there would be bedlam in college sports. From my first years of coaching, I was glad for the part that the NCAA played with sports in higher education.

My only real conflict with the NCAA was when their rules seemed to block an obvious human response. Over the years I had student-athletes come to me with the news that one of their parents had passed and they couldn't afford to get home. To help them used to violate NCAA rules. But any kind of man would reach out. I am glad the NCAA finally changed that rule with the creation of an emergency fund.

I was proud of the fact that the NCAA asked me to represent them in Congress when the Division IA schools wanted to pull away from the rest of us for their own television deal. I went to Washington, D.C., and other cities to speak against the loss of control of television. I knew the breakdown would hurt schools like Grambling and many other schools, so I was glad to be able to make my case. However, we didn't win, and the College Football Association got control of TV. Now the CFA is gone, but the TV money still goes mainly to the schools with big football programs.

I went and did these things and was really happy to help because I believed in the NCAA and in what it was doing. I never doubted that the NCAA would do right by us. We had some minor infractions, and the NCAA gave us appropriate consequences. We received two years on probation and did not lose any scholarships, TV money, or the ability to appear in postseason games.

I guess for the fifty-six years that I was the coach, everything that we have tried to do had one objective: to move the university forward. We would never cheat or use any illegal means to get an advantage. We were concerned about the people who played for us, that they got degrees. We were concerned about what kind of husbands our student-athletes would become. We were concerned about what kind of fathers they would become. Grambling has turned some great football players into great men.

I want the man who "reported" Grambling to the NCAA to know that, after all is said and done, I still believe that coaching is the most rewarding profession in the world and, as Amos Alonzo Stagg said, no man is too great to coach the American youth because what you put in is what you get out. And if you don't put the right things in there, the children are not going to get the right things coming out. We need to keep America going strong with a positive, educated group of young people moving up to take over the reins. I know the Lord isn't prejudiced, but I believe he has favored America as a nation.

I think the Lord has helped us rise to the occasion more than most other people in competition. That goes for war, that goes for games, that goes for everything. America is blessed. It is as simple as that. And I believe that athletics has had something to do with the kind of leaders we have produced.

Our young people need to have leaders to follow who they can believe in. Leaders can be teachers, soldiers, coaches—really, they can come from any walk of life. I was coach for life.

When we had team meetings, we talked about football, sure. But we also often talked about how to treat other human beings. We always watched out when we were on the road to make sure that guys didn't take girls to their room or do any other things that weren't acceptable for college men. We wouldn't tolerate that. We had parents traveling with us, and some of the mothers were young, attractive women. I really got to my guys when I told them it could be their buddy's young, pretty mamma they were inviting to their hotel room. My guys were always informed and knew what not to do. But nothing in life is guaranteed to work the way you planned.

I frequently asked our guys, "Well, what should you do if you see a situation happening in which a girl might be taken advantage of? Will you try to stop them and say it is wrong? Will you get the police to stop them? Will you and your teammates run and scream or holler and tell the guy not to do it? Will you look for the officers to come and stop it?"

We teach our guys to intervene when they see someone, especially a teammate, doing something wrong. If they know it's wrong and stand there and let him do it, then they are wrong also. I understand that they could be afraid that they might get physically hurt if they stopped it, but at least they should get some aid and tell the guy he's wrong. If you tell a guy he's wrong, he has a little time to think about it and cool down. This is just one of the things that we talk about with our players.

I know some of my guys thought I was off my rocker. But I really lectured them regularly on respecting other people, especially women. To lighten such a serious topic up a bit, I would sometimes add that they all have to learn the proper way of wooing a lady. And they would say, "What?"

Some tried to make a game out of it. "Well, Coach, what are we supposed to do?" I'd say, "You're a man. Treat her well. Tell her she's got pretty eyes. Tell her that's a nice skirt she has. Tell her you like the way she combs her hair. Tell her a lot of pretty nothings. All of this is a part of the wooing." Then they laughed and had fun because they liked to hear that kind of thing from their coach. My coaches always helped, too. Most had daughters and wives. We all had mothers. The thought of a man hurting one of our loved ones is so awful I cannot even describe it. I know no one can control the actions of another person but we sure can influence them. We constantly tried.

I would lay my body down to stop someone from hurting Doris or my daughter or granddaughters. But this isn't only my issue. I know that all other men have women or girls they love. I don't understand how there are so many cases of men being violent against women, but I know we can't tolerate it. We have to put an end to it.

I have said earlier how much I believe in discipline. We all have to face the consequences for our actions. However, I also know we all make mistakes and deserve a second chance in life.

Second Chances in Life: Strawberry, Gooden, and Tyson

I felt badly about all the criticism that took place around the Yankees' signing Darryl Strawberry and Dwight Gooden. I really believe that George Steinbrenner was trying to make the Yankees better, while giving these two guys that type of second chance.

I know many critics thought that George's attitude was win at all cost, and that he was condoning what Darryl and Dwight had done when he signed them for the team. Only a few took the position that he was giving them a second chance. There would have been no comebacks for either of them if George Steinbrenner hadn't taken a chance on them by giving them one more opportunity. I felt terrible when I heard about Darryl's arrest in 1999.

I told George that he'd made a great gesture when he signed Darryl. George responded to me, "Maybe so, but you have got to do what you think is right. But I'll tell you, Eddie, it'd be real tough to wake up any morning and know you don't have another chance in our society!"

That's a big problem for so many of our youth today. It's easy to make a mistake as a youngster. If we write such a child off, then we may have lost a great scientist or doctor. We've got to give people second opportunities. They have to pay the consequences for their actions, but then we need to give them support or we may lose the opportunity to help someone who may then help instead of hurt someone else. I am not just talking about athletes now.

If you wake up and nobody's going for you and you don't have another chance, then what are you going to do or think? Self-destructive behavior seems real likely at that point. And such behavior frequently involves hurting other people. We need to look at it like that to recognize how bad it is not to reach out and give young people that chance.

Mike Tyson may be the toughest case among athletes. Tyson's many problems seem almost insurmountable. But I have to wonder if anyone really reached out to him along the way and embraced him as a caring adult.

If Tyson changed he could make a big, positive impression on American youth. There are a lot of boys out there who admire him now. That's dangerous when he behaves so badly. But it could be positive if he really changed as a result of a friendship that helped him see the light. I don't mean just letting him fight; I mean letting him live and helping him live.

In this country boxers capture the nation's imagination, especially that part of America that struggles. Think of how black people rooted for Joe Louis or Muhammad Ali. Eventually white people also embraced them, but perhaps their greatest importance was giving hope to people who couldn't hope for themselves. Maybe Tyson could have done that if some people had helped him.

I really believe that this guy could make a contribution. With all the money he makes, he could build sports fields or gyms so young people could get off the streets and do something positive in the hours after school when so many get into trouble. He could encourage young boxers. But there has to be somebody reaching out to him so he can understand how people feel and how they want to be around him. But Mike's got to learn to say good things around young people. I think Mike Tyson's failure is partially our failure. His is a case that makes me sad because now he might have received his last chance.

American Football Coaches Association

Moral support and good advice was always there when I turned to my friends in the American Football Coaches Association (AFCA). I did that whenever I was struggling with problems with my team or the profession.

The talk about my retirement was growing on campus after our 5–6 season in 1995. People tried to couple the three straight losses at the end of the 9–3 season in 1994 to show I had lost it. There was the NCAA investigation. I was on the phone a lot that year. As they had many times in my career, I got a big lift from the AFCA.

Grant Teaff, the AFCA director, called and asked, "Eddie, are you going to be president of the United States?" I responded, "What do you mean?" It was his way of telling me that I was going to be the first coach to receive the Tuss McLaughry Award, the AFCA's highest award. I told him, "But you know, Grant, that you've never given that award to a regular coach in our association." He responded, "I know that, but we're going to give it to you this time." It had been given to three or four American presidents and several astronauts. The date was January 10, 1996.

I suggested that the AFCA wait another year and let it soak in that I was going to be in that kind of company. Grant refused. "No, Eddie, we're going to give it to you this year so you really need to be there." I guess they wanted to recognize the 400-victory mark right away.

Grant also asked me to keynote the opening of the 1996 convention in New Orleans, in my home state. I was very proud to be able to address my colleagues, especially there. And, of course, to receive the award.

I had seen Bear Bryant in this role shortly before he broke Stagg's record, so I knew what to expect. I loved what Bear had said and wanted to bring the same level of meaning to this session. I told the AFCA members that joining the association had changed my whole life and my entire view of the game. The AFCA gave me the opportunity to serve; it gave me confidence in what we were all about. It gave me confidence to face the increasing doubts on my own beloved campus so I could coach the Tigers in 1996.

When I became the AFCA president in 1976, I told Bill Murray, who was the executive secretary, that I wanted him to help me be one of the best presidents that had served under him. That post gave me an opportunity to mingle with the president of the United States and with many of the nation's leaders. I discovered that they were real and regular people.

Bill Murray asked me in the 1960s to consider serving on the trustee committee. I said, "Bill, yes, I would like to serve, but I don't want to be somebody who hangs around for the show of it. I want to really serve." I asked Bill to give me the hard things, the easy things, and the in-between things to do. I said point-blank, "I don't want to be window dressing! I want to help with any problems that the AFCA might encounter. I want to work for the AFCA to make it all it can be." A bit ruffled, Bill told me, "Eddie,

I thought you knew me. You know I won't pick out everything easy for you to do. I want you to serve; I'm going to give you an opportunity to succeed or fail." I told Bill, "That's what I really want. I want to go through it the same way the other guys have gone through it; I want the opportunity to experience the same things that the other guys have experienced." And they did give me an opportunity to do all of these things, and I love them! I mean that from the bottom of my heart. I did my best for the AFCA and was doubly rewarded when they asked me to be the keynoter and gave me the Tuss McLaughry Award in my own state! That meant so much to me and to Doris.

Mike Kornblau

As I mentioned in chapter 6 when I was discussing James Gregory, I had another white quarterback as my career came to an end. There was so much media attention on the fact that both Grambling and Southern had white quarterbacks in the 1996 Bayou Classic. It seemed like the national media liked the story, but I was on the receiving end of a lot of criticism.

Starting Mike Kornblau in 1996 stirred up some real heat. I put him in the opening game after Chiron Applewhite, who was our starter, broke his arm. Mike was from Dalton High School in New York City. Dalton was a great academic school not known for great football players. There I was, our top gun down maybe for the season, starting a tall, 6'5" white guy from Manhattan.

People were talking and writing about it almost every day. I was severely criticized that year and the next, when Mike remained as our starting QB. We started 1996 with three straight losses, including our first ever loss to Langston's Lions in a 15–14 heart-breaker. Mike threw a late TD pass to give us a six-point lead but Langston scored with just under five minutes left. Thank goodness we caught Prairie View next with a 54–12 win. We split the next two games and then experienced our worst loss ever. The Tigers of Jackson State crushed us, 52–0 at Grambling. Any confidence the team had left was gone as we fell to 2–5. Texas Southern then beat us for the first time in twenty-two years. We managed to defeat Alabama State, 7–0, when Mike had his best day that year, hitting on twelve of twenty-two passes for 129 yards. But it was our defense that gave us the win. We dropped our final two games, including our fourth consecutive loss to Southern in the Bayou Classic. We were 3–8 and the cries for my removal divided Grambling's campus in half.

Many of those venting against me said that the reason we'd had our worst year was because it was the first time that we had started a white quarterback. It was all fitting into the pattern of thinking that I had been around too long at Grambling.

When they asked me why, I told them I started Kornblau because he was the best I had. If I had anybody better than he was, I would have started that person. At the end of the season, we reviewed the game films for the year. He wasn't really bad. Heck, we dropped more passes in 1996 than we'd dropped in any previous season.

Of course, Mike didn't know about the Grambling system, since it was the first year he got playing time. He did what any first-year quarterback would do—he made mistakes and he made some good plays. We didn't do a good job on pass blocking. Mike was on his tail or on his back more than he was on his feet.

But I played Kornblau because he was the best we had, and that's what I've done for fifty-six years. That was also true in 1997. Mike transferred out of Grambling after that year and went to the University of New Haven.

I don't think Kornblau was treated as openly as James Gregory. The story was receiving a lot more attention in the national media because of several things. First of all, there was controversy about me staying on as coach. Second, both Grambling and Southern had white quarterbacks. Third, the national press was covering Grambling football more in the 1990s than in the 1960s, especially since in some people's minds, 1996 could have been my last season. Fourth, the 1960s was the decade of blacks fighting for integration. The mood on race was different in 1996 and 1997. Finally, we were winning big when James was at Grambling, but we were losing big in the late 1990s when Mike was here. That made a big difference.

As for my players, there were some who thought that playing Kornblau was keeping them from playing. And there were some, especially off the team but on campus, who felt that a black guy needed to be playing for a black school. Their sense of anger grew because they had never seen two white quarterbacks on two black teams in the Bayou Classic.

I had learned something from the experience. Greg and Mike both wanted to play, but in Greg's era, we had Harris and Reed, who were far better quarterbacks. Mike was the best I had but not so good that he made people forget he was white. The latter test made me sad that we might not have progressed as far on the issue of race as I might have hoped.

President Hicks Asks for My Resignation

I was in New Orleans right before the 1996 Bayou Classic when I was informed that what I had understood to be a campus revolt against my remaining as head coach had become more widespread. My assistants who were with me told me I looked ill. I was. I couldn't believe it.

We had just left a preclassic press conference where I had been asked if I would be back for 1997. I told those attending, "In the number of years I've worked, I've earned the right to say whether I come back or if I can't!"

I went to meet with Grambling's president, Dr. Raymond A. Hicks. Dr. Hicks had become president during the summer after serving as interim president for one year. I did not envy the role this Grambling grad felt compelled to take. He suggested that I step down and accept a job as a vice president. I told him that I was not interested and requested that I coach the 1997 season. I had never defied any Grambling president and was really shaken by the dilemma in which I found myself. If I agreed with him, then everyone who knew me would recognize that I had been forced out of a job I had held for fifty-six years. If I disagreed, many would think I was turning on or embarrassing the school I loved.

It was one of the worst weeks of my life as that meeting was aired out in the press each day. It was embarrassing for me, for Grambling, and its president. Story after story talked about the first consecutive losing seasons in our history. The NCAA investigation was in the papers constantly. There were references to my "all-time" records, but the emphasis was on the negative. Having Mike Kornblau as the starting quarterback was dropped into some of the stories. I was sick about it, and I know it hurt Doris even more deeply. That was what was the most painful part for me.

I was grateful that so many prominent people, in and out of football, made public comments in support of my continuing as coach. I know that Louisiana Governor Mike Foster's support was a big boost. Our board of regents requested that I get one more year. Even Bill Cosby wrote to President Hicks. But I surely wish that it hadn't come to that. It wasn't that I just wanted to keep coaching. I wanted to leave Grambling with all of its contracts in place for TV and the classics. I wanted Grambling to continue to be great after I was gone. I wished too that President Hicks had reached the decision for me to coach one more year on his own.

In any case, I was grateful when he made the announcement, less than one week after the controversy started, that I was still the coach.

I was, however, hurt that a handful of people who I really cared about said things that were construed as calls for my resignation. Some called for it outright. Doris could not understand why they would say such things *publicly.*

For years there had been speculation about who would replace me when I quit. There were quite a few candidates out there, including Eddie Robinson, Jr. Many of my players were coaching in the NFL or in the college ranks. My choice was Doug Williams.

I believe that the most popular choice was also Doug Williams. His years at Grambling were among our greatest. He had been First team all-American in 1977. Twenty years later, he still held our records for most yards in a season and in a career and most touchdown passes in a game, season, and career. He had represented himself so well as a professional and had always talked highly of Grambling. And, as great as so many of our players had been, Doug may have been black college football's single greatest image of success. That could surely be argued about, but when he led the Washington Redskins to their dramatic victory in Super Bowl XXII in January of 1988, an entire nation took notice. He was the Super Bowl MVP, set Super Bowl records for yards passed, touchdowns passed, and longest completion. All of the talk about blacks not being able to be quarterbacks and lead teams had been squashed. For many blacks, Doug was football's Joe Louis or Jackie Robinson rolled into one. In all my years as a coach, I still think that one day was my single proudest moment. I loved Doug Williams and was so very pleased that I was present to witness that greatest of triumphs in 1988.

He had been working hard to get prepared to coach with jobs at two high schools, in the World League, and at Navy. Morehouse was his first head coaching job.

Doug took the head coaching job at Morehouse College when my contract was extended by President Hicks just about a week after the controversy started. When I agreed that 1997 would be my last season, I supported Doug to succeed me. I still support him and wish him great success as our coach. I have appreciated the many wonderful things he has said about me since he got the job.

Just One Last Dance

The national media was absolutely wonderful once the controversy was over. They spent an entire year talking about the great years past and all that we had accomplished. They made mention of the last two losing seasons and of the NCAA investigation. They had to talk about Mike because he was our starting quarterback in 1997. But the negatives were always in a paragraph or two and the positives were spread over half and full pages. All the national press ran three big features: before our first game, for the last home game, and for our last game in the Bayou Classic.

Our 1997 squad was not deep or rich in talent. With all the speculation about my future, recruiting had become even more difficult. There were no milestones to reach. I know how hard it was on the players. Each place we played had a wonderful tribute to me. The players could see how little interest there was in the actual games themselves. City by city, America was bidding farewell to me as Grambling's coach. It was such a conflicted time. The outpouring of love was heartwarming, but I still was the head coach and our team was losing.

Every opponent made a tribute to me. Someone called it a "farewell tour," and that's exactly what it was. We played the Alabama State Hornets in Montgomery. As we entered their stadium, known as the Crampton Bowl, I couldn't help but think of Rosa Parks and Dr. Martin Luther King Jr. forty years before with the bus boycott. Like every other black coach at that time, I was coaching in a segregated South. George Wallace hadn't blocked the door to black students yet, and Bear Bryant hadn't dreamt of playing a black player. Now I was going into the Crampton Bowl for the last time. The state of Alabama had proclaimed Eddie Robinson Day all across this state, where I couldn't sit in the front of the bus before Rosa Parks made her courageous move. I was pretty sure that Dr. King and Bear Bryant were looking down with smiles. The press coverage the next day barely mentioned that Grambling lost, 20–13.

It was the same everywhere. The only disappointment in that sense was our last game at home two weeks before the season ended. We practiced hard because I knew we could beat North Carolina A&T. I pushed our guys. We were even practicing after dark the night before the game.

I exhorted them after practice, telling them that I didn't think they were giving it everything they had. Heck, I knew that at that point they were all giving more than they had. But I wanted to win. I thought we needed to win that game. I ended with saying, "If you can run, run. If you can catch, catch. If you can block, block. This is what it takes. Just come out tomorrow and win." We nearly did, scoring twenty-eight points in the second half and almost catching them. We finally succumbed, 37–35, but I was proud of our effort.

Most of the games themselves seemed less important to the public than the aspect of history that I guess I represented for them. That had to be so troubling to our student-athletes, but they never showed it. This team became a family, like so many teams before it.

One thing I will always treasure about that last squad was that nine guys had fathers who had played for me a generation earlier. My own son, who had played for me, was an assistant coach.

Ernest Sterling who, like Melvin Lee, was finishing his coaching career with me at Grambling, had his son, Ernest, on the team. Ernest had coached with me for twenty-four years. He had played for me and then in the NFL. He was like a rock and my fundamentals guy.

Robert Smith, who was our defensive line coach, and Glen Hall, our defensive secondary coach, had both played for me and then played in the NFL. Matthew Reed, who was our restricted earnings coach, had been our great all-American quarterback on our 1972 Black National Championship team. Richard Paul, our trainer, had played for me in the 1970s. Strength coach Leonard Griffin played here before a pro career. At one point in the early 1990s, my six assistants had been coaching with me for a combined 102 years!

Al Dennis was the assistant AD for business. He and his father had played for me. His daddy, who was on our teams right after the war, coached his son when he was my assistant. Fred Hobdy, my dear, dear friend, was assistant to the president for athletic affairs in 1997. Fred had succeeded me as athletics director in 1989. He also had taken over from me as basketball coach and became the winningest coach in the history of the sport in Louisiana. Fred had played for me on my very first team in 1941. Bob Piper, our new AD, had played basketball for Fred! It is easy to see why I felt at home as head coach at Grambling. I had lived and worked there since 1941 and was surrounded by family, my own and our extended family.

Down on the Bayou

We were 3–7 with five straight losses going into practice for my last game. It was ironic that President Hicks never saw that last game. He resigned under pressure a month before the season ended.

I didn't want game day to come, but I wanted to be prepared when it did. We worked hard all week, including two serious practices on Thanksgiving Day. I was short that week. I let myself get angry with my secretary the day before Thanksgiving because she forgot to type up our practice program, which we have used each day for fifty years. I knew I wasn't myself. How could I be? A huge part of my life was coming to an end within days!

There was no more Blue Bird to take us around. Our Grambling buses were loaded, and we rolled off campus one last time at 4:00 A.M. on Friday morning. I used to worry about the police in Jackson and Baton Rouge when I was a boy. Now we traveled with a full police escort. I asked myself, "Are Momma and Daddy watching?" The darkness would have allowed for sleep, but I cued up game tapes of Southern. It wasn't the first time I had seen them that week.

It was crazy in New Orleans. First there was the Bayou Classic luncheon. More than 4,500 came. It seemed as though everyone wanted a picture or an autograph or both. The state troopers accompanying me wanted to drag me away. I couldn't let them because Daddy might be watching.

Daddy had told me to take a compliment without letting it go to my head. He'd raised me to be a good person so if I did something that made people say I was a good guy, then that's what I was supposed to be doing. I referred to Doug Williams signing autographs in Japan. I taught my team that because of a lesson my Daddy had taught me so many years ago.

I had felt real good when I was first asked to sign an autograph. Then I thought back on what Daddy said and recognized that I was being asked because I was doing well at what I was expected to do well at. It was a respectful acknowledgment and shouldn't be a head sweller. On that day I decided to honor every request and try to say something meaningful to the person asking for the auto-graph. That's not always easy because you may be in a hurry when someone approaches you. But I know that whatever I do in that situation will likely be how that person remembers me for the rest of their life. If I refused, they might think coaches act like they're too good to be bothered. If it's a child asking, they may think poorly of older people. If it's a white person, they may think I'm a racist if I pass them by. It gets complicated.

Recently Doris and I were rushed by people carrying papers, photos, and pens, all asking me to sign for them. Doris was tired and hungry. In our mid-seventies, we had traveled all day to get there and the airlines hadn't served food. So I said, "Fellas, if you just give me a couple of minutes to get my wife up to our room and get things under control, I'll come back down in the lobby and sign for you all." One guy said, "It seems to me I've heard that song before." So I said, "You haven't heard this song from Eddie Robinson. . . . Just give me the time to do that then I'll come back down to the lobby." These fans had obviously had a bad experi-ence with autographs before.

So I went up, I got my wife situated, ordered us some food, ate a bit, and I came back in the lobby and I cleaned it out. The man-ager came over and said, "Mr. Robinson this is the first time I've seen this happen. It's a good way to do it, but you know the other guys haven't done it." I started to kiss him. I said if anybody else in here still wants an autograph, come on over. I especially wanted to accommodate the kids. I know if they wanted it now, they were not going to want it forever. With the kids I always write notes about life—things like, "We are living in the best country in the world," or, "Discipline isn't punishment but is showing that you care." I know the parents appreciate you if you do things like that.

No, I wasn't going to leave with the state troopers until I had signed every one's requests. There was more media to give inter-views to. *Nightline* did a full show on me that night. All the networks did substantial pieces on my career. New Orleans lit up that night with the "Battle of the Bands," a beauty pageant, a job fair for Grambling and Southern students, and endless parties.

Doris and I were exhausted when we went to bed that night. I barely slept, realizing that I was spending so much time with everyone but my players. I had been letting everything that made Grambling Grambling, everything that made Eddie Robinson Eddie Robinson, slide. Perhaps for different reasons, I don't think Doris slept much either. I was very nervous and even more tired in the morning.

We got to the Superdome early. Doris and I had a long embrace as she went up to the Grambling suite and I headed for the locker room for my final pregame talk. A few of my former players were in the room. I was really holding my feelings back. It was a very hard day.

The game was difficult to watch. Southern dominated us and won easily, 30–7. But there was an eerie atmosphere among the fans, who seemed far more interested in my last game than in Grambling playing Southern. I didn't want the game to end, yet it was painful to watch us losing so badly. I really felt for my student-athletes, who were playing their hearts out for me and the school.

When the game ended, a stage was set up at the 50-yard line. Most of the 64,000 fans in the Dome were still there, cheering for me. Doris was in my arms and chants of "Eddie! Eddie! Eddie!" echoed inside the building. I was given a new car. Then President Clinton called. I told him I was doing OK and that this was a great day for the school and for Louisiana. He replied, "Coach, I want to tell you how proud America is of you and what you have done in your incredible coaching career at Grambling. You are a great American." The tears were really flowing, and Doris was holding tight.

It was a long day that became an even longer night that didn't end until 2:00 A.M. A wonderful black-tie affair was held in my honor. The organizers had set up a couch for Doris and me to sit on during the program. The Count Basie Band was playing. I was holding Doris's hand, gazing into her sweet eyes. When I closed my eyes, we were back at the Temple Roof Gardens with Count Basie playing. Yes, a big part of my life was over but I still had the best part right there in the palm of my hands: Doris, Mrs. Eddie Robinson, the real heart of my life.

10

FAMILY FIRST

I knew that life would be so different when Doris and I woke up on the morning of November 30, 1997. No more games, no more game interviews, no athletic milestones to reach.

Fifty-six years of coaching football had flown by like it was a single season. The only time that had gone at a higher speed was that with Doris. I was content with life when we took the ferry across the river to get married on June 24, 1941. I was not a coach then and really had no prospects of being one. Grambling had been a rich icing on my life's cake but that cake was made of Doris. We are now ready for more and even richer time together for the rest of our lives.

As I said much earlier, I wanted to be with her forever from the moment I saw her in the seventh grade. I guess you can ask, "What do thirteen-year-olds know about love?" Well, if we didn't then, we do now.

I'm always concerned about Doris. I never stop thinking about her. Sometimes it is serious. A lot of times our thoughts are funny. I mentioned earlier that Doris became something of a football fan, especially after she retired. It wasn't always that way. She was being interviewed after Doug Williams's MVP performance in the Super

Bowl in 1988. I stood there in amazement as she told the reporter about what an incredible effort Doug had made and how brilliantly he played, "especially during the second inning." I was waving my arms and mouthing silently, "Doris, baseball has innings. We have quarters in football." She never saw me or, at least, didn't acknowledge that she did.

We were talking before we went to the 1996 Bayou Classic in New Orleans. I told her that I was going to the bank to get money for both of us. I was always the one who went to the bank, even when I wasn't making much money and there wasn't much to take out. I told her then that I'd been losing on this deal because when we'd return from a trip, somehow I had not spent any money and put mine back in the bank. She had never put hers back. Doris was of the opinion that she should spend it once she got it.

My Momma was real impressed with how we got along. She frequently commented on how we never quarreled and how we handled things that might lead other couples to having fights or arguments. Whatever it was, we didn't let it go so far that we couldn't talk about it. Doris and I would sit down, talk about the children, talk about our friends, and even about what we were going to say to our friends. We didn't want to brag or sound like we were bragging. I was pretty well known in our part of Louisiana, and many of our friends wanted to talk about Grambling football and how I was the coach. Because of that, I requested Doris's help right from the start to always be aware of the fact that if any time in my career she thought I was getting a big head to tell me right away. I surely did not want that to happen. She was never afraid to offer advice, and I was always ready for it.

We lived in an apartment on campus when I first went to Grambling. Doris could stand in the kitchen window and look into my office in the gym. She could see me coming in and going out. She could stand at the window and look out at us practice. That apartment put her right in the middle of everything. It was so close that

I could come home just about any time during the day. I did whenever I had a free period, and she was always there.

Doris Teaches

When Doris first came to Grambling, President Jones gave her a job counseling in a dormitory. Next she taught at the Fellowship Elementary School and then got another degree from Grambling that earned her the chance to teach at the high school.

As I discussed earlier, she taught in the segregated school system until integration came. Then she moved to the formerly all-white Ruston High School, where Doris taught English and speech.

She got along well there. A lot of the kids that she taught have gone on to be outstanding people. She knows where they all are to this day. Doris is proud of them. They write her and they just make her feel so good. When they see her, they come up and say, "This is my English teacher."

Once she started working, I couldn't just drop in on her so easily. Of course, when she got a job in the little city of Ruston, Doris had to travel some. That meant even more separation during the day. Doris left the apartment at about 7:00 A.M. and didn't get back until about 4:00 P.M. That was an adjustment, but like all the other adjustments, we made it. We just talked things through and handled them.

We also had our Mommas live with us at different times. Eddie and Lillian really adored having them around. We also decided to get help and had five young women live with us over the years to help care for Eddie, Jr. and Lillian. They became like daughters. Each still calls Doris "Mommy." We helped them all with their tuition, and all five became Grambling alums. We had reunions almost every year with their husbands and children at the Bayou Classic. They were all there for my last game.

Doris taught for twenty-five years. It is almost impossible for me to believe that she has now been retired for 25 years. Toward the end of her career, she was traveling more with us, and we were having so many good times together. The only time she had a problem traveling was one time when we were going to play a big game in Florida. The principal refused to give Doris a personal day. Doris told me she cussed the principal out. And Doris never cusses. Then she assumed her power and went directly to the school superintendent. She got the day off and made the trip. I know I never messed with Doris when she was determined. That principal learned not to mess with her after that. Doris was still young when she suddenly told me she was going to retire. I told her, "Darling, you don't need to retire. Just keep your suitcase packed!" Naturally, Doris did have more time to travel with the team after she retired. And we were flying as much as riding in the Blue Bird by then.

Mrs. Eddie Robinson

Doris likes to be "Mrs. Eddie Robinson," but maybe not as much as I liked her to be Mrs. Eddie Robinson. I write her notes and cards and say, "Dear Mrs. Eddie Robinson." If I write, "Dear Doris," she sometimes asks why am I calling her by her old name? I know she says that to be funny and to let me know she likes being "Mrs." But I love it when she says these things.

We got a red brick house that was very close to campus in 1955. We have lived there ever since. It is home, although Doris says it now looks more like a museum. People have been so kind to us. They have given us wonderful trophies, plaques, photos and other forms of mementos. They are all over the house, but we haven't really had room for them for the last decade. Doris finds places for them all. If someone was kind enough to give them to us, we were honored and wanted to keep them. I tell you that my Doris is a patient person.

We have a lot of fun together and go places together. I'm not criticizing them, but I see too many men not taking their wives with them or not taking them out to shows or dances. There are times I think my romance with Doris aggravates them because they don't look so good to their own wives when their wives look at Doris and me. We hug and kiss each time we meet, even if we saw each other only hours before. We need each other. We need to do almost everything together and let our kids see us; let the team see us. Let them see what happy can really be.

We call each other a name. I call her "darling," "baby," and "dear." Doris calls me "baby." I come home every day at noon to have lunch with Doris. No matter what, I'm going to come home to eat that sandwich with her. We are both trying to lose weight, but its not really working. Many friends want to take me out to dinner, and that's fine to go out. However, I'm going home to eat dinner with Doris first.

We try to go out to eat together regularly. Couples have to learn to get out, alone or with friends. It's just one more piece of a successful marriage. All the pieces add up to making it better.

Sometimes when we are on the road, a coach who doesn't know Doris sees me kiss her and rub cheeks. A few have asked, "Look, who's that you kissed like that?" And I respond, "Say, man, that's my wife. Do you have any objection?" The last one, a little embarrassed, offered, "Yeah you can kiss your wife! Give her a real kiss in front of the other people," and he laughed hard.

Public Speaking: Only with Doris

Doris revealed her desire to travel with me even before we got married. Therefore that had always been on my mind, and I was just trying to satisfy that urge of hers. When I go to places to speak, the organizers have to bring Doris. That's my rule. She worked out the details of many of the trips—speaking, clinics, most of the travel. She kept track of when I was committed and when I wasn't.

I always wanted Doris to be with me, especially when I'm speaking. That is even more true now that I am not coaching because the requests for me to speak have actually increased. But she can be rough on me. When I'm through speaking, I'm looking for her to say, "It was all right," or, "Good job," or, "It wasn't good." I needed to know right away. I didn't want to wait until the ride home to hear. Doris was never reluctant to respond.

I once gave a speech to a medical group and I told them, let me tell you all one thing. I want to talk to you all tonight, and I'm going to have a good time. My wife is not here and that's real rare. Now I don't want to have to worry about how long I'm going to stay up here tonight. Doris was—and still is—always telling me, "Darling, you speak too long. You should just do it, just say it, and keep it short. That's the way people like it." I don't know how long I talked that night.

She went to New Orleans with me to this sports information meeting. Doris said, "I heard you last night while you were going through your speech, and it was too long." I said, "Well, don't worry about that." She joked with me, "You know that Mac-Arthur said old soldiers never die, but MacArthur didn't know about old coaches. They don't sit down; they just get up there and talk too long."

Also, her pronunciation is much better than mine because she came from a family where they were saying things right. I came from a family where nobody was using the right pronunciation. Doris worked with me on my pronunciation.

When I came to Grambling, I knew as coaches we had to be able to do some public speaking. By the mid-1950s I was doing pretty good as a speaker. Willie Mays was a big star when he came through Louisiana at that time. I asked him to come with me to Texas on a recruiting trip. Willie was concerned about having to speak to audiences. I suggested that Willie come with me to a Grambling speech professor who could help him write some remarks he could always use. But Willie chose not to do that.

That showed me how many people, even very famous ones, don't like to speak in public. Therefore, I went to public-speaking class, and then I encouraged all my coaches and student-athletes to do the same. We all need the tools to speak well.

As for me, I would write the speech and then I'd get my director, Doris, to help me. We'd go in the living room and I'd give it to her, standing up there like the student. I'd go through it and we'd work on it. Boy, she'd send me out sometimes feeling like a coiled spring. She was a drill sergeant if she didn't like something about the speech. "Now you got to go back; you got to put emphasis here."

I remember one time something happened and she didn't get a chance to help me. She came and it was a pretty good speech. People seemed to really like it. On the way home she told me, "Well, you don't need me anymore—you get other critics to tell you about it." I understood and said, "But I do need you! I've got to have you there." She always came. I always wanted her to. I still need her. Just to see her happy means so much to me. She knows how I feel about her, how concerned I am, and that I'm always going to be there for her.

Lillian Rose and Eddie Jr.

Doris loves it when Eddie Jr. comes over. She's very proud of him and loves it when she can get her two men together. Boy, she can really strut on those days. After Eddie and I started coaching together, Doris started to rearrange the furniture whenever he came over. At first I'd ask her what she was doing. Doris would zip back with, "You all have got to talk to me. Eddie's not going to come over here and just look at these films and then get up and leave. My son is going to have to talk to me, too." We haven't had a lot of money, but we've had a lot of fun. Again, I think one of the keys to this happiness is that we can talk to each other!

And we like to do things with Eddie, his wife, Gloria, and their two children. Our house . . . their house, it doesn't really matter. It was wonderful to watch their children grow up. Sharon and Sheryl were twins. They both now live and work in Atlanta. Each has a boy. I mentioned earlier that Eddie III works for the Yankees. He also has a boy. Sharon, Sheryl, and Eddie III all graduated from Grambling.

Distance has always been the thing with Lillian Rose, since she has lived in several places. She was in Huntsville, Alabama, for a good part of her adult life. She got her M.A. from Grambling and worked in the area of early childhood education at Fort Rucker in Huntsville. She dedicated her professional life to helping children to learn, just like her mother. Now she lives in Alexandria, Louisiana, which is a little bit closer to us in the hub of the state.

She got divorced from her husband, James, after a few years. Then she remarried and moved to a new town. Doris and I offered to have her two children, Michael and Cherie, live with us so they were not moving around so much. That was some joy for us. Cherie got her degree from Grambling and now works for a computer company in Greensboro, North Carolina. Mike graduated from Howard University and is a captain in the air force, stationed in San Antonio.

All my life I heard people talk about how great it was to be a grandparent. But I often heard people who were grandparents joke that one of the best parts was that when they got tired of having the grandchildren around, they could call the parents to pick them up. Doris and I absolutely loved having two of our grandchildren live with us and having all five live in the same town with us. Now we have six great-grandchildren and wish they lived in Grambling, too. But we see a lot of them.

Over the years we have taken a lot of trips with Eddie's family. Eddie doesn't seem to mind driving. When his wife comes, Doris and I sit in the backseat, holding hands all the way.

Those trips have been even more fun in recent years because Eddie Jr. has been able to drive us around in cars that were wonderful gifts to me. First, in 1995, James Davidson of Davidson Transportation led an effort with the people of Grambling and Ruston, who bought me a brand new Chrysler. Then at the end of my last game and on the field of the Superdome, Frank Simmons of the Chrysler Minority Dealers gave me the keys to a beautiful new Chrysler. In many ways, those gifts represent the good will that the people of Louisiana and America have shown to me and my family.

Doris frequently says that "I'm in heaven when we hold hands." Me, too. I send her there as often as I can. But it is like an exclamation point to our heaven when we are with the children or grandchildren. Now great-grandchildren! But sitting in the backseat of these cars that are magnificent gifts from our friends, holding hands, quietly watching our children in the front seat: it doesn't get much better than that for me.

When Eddie was a little boy I had to come up with a half-time show for a basketball game. I loved boxing so I laced huge boxing gloves on Eddie Jr. and his friend and let them swing away. I think Eddie was then three years old. Naturally they never hit each other, but Doris let me know that was the end of such things. I always called her "Grambling's real coach." Those who know us best recognize truth in that name.

We never pushed Eddie Jr. to be involved in athletics. We hoped he would be a doctor or a lawyer. We wanted him to do whatever he wanted to do and be the best at it. But all he ever wanted to do was play and then coach. Now I realize how lucky I was that he did take to football. I was very proud of how well he did as a player but even more so as my assistant coach for fifteen years. I loved coaching with him, each and every day. He was a very hard worker. And Eddie didn't expect a free ride from me. He first coached high school ball at Webster High in Minden and Carrol High in Monroe, both in Louisiana.

Looking back now at the lives of our children, we are so proud of both of them. They are great family people, loving parents, and they couldn't have been better children themselves. It says something real special that Lillian Rose worked in her Momma's profession and Eddie, Jr. worked in his Daddy's. I am not sure how but I am confident that Eddie, Jr. and I will continue working together in some way.

Our Mommas Come to Live with Us

Doris' Momma, Lillian Mott, was such a fine lady. She came to stay with us until she died. There were many moments when I heard Doris telling her Momma, "I am your daughter! Eddie is not your son; he's just your son-in-law! You look like you are lining up against me. I'm your daughter and Eddie is your son-in-law!" When her Momma lived with us, I'd talk to her, we'd look at the programs together, ride around the area. We did a lot of things together. She even went in business with me on the housing project by investing some of her money with us. Doris's Momma liked the fact that I worked for a university. Education was a real priority for her family. All of her sisters had graduated from college. And these aunties were also good to us.

When we came up to North Louisiana, Auntie Inez took us under her wing and was a huge help. Of course, another one of her aunties, Grace Jackson, was at Grambling and helped get me the job when she let me know it was open!

I remember it wasn't always smooth sailing with Doris's Momma and me. She had been my second-grade teacher at the Perkins Road School in Baton Rouge. She knew my parents were not educated. I know she liked me, but as I said earlier, she sent Doris to boarding school in Leland during part of high school to keep us apart. That just was not possible. I covered the twelve miles between Baton Rouge and Leland by hitching a ride during the week whenever I had time, and Doris managed to get herself home every weekend. Eventually, Doris's Momma realized how much we were in love. She found out about and saw these end runs we were making to disrupt her plans. They were not effective in stopping us from seeing each other. Later, she just wanted us to be together forever. But we all had some great times while her Momma was alive. I loved her a lot.

Doris's Momma passed away in October of 1983. My mother then moved in and lived with us until she passed away in December 1991. We both handled and helped our mamas just fine, but our daddies didn't come to us before they died. It was just the mommas. And we just had such a wonderful time with them. They made our lives so much richer. Not just for us but for Eddie Jr. and Lillian also. And also for our five grandchildren. It was a hard day for me when I drove back from the 1991 Bayou Classic and Doris told me that my Momma had passed. Her death hit us especially hard since she was our last living parent. We loved all our parents so much, and they had given so much love to Doris and me, our children, and our children's children. They taught all of us how to be better parents.

The Romance Burns On

There is no parent better than my Doris. I have to put on record that Doris is one good-looking woman. She likes nice clothes, and I want her to have them. Of course, that means my pockets get lighter as I've got to go down deep to do that. But I could look at her from the time I get up until we fall asleep at night. And the romance is still burning. I wouldn't be the one to know exactly what a good marriage is and what one isn't, but I know ours is a good marriage because we respect each other so much.

We talk everything out. It can never get so bad that we can't talk. Now that's the key thing that we have had. We discuss everything. If something is bothering us, we raise it the next time we are together. And we never would say anything hurtful or mean to each other because there are some things that you can't take back. If it is out there, it might burn the other's heart forever.

I have always said that the thing I had been most proud of in my life is that I had the same job and the same wife for more than fifty years. I have a new life now, but, thank God, I have the same wife. I didn't make sixty with the job, but I will with Doris. Hopefully, we'll make a seventy-fifth anniversary in the year 2016!

She was a great teacher until she officially retired. She's still teaching me. She gave and gave, to our family, our parents, friends, and community. She's still giving. Doris helped me form my philosophy and my values. I don't know any one person more generous than Doris Robinson. She is simply the best human being I have ever met. Ever since the seventh grade, I have been at my best and most happy when I am near her, holding her hand, or hugging her. Doris Robinson is my life!

11.

MY PHILOSOPHY OF LIFE
AND COACHING

Being a Good American

Grambling has to be a university for all Americans. Whoever wants to come here must get a good education. That's why we say Grambling is a university "where everybody is somebody." We can't exclude any group. Just because blacks, Indians, Hispanics, or Asians aren't equally represented in other schools, doesn't mean the black colleges shouldn't treat everyone fairly. We have to if our students are going to get a meaningful education. This is how I see it.

There are people who have bent over backwards to bring Grambling to places we had never gone to. White people in New York; Hispanics in California. The Japanese treated us like royalty when Grambling played in Tokyo. I guess in my own way, I have been trying to create and keep a good relationship between the races.

I say that with real humility because I know that I don't know anything about theories of race relations. But I know what you need to do. I watch, I read, my wife reads, and we act accordingly. You know what it is? I'm just trying to be a good American. Sometimes I am not sure what the definition for that is, but when the Man calls me up to him, I want to be ready to answer the call of "the Big Tiger" up there. I want to hear God say, "Eddie, you have been a good person, a good husband and father, a good friend, a good coach, and a good American." That would, in the end, be the best measure of my life if I live up to it!

That's what I tell people wherever I speak. That is what I tried to convey to my players. I wanted them to understand they've got to give back. I told them as often as I could how fortunate they were to be at Grambling and added, "To whom a lot is given, a lot is expected." I really believe a lot has been given to Eddie Robinson and I don't want to be a fake.

I wanted to be good enough to coach the sons of mothers and fathers. I didn't care whether the son was white or black. I wanted to be a man who could help anyone, who could coach anyone. I wanted to tell them the right things and help them develop the best values.

Grambling wanted to have a great American football team. We wanted to play like the Notre Dames and the Michigans. I grew up under the shadows of LSU and Southern University. I looked at them in the early years and began to understand what I wanted for my guys and my school. We always had less, but we never could do less for Grambling students. They were part of America's future. Some of them might have thought that part of America did not see them in their future, so we tried to convince them otherwise.

When guys like Willie Davis came back and told me that I had helped them, man, that really made it all worthwhile. If I had done anything that helped anybody who played for me, that's what it was all about.

Coaching's Highest Compliment

Some of the players I had in my last twenty years at Grambling were the children of former players. Nine on my last team! The young ones told me that their daddies shared so many stories with them that they wanted to experience it for themselves. That was the highest compliment for what we were trying to do at Grambling. If the boy's father had played here and chose to send his son to be with us, then we must have done well by the daddy. We tried, of course, to do well by everyone.

I received one of my biggest compliments from a woman I didn't know after making a speech in Lubbock, Texas. She was a member of a civic group I addressed. There were a few people who came up to me to thank me afterward when she grabbed my hand and told me, "If I had a son, I would want him to play for you." I held her hand and I said, "Now, look, do you realize you've paid me the highest compliment a coach can receive?" She asked, "What do you mean?" I went on, "If you had a son, then he would be your most precious possession. If you think I'm good enough to coach him, then you couldn't give me any higher compliment than to say that you would want me to coach your boy."

I think about that all the time. When you are coaching these guys, they are somebody's baby, somebody loves them—I don't care how big he is, how small he is, somebody at home loves him. You can't coach him unless you love him. You coach him as though he were the boy you want to marry your daughter. You want him to be the greatest. And this is what a coach has to understand. Coaches need to govern themselves by these principles.

I mentioned Al Dennis earlier. This was Al Dennis III, and he became our business manager in my final years as coach. His daddy, Al Dennis II, was the captain of our team right after the war years and was my assistant coach when Al III arrived as a highly touted freshman.

We had a press conference and the reporters were interviewing Al III. His father was amazed by the scene and how things had changed over the years. He said, "That's my son over there; he's never caught or kicked a ball or tackled anybody in college, and they've got the media wrapped around him, making him an all-American before he even starts. I was here four years and didn't get the coverage in four years that he got today!"

Al III did become a fine player and had some good years in the NFL with Cleveland and Dallas. But his daddy sure didn't like it that first day, and he was right in some ways. Having all these expectations on a young person can be unfair. In an ideal world, you ought to let him play first. That's how you learn ball. But now everyone wants the hype. Too bad. We always tried to balance that for our own student-athletes. It was easier when the daddy was on the coaching staff to help.

Al III went into business after his NFL career, but then we brought him back as Grambling's business manager. He is a good man, just like his daddy was before he passed away.

Motivating Student-Athletes

We not only try to motivate our guys to be better players but also to be better people. We talked a lot with the players. We asked them to watch what other people were doing and what they were experiencing. We used everyday happenings on the campus as examples. If a student got into trouble, we talked about that. If a student got an award, we talked about that.

We were always discussing grades and what they would mean to their future. We used everything that we could to educate them and motivate them. We talked about whether the student-athletes went to church or not. We talked a lot about relationships. They saw me and Doris. They saw the other coaches and their families. We used whatever we could to pick them up and get them motivated.

Of course, what works has changed over time. It is definitely harder to do that now than forty or fifty years ago. Nobody chooses to be lectured to, but in the end, even the student-athletes on my last team appreciated it. That's harder, partly because they have more material things, more information from television, and are living in a smaller world. But we had to keep at it because, in many ways, coaches were closer to their student-athletes than teachers were to their students.

Parents

Even parents seemed to expect more out of the coaches than they did of other people on campus. I tried to make parents feel obligated to be more responsible than many were. Some fathers came to me, saying, "Take my boy, Coach. I can't do anything with him." The father had him for eighteen years; then he expected me to do the job he didn't do.

It disturbed me that some parents and schools allowed youngsters to disengage from academics because of athletic talent. If a boy can't tackle, we show him how. I sometimes wondered if anybody cared enough to teach him to read?

Coaches had a big advantage. We were with our student-athletes every day. We lived closer. We rode with them on the bus. If there was a tense situation with a student-athlete, we could arrange for him to sit next to us on the bus. After a few curves in the road, the young man eventually relaxed and opened up. Most professors don't get the same opportunity to be close.

Discipline

I believe in discipline. It shows you care enough to be involved. I learned that from President Jones with my very first team. I might warn a player a few times. If he didn't come around, I would tell him to find another team! I almost never had to do that after my first season.

I began every team meeting with a talk about the importance of education. I would even correct players' grammar on the practice field. If a player damaged his room, I would talk to the entire team about character and pride and being a real man. If the players didn't do the right thing, they had to deal with me by running the stadium steps.

I required that my guys all wear suit coats and ties to interviews with the media. I didn't allow jewelry. When I packed up my old office, I found a bunch of earrings. I had to laugh at myself. Looking around at how many men now wear earrings, I thought I might have become that dinosaur my players sometimes suggested that I was.

A whole lot of times people in our society stand back and just talk. I don't believe in standing back and talking but in changing things. Go out and change it and make your contribution. That was, in part, why I started with the cow bell. I wanted to change the pattern of my guys' lives to make them better.

I was in my mid-seventies, ringing cow bells in the dorm at 6:30 A.M. to make sure they were out of bed, getting breakfast, and making it to class. A lot of people at Grambling thought I was crazy. But I always was convinced that my team needed to see me actively involved in their lives and in their education. And I thought our student-athletes appreciated knowing that we cared that much about their schoolwork.

If a player didn't get up and go to class, we'd take his meal card for that day. In effect, it cost him money because he would usually buy some food. Nobody likes to lose money, especially if you don't have much to lose. However, in my last few years we had a problem because the guys were scattered in four dormitories. I couldn't do it alone anymore. In that way, the new NCAA rule banning athletic dorms hurt us.

Academics and Athletics

If we found out that a player missed class, he ran the bleachers. Losing money was bad, but running the bleachers was worse. A few of them burned the bleachers up. Sometimes we would not let them attend events on campus. Most importantly, and as our ultimate weapon, we didn't let them dress for a game if they didn't do what was expected of them. We did whatever we could to keep their attention focused on getting their degrees, class by class.

Because they were new to college life, we spent a lot of time with the freshmen when they arrived about five days before the upper classmen got to campus. The president spoke to them the first day. Then all the academic deans and chairs met with them about Grambling's great academic programs and offerings. Others, like the registrar and dean of students, discussed the "how tos" of Grambling. Last, but perhaps most important, we started having the freshmen spend a day in Grambling's library to learn how to use it as a resource for their education. Leland had a tiny library with only a few books when I was a college student. But when I went to graduate school at the University of Iowa, I honestly would get lost in their library. It was embarrassing. I didn't want my guys to be embarrassed. I knew they would need the library to go to class prepared.

We gave awards to student-athletes who did exceptional things in class. We wanted to use positive motivation, not negative. That's always better. Always. But success doesn't happen automatically. At Grambling our coaches were committed to making it happen.

My boys meant a lot more to me than touchdowns. For me, a huge highlight of the year I won number 324 was that twenty members of the team were on the honor roll! Over all my years, I found that most student-athletes were smart. It's just that society doesn't ask them to be smart often enough. My mission was to produce good people and to make certain our boys took full advantage of their educational opportunity. When they left Grambling, I kept in touch. I wanted them to know that if they ever had a problem, I'd be there for them.

Faculty and Student-Athletes

Some student-athletes felt that teachers didn't give them enough credit as students. I think that may have been true of some professors but certainly not most. There was more than one kind of professor. The best just treated our student-athletes like any other students, applying the same standards and expectations to everyone. I think most professors did that. There were others who thought of our student-athletes simply as athletes on their way to the NFL. They wanted to help them achieve that goal and did so by not demanding as much academically from a player. They mistakenly believed that tough academic standards would only get in the way of an NFL career.

Then there were professors who resented the notion that a Grambling football player might make $10 million as a player in the NFL when they couldn't even make a fraction of that amount in their entire teaching career. That resentment could affect how the professor treated a student-athlete in class. There weren't many professors in the last two groups. But there were enough to derail the intellectual confidence of some student-athletes.

That's why we tried very hard to get our Grambling faculty to know the players as athletes, as students, and as people. We invited them to see our guys perform on the field but also to meet with them afterward and learn more about the students behind the face masks on their helmets. Life has too many obstacles. We didn't want to add any at Grambling. We always assured the faculty that whatever their guidelines and requirements were in their classes, our student-athletes had to meet them.

I also knew that some student-athletes brought on their own problems by overemphasizing the "athlete" and not the "student" in themselves. I always asked those having academic issues if they were really trying in class; were they putting in the time to understand the work, learning things to help them in the future, or were they just trying to pass to stay eligible?

The material expectations of today's young people became a complicating factor. Of course they want things we never had. I began to see so many more kids coming into college with money, a car, and good clothes. But this was what was happening all across America. So many young people seemed to expect these things without having to earn them. I'm afraid the dedication to hard work may be diminishing today. I hope I am wrong.

As coaches, we had to talk more about it and let student-athletes know that if they didn't get their degrees, then they would be the losers. When they lost that way, so did their community and their country. Student-athletes need to get their class work done and graduate. Only then can they really see what they are actually able to do. Grambling has had some brilliant minds on our teams. Occasionally, we saw a student-athlete's intelligence when he didn't. Then we had to push him to develop self-confidence.

If a student-athlete left here without graduating, I considered it my job to never let him off the hook. Along with my assistant coaches, I would push until he gave in, came back, and completed the work he'd begun. This was the case with one of our greatest players ever. Buck Buchanan starred here and then for thirteen seasons in the NFL. He won a Super Bowl ring and just about every honor but his Grambling degree. I never let him forget it until he finally came back. The entire university was so proud on that afternoon when Buck wore his cap and gown.

We see examples every day in our nation where children feel

alone and become antisocial. Now we are spending more money keeping them in prison than if we got them a good education. A lot of coaches say they don't have time. You've got to make time. If you don't have students, you don't have a school. I walked around with all my players' updated grades in my briefcase. We checked on their academic work daily. Because a guy was a football player didn't mean he was a dummy. Just the opposite. You had to be smart just to understand our system.

We had to put the whistle down every so often to get after them and tell them what they were supposed to do. I wanted each of my student-athletes to be good family men and good citizens. I was rarely disappointed.

As a youth, football was all I had. I learned the American way from football. I want to give something back to America because so much was given to me. When I autograph things for the youngsters, I always write that football teaches the lessons of life.

I don't guess Michael Jordan knew he would play basketball as well as he did; I doubt that George Washington Carver, the professor at Tuskegee, thought that there could be so many different products from the peanut. Life is a process of discovery.

We taught our student-athletes not to let anyone, from teachers to advisors, create limitations for them. I think of how Willie Davis's advisor almost messed him up. Some students listened carefully and absorbed our messages. A few didn't want any part of what we were saying if they thought we were pushing too hard. As coaches, we always had to find that oh-so-fine line.

Prop 48 and Other NCAA Academic Standards

Grambling has an expert admissions staff. If that staff admitted a student-athlete we recruited, that meant they were convinced that he could graduate. But in recent years, many young black high school students have been having problems passing standardized tests used by the NCAA to determine eligibility. Many educators hold these tests are more difficult for people who come from families with low incomes.

I thought that if these standards were going to improve the student-athlete, then I was for them. Still, I clearly remember that when the NCAA was ready to raise the scores, I just didn't believe that you could take a test to say who could and who couldn't go to college. However, the way it turned out, I think Prop 48 may have helped. But these new standards may be too much.

However, I can tell you something I saw too many times. If a young person came to Grambling—or any other school—branded as a Prop 48 student, then that entire confidence-building process was at least set back and, maybe, even sabotaged. Our work doubled because we had to help him rebuild that confidence.

We've had kids whose test scores didn't predict success when they came to Grambling, but who discovered they could do well in school because they had to if they were going to play here. I didn't pretend that we were Harvard, but our standards were good and we lived by them. Still do.

I was a football coach so I talk mostly about boys and men. But I know these things are just as important to girls and women.

Some Final Thoughts

A lot of my guys have come back years after graduating and disclosed to me, "There are many times when you said things that I wasn't completely in agreement with. I often didn't know where you were coming from. But with my experiences since I've gotten out of school, I can understand better." We had many conversations about America when they came back. I always preached hard that they had to be part of America and not use racism and hard times for blacks as a reason for them not to excel.

I could tell that when I told them the importance of voting, a few just did not comprehend the pain and sacrifices that so many went through so we could vote. Most of the guys who come back now tell me they vote in each election. "Coach, you were right; now I understand the importance of the vote. You used to say, 'One vote can make a difference. You've got to start with one.' I believe that now."

The thing I stressed most often was how they, as blacks, had to love America just as well as anybody else loved it. That was harder to get through at various times in our history, especially when there were racial tensions running high somewhere. I can tell you that there are lots of Grambling graduates out there now sermonizing about being proud to be Americans—and contributing to making this a better nation for all of us. Knowing that makes me feel so good.

It's funny. People sometimes seemed to be waiting for me to brag about how great a coach I was or how much I accomplished. They were going to the wrong person. My record belonged to everybody at Grambling. The attention on me was often embarrassing. An example of that happened when I got to New York in the summer of 1997 to do a commercial for Burger King. This is a company that was very good to me, to Grambling, and to college football.

As soon as I read the script, I knew I was faced with something that I didn't want to say. The writers had played me up having won more games than anyone in history. I didn't want anyone to think I thought I was better than other people and tried to get them to rewrite it. This was for Burger King and I wanted to have it my way, but Burger King wanted to brag about my 400-plus wins. I didn't feel that it was necessary for me to brag about my career.

The producer was laughing at me. "Coach, you did this—you are a football coach and you broke the record."

There were twenty-five or so people in the film crew. I knew they had worked hard to get ready for me. This was my commercial, but these were their jobs and I was getting in their way, keeping them from getting home to be with their own families. I just didn't want to be the person holding out on all of these people. So I decided to do it their way, but I got some things softened up.

After it was over, I called Grant Teaff, the head of our American Football Coaches Association. I felt I needed to apologize in advance so my fellow coaches wouldn't think I was bragging on my own in the commercial. Grant told me not to worry. I always did.

I've never gotten up to talk to people and told them about how many games I've won. You won't find that anywhere in a newspaper because I don't talk about my accomplishments to the press. We won those games because so many great young men played hard and because I had so many brilliant assistant coaches helping us figure out how to win. Those wins didn't belong to Eddie Robinson but to all who helped us get them.

I've always worked on my head to keep my hat size normal. I want to be real and give the other guy the same thing I'd want him to give me. I just wished that more of the attention had been directed toward the team and our coaches.

I'm not concerned about personal records. All they mean is that I was around a long time. I didn't block or tackle anybody. I just tried to give encouragement to the young men who have played for me. The record belongs to everybody.

I got so many letters from my former players who wrote to tell me how much I had done for them. What they didn't understand was that they've done more for me than I'd ever done for them.

Sometimes I wondered what it would have been like to be at a big Division IA school. Sure, I could look up at our stands on game day, and wonder to myself what would it be like to look up there and see 60,000 or 70,000 faces. But I had the best student body, the best student-athletes, the best faculty, and the best administration. Above all, I had the best group of coaches by my side for over fifty years. I always knew I was exactly where I wanted to be. At home it always has been Doris . . . Doris . . . Doris! At work, it has always been Grambling . . . Grambling . . . Grambling!

I believe Dr. Steve Favors is the man to move Grambling forward. He gets up working and goes to bed working. It is exciting to work for him as his senior advisor for institutional advancement. He gives me the opportunity for real input. It is surprising to me that after all these years I am learning even more things about this great university. I will work hard in the years ahead to help Dr. Favors have our alumni put their arms around him. It is still Grambling . . . Grambling . . . Grambling!

Now I want to offer hope and encourage this generation of children. My vision of America is of one people working together to make things better for all of us. I have already started the new phase of my life traveling across this land, devoting my energies and the knowledge that has come from my experiences to helping all of our children. I tell young people that I was raised in a segregated society in which people told me I couldn't do most of the things I did. I tell our youth that they can make their dreams happen.

People say I touched lives. Well, they have touched me. I've got a piece of every boy who ever played at Grambling in my heart.

My fifty-plus years in football seemed like we had one long-running play going. If I had the chance, I would call for an instant replay of my entire life—in slow motion—so I could savor every second as I continue to work on the next stage of my life. If I could have created a game plan for my own life, I'd want to be born in America to my same parents, marry Doris, go to work for Grambling, and have Eddie and Lillian as our children, their children as our grandchildren, and their children as our great-grandchildren. I have a great life.

When all is said and done, there can be no doubt after reading *Never Before, Never Again* that Coach Robinson was one of a kind.

In a time when racial issues can divide the nation, Coach brings people together. At a time when coaches leave for the next greatest jobs, Coach stayed at one school for fifty-six years. Being at Grambling all his life was a feather in Eddie's cap. For him, the grass was not greener on the other side. He never had to have his ego massaged. Eddie Robinson was happy being Eddie Robinson at his institution. And he helped make it a great name in higher education.

After the integration of the previously all-white colleges and universities, Coach helped invent the "Classics" that kept games between the historically black colleges and universities in the public limelight.

At a time when there is so much negative publicity about coaches and athletes, Coach shows America how much good sports can do for us as a people.

We talk about being mentors to young people. Coach has spent a lifetime doing that for his own players. They were his sons, a part of the family. He took so many young men from a variety of circumstances, including those from broken homes and many who were away from home for the first time. The background didn't

matter to Eddie Robinson. As a coach, he went far beyond football. He was more concerned about the total person than just the
football player. His graduation rate was remarkable. He developed
minds before he developed muscles.

This book is not only a story about sports but is a social history
of race relations and the civil rights movement as viewed by a
pioneering sportsperson. He helped break barrier for African-
American people. First, many whites believed African-Americans
couldn't be great coaches. He was perhaps the greatest coach ever.
They said African-Americans couldn't be leaders in teams' front
offices. So many Grambling grads have been NFL executives. They
said African-Americans couldn't be corporate leaders. Willie Davis
may be the number one graduate of both Coach and Grambling.
The breakthroughs provided by the work of Coach Robinson
might have been less dramatic than the day Jackie Robinson
donned the Dodger uniform; However, they were no less meaningful. Two men named Robinson changed American life forever.

The love story between Coach and Doris contained in these
pages as well as the closeness of the Robinson family will inspire
people to work harder and love better.

Having Coach tell his story with Richard Lapchick was a great
idea. Lapchick's own life experiences make him uniquely qualified
to help chronicle Coach Robinson's life. He has been a civil rights
activist, scholar, and an author for more then thirty years. North-
eastern University's Center for the Study of Sport in Society,
which he founded in 1984, has been a social conscience for sport.

Lapchick has worked with me and the Rainbow Commission
on Fairness in Sport. He knows the issues Coach talks about.

Never Before, Never Again shows why Eddie Robinson has always
been a hero in my eyes. Without question, Eddie Robinson is an
ambassador for our people, not only African-Americans but all
the American people. That's why I have such respect for Coach
Robinson.

—Reverend Jesse Jackson